What others are saying about

Smith and Kai's T4T: A Discipleship Re-Revolution

"This is a breathtaking read with its mix of biblical principle and human experience. An adaptation of the principles set forth in this book have transformed our church-planting work across the world and enabled 4,000 new churches to be planted in an African country in a two-year period by ordinary believers experiencing God working with them. I highly recommend an in-depth read."

> — Rev. Raymond Belfield, Executive Missions Overseer, Victory Family Centre Singapore, Emeritus Board Member of Assemblies of God World Ministries Council in the UK

"T4T addresses the most fundamental, but often missed activity of a disciple maker who desires to see a Church Planting Movement. This is the intensive, focused, ongoing training of disciples. I highly recommend this book to those who long to see God move in amazing ways among a people group."

> — Richard Schlitt, International Director, OMF International

"A 'must read' for every mission-minded person and CPM practitioner! T4T: A Discipleship Re-Revolution is highly practical and biblically sound, giving inspiration for trusting God today for the impossible, church-planting movements sourced in God alone."

> — Alvin W. Hull, Director of New Ministries,
> SE Asia and Pacific Region Pioneers

"God is moving in unprecedented ways to fulfill His global mission as we move deeper into the 21st century. Through His divine providence and power, an expanding indigenous witness and church multiplication is occurring through a reproductive methodology called 'Training for Trainers.' Steve Smith and Ying Kai present this phenomenon from the perspective of practitioners who have personally led this thoroughly biblical and effective approach to evangel

> — Dr. Jerry Rankin, President Emeritus
> International Mission Board, SBC

"Revolutionary in its elegant simplicity, and ruthless in its focused commitment to bring people to Christ who can bring other people to Christ, T4T contains best practices in pioneer missions. If there were a "Top Gun" for missionaries, T4T and CPM would be the curriculum. However, teaching only the best to get better misses the point of T4T, it can help every Christian witness to everybody they know. Try it yourself! Share it with friends! I want to use this as a textbook ASAP!"

— Dr. Bob Garrett, Director, MA in Global Leadership,
Dallas Baptist University

"II Peter 3:9 tells us that God's desire is that none should perish, but that all should come to repentance. He blesses us by allowing us to serve as His instruments to bring others to Him. Steve and Ying have recorded for us an eminently practical yet thoroughly biblical guideline to doing the right things to be effectively used by God as He brings about church-planting movements. This book will inform, encourage, and inspire you, as you realize that you can obediently and effectively reach and train others to train others, and see what our mighty God will do!"

— Dr. Clyde Meador, Interim President and Executive Vice President,
International Mission Board, SBC

"The contents of this book are clear, practical and proven. More importantly, the authors are faithful and fruitful as people who live out these practices and pass them on to successive spiritual generations. Many people hear about Church Planting Movement (CPM) principles and are confused about how to get started. T4T is a valuable tool that embodies many of the principles at play in CPMs and provides step-by-step guidance on how to implement those principles. I have known both Ying and Steve since their own CPM training and highly commend them to you as exceptional servant leaders. It has been said, 'Experience is a good teacher, but success is a great mentor.' In that spirit, take these men as mentors!"

— Dr. Curtis Sergeant, Vice-President, Global Strategies, e3 Partners
Ministry

"Working in the hardest parts of the Muslim world we found the practical insights from T4T provided an answer to our prayer for how we could experience the Spirit-driven multiplication of churches. Steve and Ying have shared the gift of multiplying churches that works even among very resistant people. One caveat: reading this book is not enough. If you put into practice the principles you will find in T4T, you will find the gift. Don't miss out on what the Lord is teaching us through these brothers."

— John, Affinity Group Strategy Leader for North Africa and Middle East Peoples, International Mission Board, SBC

"The principles in this book are sound, biblical, reproducible, easily applicable and universal in their application. God is up to something in our generation that will be studied and talked about for generations to come. This book will give you a glimpse of what He is up to. A word of warning though: it is hard to read about this and not want to be a part of what God is doing in the world today. Read at your own risk."

— Neil Cole, Founder and Director of Church Multiplication Associates, author of Organic Church, Cultivating a Life for God, and Journeys to Significance.

"An outstanding book from two men who understand church-planting movements from the inside out. Inspiring and instructive for anyone with a passion to make disciples."

— Steve Addison, author Movements that Change the World

"Steve Smith not only writes with biblical authority but with deep life experience. All the churches I am involved with around the world have been transformed by Steve's leadership, teaching, and life. My prayer is that this book will not only stir your heart, but empower you to change the world. Thank you, Steve, for sharing proven and biblical truths that will change lives."

— Dr. Jimmy Seibert, Sr. Pastor, Antioch Community Church and President, Antioch Ministries International

T4T

A Discipleship ReRevolution

T4T

A Discipleship *Re*Revolution

by Steve Smith
with Ying Kai

WIGTake Resources
P.O. Box 1884
Monument, CO 80132
1 (719) 646-3190
www.churchplantingmovements.com
www.T4TOnline.org
Printed in Bangalore, India
© 2011 by WIGTake Resources

T4T: A Discipleship *Re*-Revolution
by Steve Smith
with Ying Kai

WIGTake Resources
P.O. Box 1884, Monument, CO 80132
1 (719) 646-3190
www.churchplantingmovements.com
www.T4TOnline.org

ISBN-13: 978-09747562-1-9
1. Missions. 2. Church planting. 3. Discipleship.
Smith, Stephen Robert., 1962 –

First printing, February 2011
Second printing, July 2011

Printed by Brilliant Printers, Bangalore, India
Page Design by Megan Chadwick
Cover Design by Mike Mirabella

Smith, Stephen Robert
    T4T: A Discipleship *Re*-Revolution/by Steve Smith with Ying Kai

Dedication

To my precious wife Laura whose insights shape and pervade all my teaching!

Table of Contents

Ying Kai Vignettes
Table of Contents

Acknowledgements

I give complete credit to the Lord Jesus for anything of value in this book and take complete responsibility for anything that's off base! The King has put this book on my heart for years, and I have finally gotten around to writing down the insights I have learned from His Word and works.

This book would not have been written without the unwavering support of my precious wife Laura. Outside of Jesus, she is my greatest counselor and advocate. Much of what you see in these pages comes from the countless daily conversations we have about life, godliness and ministry.

I also want to thank David Garrison for believing in the project and laboring to make it a reality.

Ying Kai graciously supported the book and contributed so much content from audio recordings of our trainings together.

Several people have read every word and given insights and corrections based on their extensive knowledge of CPMs and T4T: Bill Smith, Stan Parks, Bill Fudge, Hal Cunnyngham, Allen James, Neill Mims and David Garrison. Stan Parks and his two sons Kaleb, and Seth spent hours transcribing recordings of Ying Kais' teaching and worked on many of the logistics of this book. I want to thank Mike Mirabella and Megan Chadwick for their excellent work on the graphics and design of this book. My mother Jean Smith, an English professor, meticulously combed through every word editing grammatical mistakes.

Many others have contributed ideas, case studies and vignettes that are included in this book. I have tried to cite them where security allows. I cannot express deeply enough my debt to Dr. Thom Wolf and Carol Davis whose insights fill many of these pages.

I give special thanks to my three sons (Cris, Josh and David), the team, the national partners and the leaders of the "Ina" CPM of which we were a part. Together, we re-lived the book of Acts.

FOREWORD

Rarely have I been so excited about a new book. For the past two decades I have been immersed in the world of Church Planting Movements (CPMs), the rapid multiplication of new churches that sweep through a people group or city. My investigations have taken me into virtually every corner of the world. Of the many movements I have investigated, though, none has better earned the title of "CPM Best Practice" than the remarkable T4T or "Training for Trainers" movement that has exploded across a closed and crowded country in Asia.

Since its inception in 2001, this movement has documented more than 1.7 million baptisms and more than 150,000 new church starts. Truly we have never seen anything quite like this movement that is now influencing other mission efforts throughout the world.

Thanks to Steve Smith, for the first time, we are now getting an insider's look at how and why this movement is multiplying so rapidly. Steve has earned a reputation as one of the IMB's finest CPM trainers. In this insightful book, Steve teams up with Ying Kai, the father of the T4T – Training for Trainers – movement to give us a deeply spiritual, solidly biblical and immensely practical insight into just how God is at work in this extraordinary movement.

T4T: A Discipleship *Re*-Revolution promises to shed light on the ways that God is multiplying new life in Christ and communities of faith, but it does more. This book promises life and ministry lessons that can be applied anywhere, and are already transforming ministries around the world.

I am honored to be associated with this book and pray that God will use it to enrich and expand His kingdom where you serve.

David Garrison, Ph. D.
Author, *Church Planting Movements*

Part One
THE FOUNDATIONS OF T4T

CHAPTER I

Kingdom Come!

I've finished my CPM plan. What do I do next?

At the dawn of the 21st century, God began to unfold an amazing story of kingdom advance in a densely populated corner of Asia. Ying and Grace Kai were laboring in an urban sprawl of crowded factories packed with 10,000 to 100,000 workers, a mad mix of highly educated college grads and barely literate villagers who had migrated into the factories.

Within weeks of arriving, Ying began to see results we could scarcely have imagined. God was orchestrating an incredibly explosive movement in the Kais' part of the country.

> In all my years of training others, I have never seen a missionary fulfill the vision in his church-planting movement plan – until Ying.

For years our organization has trained missionaries and church leaders how to cooperate with God to experience church-planting movements (CPMs) – the Spirit-empowered rapid multiplication of disciples and churches generation by generation. At the end of the training each participant develops a CPM Plan. Their plans begin with God's vision for a movement, but majors on the practical ministry steps they will need to take to move toward that lofty vision.

Over the years, we have seen missionaries and church leaders make great progress and breakthroughs in the ministry to which God has called them. Yet in all our years of training, we had yet to see a missionary or church leader fully reach the vision and goals set out in his CPM plan. The purpose of the vision is that it is so God-sized that it guides the missionary and his partners for many years to come. That end-vision drives them to attempt things in faith they never would otherwise have attempted.

Three months into his CPM plan, Ying called the regional leader for our mission organization.

He said, "Bill, I have finished my CPM plan. What do I do next?"

Once Bill picked his jaw up off the floor, he responded, "Ying, just keep going!"

Ying's CPM plan called for a goal of 200 churches in his end-vision.

Ying reached his goal in *just three months!*

That made all of us turn our heads and pay attention. As the months flew by, the hundreds became thousands of new churches,[1] most of them meeting in homes, restaurants, parks and factories. Tens of thousands of people were coming to faith and passing this faith on to others in an Acts-like explosion of discipleship.

The movement grew every day. Ying and Grace kept meticulous records as the many emerging leaders in the various networks of the CPM reported to them each month. These numbers were logged in faithfully and then recorded in the most conservative manner (discounting for possible discrepancies). In 2005 an independent assessment team visited various groups of believers and leaders to better understand the nature of this rapidly multiplying CPM. They not only affirmed the accuracy of the movement, but realized that the numbers being reported to Ying and Grace were just the *leading edge* of the movement. The numbers didn't portray the full extent of God's kingdom growth there. In any movement of such magnitude contact is eventually impossible with distant generations of believers and churches.

---

[1] In this book, I will frequently refer to churches. I will define this more later, but these are Acts 2 type churches that display the basic covenant and characteristics of that Acts 2 community whether they meet in homes or in dedicated buildings. Usually I am implying house churches or church-like small groups of a larger worshiping community.

Yet in one random sampling the assessment team met representatives of 18 generations of believers who had come to Christ over the course of the 4-5 year time-span. That meant that the first generation in the room was responsible for leading the second generation to faith and discipling them. The group was able to track 18 generations of discipleship and church planting down to the 18th generation believer sharing a testimony. As they listened to this 18th generation believer, they were struck by how similar his evangelism and discipleship pattern was to that which was taught in the first generation.

Ying and Grace's ministry has emerged as what is probably the fastest-growing church-planting movement in recent history. Below are compilations of monthly reports from leaders in the movement. The numbers below conservatively track the leading edge of this movement of God. Within a few months of the beginning of the movement, over 12,000 people had been baptized and 908 small churches formed.

	Baptisms	**New Churches**
Year One	53,430	3,535
Year Two	104,542	9,320
Year Three	90,648	9,307
Year Four	121,859	12,548
Year Five	153,625	15,193
Year Six	204,055	18,194
Year Seven	210,951	19,921
Year Eight	313,598	28,602
Year Nine	279,231	24,005
First 9 Mos Year Ten	206,204	18,368
TOTAL	**1,738,143**	**158,993**

Today the movement might best be described as a sort of *super* church-planting movement. It has become so large that it is impossible to track all that is going on. But it is clear that an entire Asian region has been saturated with the kingdom of God, and the ripples of its effect are now touching people groups in other countries and continents.

At last count, more than 1.7 million people had been baptized and more than 150,000 churches started!

As believers were faithfully following Jesus as obedient disciples and passing on the gospel and discipleship to others they led to faith, a discipleship revolution emerged. Ying called it *Training for Trainers (T4T)* because he expected every disciple to train others. This discipleship revolution looks very familiar to readers of the book of Acts. It harkens back to Jesus' prophecy that His disciples would do greater works than He did.

> Truly, truly, I say to you, he who believes in Me, the works that I do, he will do also; and **greater works** than these he will do; because I go to the Father. (John 14:12, NASB, emphasis added)

Out of love for Jesus, the early apostles sparked the original discipleship revolution with the expectation that new believers, filled with the Spirit, would follow Jesus wholeheartedly and fish for souls. They ignited a discipleship revolution that moved beyond the old covenant to spread the King's reign throughout the Roman Empire and beyond. It was indeed a greater work – a greater extent of the King's reign!

The CPM that has emerged in Ying's ministry has challenged common discipleship and church-planting expectations of today. It harks back to the original discipleship revolution. As a return to the original revolution, it is a *RE*-revolution!

Simultaneously with the Kais' *super* CPM, another work of God was unfolding, this one in our own ministry.

3 ½ Years!

Our work among the remote people group we call the "Ina"[2] was finally taking off. In this oppressive Asian country, we had labored for five years to get to this point. The Ina were the poorest people group in the country, most of them uneducated and illiterate, and days away from most population centers. Five thousand of their villages dotted the haze-covered emerald mountains as far as the eye could see.

We were desperate for a movement of God's kingdom to break loose among this animistic people entrenched in their fear of demonic powers, but even accessing them was difficult.

I had tried sneaking into Ina villages to share the gospel. With my coat collar pulled up, hat pulled down and sunglasses on, I would slip in at dusk and out at dawn. My team and I would share in homes privately about the gospel as we sipped murky tea and ate bee larvae. Then shortly after we departed, the police would raid the village and crush the work. We felt so helpless. "Father," I prayed, "even if they believe, how will they ever have a chance to grow in faith before they are crushed?!"

Through repeated readings of Matthew 10, Luke 10 and the book of Acts God led us to a different strategy. If people who looked like the Ina – other Asians – could discretely enter the Ina villages to share the gospel and disciple them, perhaps the authorities would not notice for a while. And *if* these new Ina believers could then pass on this witness, discipleship and church planting to new villages themselves, then perhaps they could go places we and our other Asian partners couldn't. And *if* the kingdom expectation of each new obedient disciple becoming a witness and each church becoming a church-planting church could catch on, there was a hope that the movement could sprout up as a mustard tree in each place until nothing could stop it.

---

[2] The name Ina is a pseudonym I use in this book for the previously unreached people group we worked with in a limited access nation. For security reasons, many real names will be changed in this book.

So we mobilized and trained Asian partners who trekked into the remote mountain homeland of the Ina people. Many of these partners were arrested, thrown into jail and beaten, but they also were able to share the gospel, disciple new believers and plant churches among the Ina.

In two short years, they planted the first churches among the Ina that launched into a kingdom movement! The outside Asian partners had started a few churches, but what was most thrilling was that the discipleship revolution was catching on among the Ina themselves. The *majority* of the new churches were being started by new Ina believers anxious to spread their love for the King to other villages.

I was thrilled. Yet, there was something troubling my soul. "Lord, this is not enough! We have only reached 80 villages. There are still more than 4,900 villages yet to be touched by the gospel! Don't let us become satisfied with the good and miss what it will take to see all 5,000 villages reached!"

I sat in a small room in a secret location with 12 new Ina leaders and three foreign partners. These Ina leaders rode buses on perilous mountain roads to represent the 80 new churches at our first leadership training. As the week went by, we gave them some basic leadership training to take back to the churches they represented. We discussed many topics in that secret room that week – marriage, discipleship, leading well, loving well, enduring persecution, understanding the Bible, etc.

But most of all we discussed the kingdom revolution that has spread from country to country, from people group to people group since the time of Acts. It was God's time for the Ina to be reached and for them to take their place in God's relentless plan of spreading His kingdom to every people group.

Although these brothers and sisters had been so faithful in starting new churches, 80 churches weren't enough! These 12 leaders needed a bigger vision, a vision that would drive them to all 5,000 villages and beyond to other people groups and nations.

I had that vision.

My Asian partners had that vision.

But did the Ina churches have that revolutionary vision?

I spent many hours teaching the group about church-planting movements. About how God could use them to reach the whole people group and beyond. About how every obedient believer could become a witness and discipler of others. About how every church could start churches. About how new generations of disciples and churches could begin every few weeks or months.

But still it wasn't sinking in.

One morning, I cast the vision once more for how a church-planting movement could expand to all 5,000 villages. As the morning progressed, and confusion continued, I almost gave up. In exasperation, I told the group:

> It's lunchtime, and I have to leave for an appointment. Over the lunch break, I want you to come up with *a plan for how 80 churches can reach 5,000 villages in five years or less!* When I come back, I am going to ask you what you are thinking.

I could see the nervousness in their eyes, but I didn't know what else to do. I walked out the door and left them with each other – and the Holy Spirit.

Two hours later, I returned to the training room and was amazed at the visibly different atmosphere in the room. They were jubilant! The 12 Ina leaders were beaming with excitement.

As I looked around the room, my eyes rested on the white board where they had written these numbers:

80
160
320
640
1,280
2,560
5,120

The movement came to life. A couple of years later, my supervisor responded to my monthly report: "Steve, this sounds like the book of Acts!"

One of the Ina leaders approached me jumping up and down with excitement. He was the spokesman for the lunch work group.

Brother Steve, you'll never believe what we discovered! *[Continued jumping.]* As you know, we represent 80 Ina churches. *[Jumping.]* We can easily go back and train each of our 80 churches to start a new church in six months or less. In six months, before the harvest season, we'll have 160 churches! *[Him jumping. Me feigning ignorance.]*

That's not all! We can train all 80 **new** churches to start a new church in six months or less. And before the planting season six months later, we'll have 320 churches! *[Jumping higher; me feigning shock – though real shock is beginning to set in.]*

That's not all, every six months we can help the new churches to repeat the pattern so that every six months we double in number from 320 to 640 *[pointing to the numbers]* to 1,280 to 2,560 and finally to 5,120!

Now all the Ina in the room were jumping up and down, smiles on their faces. It was beginning to occur to me that the Spirit had finally opened their minds to understand church-planting movements and their part in them. Hope welled up in my heart that the Ina could indeed be reached in my lifetime. They really were grasping the idea that every new believer could be trained and expected to live out a lifestyle of witnessing and training other new believers.

I thought the presenter had finished but he had one more thing to share. In large writing he drew on the board a number and exclaimed in a loud voice:

$$3\frac{1}{2}$$

"Brother Steve, we are going to be finished in 3 ½ years!"

Now I **knew** that the vision of God's kingdom coming had caught on. Their spiritual DNA was becoming the kingdom DNA. They understood it. They owned it. "Spirit of God!" I prayed, "Empower them to fulfill this vision!" These Ina leaders became trainers who trained other believers who trained other new believers who kept repeating this generation by generation.

The movement came to life. Though the Ina fell short of their goal to reach all 5,000 villages in 3½ years, they began diligently moving toward that vision. Over the next three years the number of Ina churches more than doubled to 176. In the years since, the movement has hit many bumps and overcome many roadblocks, but today the Ina continue to plant new churches and recently sent out their first long-term international missionaries. What had begun as the vision of a foreign missionary was now being pursued by hundreds of Ina believers, prompting my missionary supervisor to say: "Steve, this sounds like the book of Acts!"

Indeed, it did. It was truly "God's kingdom come." It was a return to the original discipleship revolution—a *re*-revolution.

Enter and Discover

The spiritual principles that God is teaching us from the Kais' T4T movement and our own CPM experience among the Ina are now informing and enhancing the work of many other CPM missionaries and church leaders around the world. The King has many deep principles and practices to teach us from these church-planting movements – these discipleship *re*-revolutions – that can be applied in your own community.

Ying and I invite you to enter these pages and discover what those principles and practices are.

CHAPTER 2

It's Happening Again!

So then, those who had received his word were baptized; and that day there were added about three thousand souls. (Acts 2:41, NASB)

And the Lord was adding to their number day by day those who were being saved. (Acts 2:47, NASB)

Many of those who had heard the message believed; and the number of the men came to be about five thousand. (Acts 4:4, NASB)

And all the more believers in the Lord, multitudes of men and women, were constantly added to their number. (Acts 5:14, NASB)

Now at this time while the disciples were increasing in number . . . (Acts 6:1, NASB)

The word of God kept on spreading; and the number of the disciples continued to increase greatly in Jerusalem, and a great many of the priests were becoming obedient to the faith. (Acts 6:7, NASB)

So the church throughout all Judea and Galilee and Samaria enjoyed peace, being built up; and going on in the fear of the Lord and in the comfort of the Holy Spirit, it continued to increase. (Acts 9:31, NASB)

And the hand of the Lord was with them, and a large number who believed turned to the Lord. (Acts 11:21, NASB)

And the word of the Lord was being spread through the whole region. (Acts 13:49, NASB)

After they had preached the gospel to that city and had made many disciples, they returned to Lystra and to Iconium and to Antioch. (Acts 14:21, NASB)

So the churches were being strengthened in the faith, and were increasing in number daily. (Acts 16:5, NASB)

And he entered the synagogue and continued speaking out boldly for three months, reasoning and persuading them about the kingdom of God. But when some were becoming hardened and disobedient, speaking evil of the Way before the people, he withdrew from them and took away the disciples, reasoning daily in the school of Tyrannus. This took place for two years, so that all who lived in Asia heard the word of the Lord, both Jews and Greeks. (Acts 19:8-10, NASB)

So the word of the Lord was growing mightily and prevailing. (Acts 19:20, NASB) You see and hear that not only in Ephesus, but in almost all of Asia, this Paul has persuaded and turned away a considerable number of people, saying that gods made with hands are no gods at all. [Demetrius the idol maker] (Acts 19:26, NASB)

And he stayed two full years in his own rented quarters and was welcoming all who came to him, preaching the kingdom of God and teaching concerning the Lord Jesus Christ with all openness, **unhindered**. (Acts 28:30-31, NASB, emphasis added)

Discipleship Revolution

In the story of the *Acts of the Spirit of God*[3] through the apostles, Luke delights in showing the power of the kingdom of God breaking loose in previously unreached areas. Acts is the

---

[3] The title of Acts in the Greek is simply "Acts." It can be interpreted as the Acts of the Apostles. Or, as we study the theme of the book, perhaps it is more appropriate to call it the "Acts of the Spirit through the Apostles."

triumphant drama of the King's reign overcoming every obstacle it encounters in the provinces, cities and towns of the Roman Empire. Read the verses above and ponder the incredible growth of disciples and churches *in a span of twenty years*. The exclamation mark that Luke adds to the book is the very last word of the Greek text: "unhindered!"

Scholars of Acts agree: This movement took place in the power of the Holy Spirit through the lives of ordinary, months-old and even weeks-old believers as they were equipped by the apostles and other believers. A discipleship revolution ignited a firestorm of loving evangelistic zeal and fervent obedience that took the kingdom into the remotest corners of the known world in a period of years and decades, *not* centuries!

> This was the original discipleship revolution. Disciples of Jesus learning to live out the universal twin call to **1) follow Jesus and 2) fish for men** (Mark 1:17). Their love for their Master and desire to see His Name glorified in all the earth inspired them to sacrificial commitment that transformed daily life and interpersonal relationships.

Pliny, the governor of the *distant* province of Bithynia wrote to the emperor Trajan about 50 years later:

> I therefore postponed the investigation [of Christians] and hastened to consult you. For the matter seemed to me to warrant consulting you, especially because of the number involved. For many persons of every age, every rank, and also of both sexes are and will be endangered. For the contagion of this superstition has spread not only to the cities but also to the villages and farms. [Pliny, governor of Bithynia to Emperor Trajan about AD 111]

Pliny later noted that many of the pagan temples were almost deserted. A discipleship revolution shook the foundations of the empire and seeped into every crevice of society: rich-poor, young-old, urban-rural.

By the year 197 Tertullian, the early church apologist, wrote about the spread of the disciples to the Roman rulers:

> We are but of yesterday, and yet we have filled all the places
> that belong to you — cities, islands, forts, towns, exchanges,
> the military camps themselves, tribes, town councils, the
> palace, the senate, the market-place; we have left you nothing
> but your temples. (Tertullian's Plea for Allegiance A.2)

The discipleship revolution is magnificently depicted in
Ephesus in Acts 19.

- **Paul won a few:** Paul won a number of people to faith
  and began to disciple them (Acts 19:1-9). He spent about
  three months mainly in an evangelism role.

- **Paul trained them:** As opposition developed, Paul
  withdrew to a place where he could train the disciples
  in earnest without drawing too much persecution. He
  trained them regularly, perhaps even daily for some
  (Acts 19:9).

- **Movement spawned by new believers:** These
  disciples, ignited by their love for Jesus and filled with
  the Spirit, took this message to every city, town and
  village of the Roman province of Asia (Asia Minor – the
  western part of modern Turkey) over a two-year period
  of time so that **everyone** heard the Word of the Lord.

This took place for two years, so that all who lived in Asia heard
the word of the Lord, both Jews and Greeks. (Acts 19:10, NASB)

- **Training base for kingdom advance:** Paul used
  Ephesus as his training base for three years (the initial
  two years plus one more) while he sent out these new
  believers. *They* were the front-edge of the kingdom
  advance. This meant that Paul had to trust the Spirit's
  guidance in young believers. But his pattern since his
  first trip had been to allow the young believers to begin
  serving and leading at an early stage in the power of the
  Spirit (Acts 14:23).

- **From a pagan base:** This kingdom advance was not
  primarily through converted Jews. The great majority
  of these new disciples were as pagan as they come –
  idolatrous worshippers of Artemis (Acts 19:27) and

practitioners of magic (Acts 19:18-19). God performed this discipleship miracle with people who had huge barriers of false teaching, high levels of illiteracy, and strongholds of sin in their lives. This was not an "easy" field!

- **The vast majority of people who came to faith – thousands and thousands – were won to faith through the witness of fairly young Christians excited about their newfound faith.** This process of winning new believers and training them to witness to others who believed and witnessed to others cascaded out in ripples that touched the farthest reaches of the empire.

Truly new, yet rapidly maturing believers were reaching out to others in the model of 1) follow Jesus and 2) fish for men. Paul carried on the same pattern his Master Jesus had taught. He trained new believers to witness to others and train them, who witnessed to others and trained them – generation after generation after generation. In the process, they purposefully gathered new believers into new churches. In the book of Acts, disciples did not just receive what they had been taught. They also *passed on* what they had been taught. They became trainers of others. Each subsequent wave of new believers also trained others. It was based on their passion for Jesus and a desire to obey all His commands – including the Great Commission.

What occurred in Acts through the hands of the apostles and ordinary believers led by the Spirit of Jesus was nothing less than a *discipleship revolution.* It challenges our stereotypes of what God can do through ordinary believers. Throughout history that revolution has been repeated again and again. Today, we call such a discipleship revolution a *Church Planting Movement.* All over the world, the Spirit continues to spark discipleship revolutions. But since they are just a continuance of that first Acts revolution, it is more accurate to call them "re-revolutions!" As more and more missionaries, pastors, and lay people are learning how to position themselves in some of the kingdom principles from the Bible, the *re*-revolution is being repeated in almost every type of context imaginable.

Discipleship *Re*-Revolution

The T4T Movement: 1.7 Million Believers

To ignite the T4T movement described in the previous chapter God had to convict Ying Kai that an entirely different model of discipleship and church planting was needed than the one he knew and felt comfortable with.

Ying Kai was the son of a church planter and pastor from Taiwan. By the year 2000, Ying had already proven himself a successful church planter serving as a missionary in Hong Kong. Together Ying and his wife Grace had been able to start one new church every year, quite an accomplishment for a place like Hong Kong.

But now God was calling the Kais to a new assignment: 20 million lost people in a congested group of cities in Asia that was teeming with migrant workers, displaced farmers, crowded factories and wealthy investors. In a typical year, Ying and Grace reflected, they could lead 60-80 people to faith personally, but what good would that be among the millions of lost souls in this area? Their new assignment was of such magnitude, that ministry-as-usual would never be sufficient. How could they reach the millions who were flooding into the cities and factories of their area?

In October 2000, as Ying sat in CPM training, his eyes and mind were fixed on a poster on the wall that read: "How many of my people will hear the gospel today?" Ying knew that ministry as he had practiced it before was not adequate to win the millions of lost in this new assignment. Something had to change.

As Ying prayed and meditated, the Lord brought the words of the Great Commission to mind.

> Therefore go and make disciples of all nations, baptizing them in the name of the Father and of the Son and of the Holy Spirit, and **teaching them to obey everything** I have commanded you. And surely I am with you always, to the very end of the age. (Matt. 28:19-20, NIV, emphasis added)

The Lord gave Ying these insights:

- **Go, not come:** The Great Commission says we are to go, not invite people to come to us. We must go to where the lost are, and train the new believers to also go where the lost are. This was going to mean an ever-expanding wave of evangelism into factories, homes, shops and neighborhoods.

- **Everyone, not just some:** The verse says to make disciples of all, not just a few. We typically choose whom we want to share the gospel with. We try to pre-judge who might accept it. But God said to share with everyone. *We cannot predict who will accept the gospel and whom God will use to birth a movement.*

- **Make trainers (disciples), not just church members:** We are often satisfied if someone will believe and join our church. But the command Jesus gave us is so much more. He wants these new believers to be true disciples. And what do disciples do? Every disciple is to learn how to obey Jesus' commands, including witnessing to others and then training these new believers to repeat the process. Every disciple should be a trainer.

Ying and Grace began to see that, though their previous ministry had been good, it might also be the enemy of what was needed to reach the people to whom God had called them.

Ying and Grace entered their new assignment determined to see people in only one of two categories: **lost or saved**. If someone was lost, then Ying and Grace witnessed to them. If they were saved, then Ying and Grace offered to train them. As they met existing believers, they began to schedule times to train (disciple) them every week or two. Everything that Ying taught, he expected these trainees to reproduce by witnessing to numerous people and training those who believed.

Ying called this disciple-making process Training for Trainers (T4T). T4T trains believers to witness to the lost and then disciple them in a reproducible pattern that cascades out for generations. Trainers and disciples together hold one another accountable to witness to the lost and train new believers to form reproducing discipleship communities led by rapidly maturing leaders generation by generation. T4T is training trainers to train trainers to train trainers.

Over time, Ying and Grace were training groups of believers morning, afternoon and evening. In an average week, Ying and Grace might invest in 20 to 30 different groups. As the number of groups continued to grow, Ying and Grace began to meet with groups only once every two weeks. This enabled them to add another 20 to 30 groups on the second week of their training cycle.

As the Kais trained these believers to be trainers of trainers, they found that many would witness, some would start new groups, and a smaller number would go on to train their new group members to repeat the process. By living out this spiritual principle of training people to be trainers of others who would in turn train others, hundreds and then thousands began to come to faith according to the this biblical pattern:

> The things which you have heard from me in the presence of many witnesses, entrust these to faithful men who will be able to teach others also. (2 Tim. 2:2, NASB)

As mentioned in the first chapter, more than 1.7 million disciples have been baptized and formed into over 150,000 churches. Each month, some 2,000 new house churches and small groups are being started in villages, urban high-rises and factories among the people where Ying and Grace serve.

T4T is an all-inclusive process of training believers over the course of 12-18 months to witness to the lost and train new believers to form reproducing discipleship communities generation by generation. T4T truly is a discipleship *re-*revolution – a return to the original discipleship revolution of the New Testament.

In less than a decade, the ministry and insights derived from Ying and Grace's T4T training has influenced the ministry of thousands of co-laborers around the world. Many of the ministry tools and models you'll find in this book have been birthed in the crucible of their ministry.

Ina Breakthrough

As my family and I faced the challenge of reaching the remote, illiterate Ina people group, I began reading the book of Acts over and over again and contemplating the verses at the beginning of this chapter. I knew that the God I served was the same yesterday, today and always. I just knew there had to be a way for him to reach all 5,000 villages, but it would have to be very different than the way we had planted a church in Los Angeles.

Early on I heard an example of God birthing a CPM in an unreached area (pre-dating Ying's CPM). It sounded so Acts-like that immediately I knew in my spirit that this should be normative for our mission work. The Word said it and *now* I was hearing a real example of how it could happen again.

That story of a discipleship revolution taking place in Asia inspired me. Previously, I had had a fairly successful ministry in Los Angeles. But the good ministry tools *I already was comfortable with* threatened to become the enemy of *what was essential* to finish the task in my new people group. Something *different* was needed. I was learning that the shape of my ministry had to be dictated by the **end-vision** we were trying to get to, not by what we **enjoyed** doing or what brought personal fulfillment.

For 3 ½ years, my team and I labored with almost no fruit among the Ina, seeing only 1-2 new believers and no churches started. Yet we continued applying biblical CPM processes. We mobilized national partners and trained them to win the Ina to Jesus. We learned how to help ordinary new believers get excited about true discipleship – following Jesus and fishing for men – loving God above all else and loving others as themselves. We began to train them to not only start churches in their villages, but to cascade out to new villages and valleys to reproduce what they were learning. The new believers they won would then repeat the process.

Then, after 3 ½ years of no churches, we saw a breakthrough as 25 new churches were started in extremely remote villages. The next year the number grew to almost 80 churches. The next year the number grew to 176 churches despite fierce persecution that ravaged the churches. Their love for Jesus was stronger than their fear of man.

We were witnessing a discipleship *re*-revolution, a *recovery* of kingdom principles from the original revolution in Acts. We didn't know what to call the spiritual processes we were learning, but since it was simultaneous to Ying's movement, it became known as *TRT – Training Rural Trainers*. Every rural believer was trained to 1) follow Jesus and 2) fish for men, and then to train the next generation of believers to live this way, who trained the next generation of believers to live this way – several generations deep.

*T4T is not a silver bullet to give you a church-planting movement; **only a move of the Holy Spirit** can cause a CPM. But when understood and applied appropriately, the principles and tools of the training process can help you position your ministry to live out kingdom principles God delights in using.*

Nine Urban Church Planting Movements

Over the last few years, many people have been emulating the T4T process[4] of these discipleship *re*-revolutions. When they have understood the process and adapted it to their context, they have often seen significant growth in their ministry. Where believers have just copied the exact method without understanding the process or adapting it adequately, the results have been mixed or even dismal. **It is the process of training trainers, which must be understood and adapted appropriately for each cultural context that empowers believers to implement the kingdom principles of T4T.**

In 2009 we convened a meeting of practitioners from nine urban CPMs. The criterion for attending this summit was that the work in the city had to have at least 100 new churches at the level of at least the third generation. [Third generation

---

[4] Though many names and variations have been adapted around the world, in this book we will simply refer to the process as Training for Trainers (T4T).

means that the outsider (missionary) started the first church (1st generation) and trained them to start a new church (2nd generation) which then started a new church (3rd generation).]

Missionary church planters from nine cities in Asia gathered for the summit. Each of them was seeing significant numbers of conversions, baptisms and new church plants. Each had a process in place that would quickly disciple new believers, training them to witness, and then disciple the people they won to faith. In the process, they formed the new believers they were training into new churches.

They reported a number of common factors contributing to their success, but perhaps the most revealing was this: Each one of them had learned T4T, adapted it to their own context, and were training believers using the T4T process.

T4T is not a silver bullet to give you a church-planting movement; only a move of the Holy Spirit can do this. But when understood and applied appropriately, the principles and tools of the T4T training process can position your ministry to live out the kingdom principles God delights in using.

For these nine practitioners, it was a discipleship *re*-revolution echoing the great first-century urban movements in Ephesus, Corinth and Philippi.

Around the World

Middle East

In late 2005, a courageous missionary family working in the Muslim world attended a training that my colleague Bill Smith and I hosted. They were serving God in one of the darkest, most difficult places on earth in the heart of the Middle East. Over the course of six years of labor, they had started six small underground groups or house churches among Muslim-background believers. Most of the members of each church were members of the same family because of the security concerns. This is a country in which both missionaries and national believers have been martyred.

As the couple worked through the training, they wrestled with what needed to change in their ministry. By anyone's reckoning, they had already had a very good ministry. But again they recognized that good ministry can be the enemy of what is most essential – especially if the goal is for everyone having a chance to hear and respond. There were a number of lessons the couple applied in fresh ways to their work among Muslims.

A key lesson they learned was that they needed a training process that would empower any new believer to grow in discipleship, witness lovingly to others, then train new converts to do the same while starting new churches as a part of the process. They took the T4T process and wrote their own set of contextually appropriate evangelism and discipleship lessons.

Armed with a practical, culturally appropriate tool, kingdom principles to search for people of peace, strategic prayer and renewed vision, this family returned to their work. Then the discipleship *re*-revolution exploded. Over the next eight months they saw *50* new house churches started among new Muslim-background believers. In one stream of discipleship, they were able to track five generations of believers!

South Asia

As missionaries in South Asia began to learn about T4T, they wondered if this might work among Hindus and Muslims as well. Again, as they understood the process, they began to adapt the content to their own cultural contexts. From the tsunami-ravaged coast to the Himalayan mountains, they found that the T4T process became a foundational building block on which hundreds of churches resulted.

David Garrison, who formerly led the work of the IMB in this region, incorporated T4T into the basic training he recommended for any practitioner hoping to initiate church-planting movements reminiscent of the book of Acts.

Elsewhere

In the last decade, T4T has been taught on virtually every continent. One missionary in Japan said that he had **never** seen a Japanese believer win another Japanese person to the Lord. But the very next day, a colleague of his shared that he had been applying T4T in his community and had seen several generations of Japanese win friends and family to Christ!

Even in the U.S.! The status of decline in many American denominations and churches is alarming. Churches are reporting fewer and fewer baptisms and new church starts. But around the country there are signs that a *re*-revolution is brewing.

In Waco, Texas, a dynamic church is being used by God to birth a movement worldwide. Antioch Community Church has planted many churches in the USA and supports over 200 missionaries and church planters around the world through their ministry: Antioch Ministries International (AMI). By anyone's standard, AMI is a "success" in terms of authentic prayer and worship, radical obedience-based discipleship, fervent evangelism, living-on-the edge church planting and missions in very tough contexts. Yet, AMI became aware that the many good things could easily lull them into missing what is most critical in finishing the task of world evangelization. Over the last three years, AMI has been re-tooling teams overseas, throughout the US and at home in Waco to incorporate the T4T principles of this book.

The results have been very encouraging for them worldwide. The first year after re-tooling they saw more than 300 salvations in Waco alone. What is even more encouraging are the 2nd and 3rd generations of believers, groups and trainers arising from these adaptations of T4T. (See Chapter 9 for more details.)

In the 12 months leading up to the publication of this book another movement has been emerging in North Carolina using a T4T approach. A key CPM initiator has taken what he learned about the T4T process in Asia and now applied it to the Bible Belt of America. Starting from virtually nothing, the movement is currently seeing its third generation of groups forming with almost 40 T4T groups started in 12 months. The majority of the believers in these groups were previously non-believers and/or non-churched. (See Chapter 20 for more details.)

Come Journey with Us

Jesus taught His disciples not only to baptize but also "to obey everything I have commanded you" (Matt 28:20, NIV). In obedience to this Great Commission, each of us **must** have a way to witness, disciple, start groups or churches, develop leaders, and mobilize other believers to do the same. Otherwise our ministry is just theories that sometimes get implemented. T4T is not a magic solution, but it **does offer** a clear process that effectively applies many kingdom principles that too often get neglected. T4T implements New Testament kingdom principles that can:

- Mobilize existing Christians to live out God's calling on their lives

- Teach believers to witness appropriately as a lifestyle

- Disciple believers to grow in a genuine love relationship of obedience to Christ

- Start new small groups or churches (usually both)

- Develop maturing leaders quickly

- Cascade out into multiple generations of disciples and churches/groups

- Equip missionaries or church planters to appropriately phase out of leading the movement themselves and help the indigenous movement stand on the Spirit of God alone once the discipleship and training process has taken root

In this book, any adaptation of this basic process is called *Training for Trainers (T4T)*. Ying Kai and many other T4T practitioners specifically use the word "trainer" instead of "disciple" because there are so many preconceptions and misunderstandings associated with the English word "disciple" that hinder our understanding of the biblical mandate.

The New Testament Greek word for "disciple" is *mathetes* (μαθητης). It simply means a "learner" or student of a master. But Jesus strengthens the term to describe those who live out his teachings and follow his example:

[24]"A disciple is not above his teacher, nor a slave above his master. [25]It is enough for the disciple that he become like his teacher, and the slave like his master. If they have called the head of the house Beelzebul, how much more will they malign the members of his household!" (Matt. 10:24-25, NASB)

We should use any English term that describes the true essence of the original Greek and Hebrew languages of the Bible. In this case, we use the word "trainer" instead of "disciple" to denote that the follower of Jesus should be like his Master and emulate Him in all respects. Too often, our current understanding of the word "disciple" or the phrase "being discipled" connotes an idea of *receiving* not *giving*. Jesus taught His followers to pass on all they received:

Freely you received, freely give. (Matt. 10:8, NASB)

We hope the word "trainer" will give more of that original idea than the word "disciple" does at times. So, in this book we purposefully use the word "trainer" to convey the idea of someone who both grows in his loving obedience of Jesus and also passes on what he learns to others through his witness and training.

As Ying describes it, this is the difference between "teaching" and "training." Teaching conveys the idea of transferring knowledge, but training conveys the idea of changing behavior:

But prove yourselves doers of the word, and not merely hearers who delude themselves. (James 1:22, NASB)

It is doers of the word who generate a discipleship *re*-revolution.

An All-Inclusive Process

In ministry, many of us have a certain tool for evangelism, another for discipleship, maybe one for church planting or starting new groups, another for equipping leaders, etc. There is nothing wrong with that. What we have found with T4T, though, is that it can be an all-in-one process of accomplishing all of these things well. It helps bring all of these together in a balanced process that builds *sustained* church-planting movements. It helps believers to know what to do at each stage when people say "yes" – yes to listening to the gospel, yes to following Jesus, yes to baptism, yes to becoming church, yes to witnessing to others, etc.

T4T is not a set of lessons, though T4T does include lessons. T4T is not a six-week outreach, though it does include outreach. Instead, T4T is a comprehensive process of training believers over the course of 12-18 months to witness to the lost and train new believers to form reproducing discipleship communities generation by generation. As each generation emerges, believers are discipled, new groups or churches are started, and leaders are developed. T4T truly is a discipleship *re*-revolution – a return to the original discipleship revolution of the New Testament.

Perhaps you just need a slight adjustment for the next stage of kingdom advance. T4T may provide that 10 or 20% tweak that God will use to spark a movement. Perhaps you need a complete overhaul! No matter where you are between a tweak and an overhaul, T4T can help. It's amazing how over the years, decades, even centuries, kingdom DNA gets diluted and our expectations for a true movement of God wane. **What we all need is a discipleship *re*-revolution – a return to the original revolution!**

Come journey with us as we learn how to live this out together. To hear Ying's own story, read the next chapter.

Be a Doer, not just a Hearer!

T4T will call upon you to be more than just a hearer of the word. Take a minute to write down in the margin or back of this book how God has spoken to you and what you need to obey as a result.

CHAPTER 3

The T4T Story

By Ying Kai

[From Steve: This chapter is in Ying Kai's own words. Since Chinese is his first language, I have generally left the English as he spoke it with only slight edits.]

Personal History

My name is Ying Kai. My family was from China, but I grew up in Taiwan. My father was a pastor for 28 years, and he started 28 chapels (new church plants) in those 28 years. I learned a lot from him. I thought that his work was a very good model.

Like my father, I became a servant of God and attended seminary in Taiwan. In 1978 I moved to the US. At that time in my town in Texas, there were no Chinese churches, so I started a new Chinese church and began to pastor it. In the first year our congregation went from 0 to 100 people very quickly. In the second year there were over 200, and I was so happy. In the third year I said to my congregation, "Every year, we have 365 days, so you have that many opportunities. This year, I would like for each of you to lead one person to join our church. By the end of this year, our church will double in size." From 0 to 200 is very easy, but from 200 onwards is very hard. That year, 25-30 people joined our church. But we lost another 20 people. Some moved, some changed jobs, some just didn't like this pastor! So I was very sad that our church did not grow.

Serving Overseas

At the end of 1994, I became a missionary to Hong Kong. The first year I spent learning Cantonese. I was born in Taiwan, so my mother tongue is Mandarin, but Cantonese is so different.

Though I studied Cantonese and used it in my ministry, my Cantonese was not very good.

At that time in Hong Kong, the mission told all the missionaries that we needed to plant one new church at least every five years. In 1996, I started the first church plant. In the second year, I started a second church plant. In 1998, I started a third church plant. Every year I started one new church. I kept good records all during these years and discovered that every year my wife Grace and I could lead 40-60 people to the Lord and start a new church. I felt like this was pretty good. The mission said, "In five years, start one new church plant," but we were starting a new one every year.

In 1999 we took a yearlong furlough. When we came back, everything had already changed in our mission organization. We had a new regional leader. He came to Hong Kong and said, "Hong Kong has 147 Baptist churches, and they're already sending missionaries to other countries. Hong Kong doesn't need you anymore. In other places in Asia there are much greater needs."

He mentioned to us one nation[5] that was very opposed to mission work. But at that time, I didn't want to work there for many reasons.

A New Burden

So I stayed in Hong Kong. But in 2000, when we came back from the States, the first Sunday we were back, I went to my church. A member of the church asked us to consider going to that same country to share the gospel. He was a businessman who owned a factory there.

I responded, "No, I don't want to."

He said, "Why not?"

---

[5] For security reasons, the name of this country will not be used. The movement there has undergone great persecution and identifying this place in print could invite increased persecution.

I said, "I worry about the oppressive government there."

He said, "Today things are different. If you'd like, I'd love to take you and Grace to visit. You can try. If you listen, maybe God will talk to you."

After getting our visa, this businessman took us to the city where his factory was located. As we rode the train, we passed many factories. The man told us about every factory we passed. He would say, "This factory has 3,000 workers. I know the owner. He hopes that someone will come to share the gospel, but we cannot find anyone who will come." As we passed another, he would say "That factory has 10,000 workers." The biggest factory we passed has 70,000 people. When we saw all of the lost people of these factories, God opened our eyes and our minds. I realized, "These people need the gospel." So we went back to Hong Kong and prayed. After two weeks, we talked to our regional leader and said, "We've been considering transferring to work in that country." He said, "Okay, good. We've been waiting for this a very long time."

How many will hear?

At that time, I didn't know anything about this country, so people told me, "In one particular area, there are a lot of factories. The factory workers come from many different places across the country. In that area, there are several fast-growing cities all clustered nearby each other." So we asked to be the Strategy Coordinators (SC) for those three cities. A Strategy Coordinator is a person who oversees a CPM (church-planting movement) strategy to reach a people group or city. At that time, there were only 5.8 million local people in those cities, plus 15 million immigrant factory workers from other parts of the country – a total of 20 million people.

At the beginning of our ministry, we attended a four-week CPM training. In the training room, there was a sign on the wall with this question: "How many of my people will hear the gospel today?"

In our previous ministries Grace and I could lead 40-60 people to become Christians every year. Now, there were 20 million. How were we going to share with everyone? I did not know what to do for my CPM plan. At that time, it was very difficult for us, and our English was very limited, so we were very nervous. We didn't know what to do, so every night we prayed, and prayed, and prayed. At night, when everyone else went back to the hotel, we stayed to work, pray, and think. We would usually leave at around midnight. We looked at that sign ("How many of my people will hear the gospel today?") and prayed a lot asking God how we could help the people in our area to hear the gospel.

Jesus' Great Commission

Therefore go and make disciples of all nations, baptizing them in the name of the Father and of the Son and of the Holy Spirit, and **teaching them to obey everything** I have commanded you. And surely I am with you always, to the very end of the age. (Matt. 28:19-20, NIV, emphasis added)

Go, Not Come

Then we read Jesus' **Great Commission** in the Bible, and saw that Jesus had already given a battle plan for us. We didn't need another strategy. Jesus had already given the strategy. What was it? Jesus said, "Go!" Something stirred in my heart. Before, when I pastored the church, we said to people, "Welcome, our door is open." We prayed for people to come. But Jesus said, "Go!"

It is very difficult to invite people to come. People don't know what your church is; they don't know you. They don't know anything. It's very difficult to get people to come. But Jesus said, "Go!" I was wrong. Instead of inviting people to come, I needed to go out and find them, to touch them, to talk to them. I think the first key word is **GO**, not come.

Everybody, Not Just Some

What does Jesus say next? He says to go to all nations. That means everybody. But before, we always chose people. We would think, "This person is very ugly. Don't give anything to him. But this other person is very nice." We tend to choose who we think will respond to the gospel.

Jesus said, "Don't just choose some. Go to everybody." Jesus gave the example: one farmer went outside to sow the seeds. He is a farmer; he knows which soil is good and which is bad. But this farmer is very strange. He throws the seeds everywhere. Some of the soil is very shallow, some of the soil is very hard and some of the soil is choked with weeds. However, some of the land is good, and God multiplies the fruit 30, 60, and 100 times. Sowing the seed is our responsibility. Only the Holy Spirit can make the seeds grow. So don't miss any chance. Don't miss anybody. Even right now, the soil may not be good. But one day, God can change the soil; we never know. We can't miss any chance. The second word is **EVERYBODY**, not just some.

Make Trainers, Not Just Church Members

Third, what did Jesus invite His followers to become? Disciples. Not simply church members. A disciple must learn everything that his teacher teaches him. Then he needs to follow and to teach other people. My previous way of doing things was different. As a pastor, I had hoped for my congregation to double in size, but that's not what Jesus commanded. If you have many church members, you know that you only see some of your church members once a year. A lot of church members will try to find you if they are having a difficult time, but the rest of the year, you have little direct contact with them.

But this wasn't what Jesus had in mind. He wants every person to become His disciple. So go, share the gospel with everybody, and lead them to become disciples. Essentially Jesus said, "What I teach you, you need to teach them, and let them obey." Jesus teaches us to obey, then to teach the disciples to obey also. They must obey all the commands, including the Great Commission. Then Jesus said, "I will be with you until the end of the world." This is a promise. If we want God's promise, then first we need to obey Jesus' Great Commission. A disciple should be a trainer of others. So the third key word is **TRAINER**, not just a church member.

This stirred something in my heart, so in my CPM plan, I wrote, "I hope I can train every Christian or new believer to become a trainer." Even though my wife and I could only lead 40-60 people to faith every year, we could train the people that we led to faith, then they could lead 40-60 people to faith every year, too. Even if only half of them succeeded, it would still be a lot of conversions. So in my 3-year CPM plan, I put as my main goal: "We want to see 200 churches start and 18,000 people come to faith."

The First T4T Group

On November 1st, 2000 I went back to my assigned area, but I didn't know anyone there. But a Christian from a neighboring country introduced me to a pastor of a government-registered church in one of the cities in my area who was looking for a pastor to help train his congregation. So I visited the church, and the pastor said, "What do you want to teach us?"

At that time, I could not say church-planting movement because it carried a very negative political idea. So I said, "I'll teach you a fast way to share the gospel."

He said, "Oh, good!"

But as I thought about my CPM plan, I asked, "What is the population of your city?" He told me that the population was 618,000. Then I said, "How many districts?"

He said, "22 districts, and every district has 100 or 200 villages. Small villages have 30-40 families. Large villages have over 100 families."

Then I asked them, "Where can you share the gospel?"

"Oh, we obey the Great Commission, so we can share the gospel anywhere."

I said, "Okay, how do you share the gospel?"

He replied, "The church has many meeting points, and every member can have family Bible study groups in their homes."

I said, "Really?"

He exclaimed, "Yes! Why not? We can learn the Bible at home."

I said, "Good." When I heard that, I was very happy. I said, "We need to make a goal, an end-vision. In three years, I hope that every village will have a family Bible study [i.e. over 3,000 family Bible studies]." He and the other staff members looked at me as if to say, "That's impossible." After a lot of arguing and discussing, I said, "If you want to try it, I will show you a fast way to share the gospel."

But on that day, we were not able to resolve anything, and finally the pastor said, "Okay, you should go back home. I will let people register for your training. If enough people want to learn from you, I will call you so you can come."

I went home, not expecting much. But after two days, he called me. He said, "Right now, almost 30 people want to join your training class. Can you come this weekend?"

I said, "Yes, sure, we want to." So, that Friday night, Grace and I went over there. That was the middle of November. When we arrived, there was one person waiting outside the church. He said, "It's not in this church building. We will go to another church building, in the rural countryside. We will ride a motorcycle for one hour." So Grace and I took one motorcycle with him. Three people on one motorcycle for one hour. It was very tight!

The 60-member church was very small, only half the size of the other church. When we arrived there, around 6 p.m., there was only one person waiting outside the church, who said, "Not everyone has come back from the fields. We need to wait for them. Some of them are riding bikes, some of them are riding motorcycles, and some of them are walking. Maybe it will take 1½ hours, so we need to wait for them."

Why Christians Don't Share

Grace and I waited and prayed together until 8 p.m. Finally 30 people came. They were very excited. They were all farmers. Many of them hadn't even had dinner, but we hadn't had dinner, either. Thirty people had come, so I started to share with them. I told them, "Today, not all Christians can share the gospel. Why? There are **three reasons**. The first reason is '**why?**'" I began to explain *why* these existing believers should share the gospel. I cast vision to them using Jesus' **Great Commission** (see above). I told them, "Jesus commanded us to share the gospel." Everybody agreed with me. God was convicting their hearts about being witnesses.

The second reason is that we don't know **whom** to share with. There are many people, in our homes and outside, but we don't know *whom* we can start to share with." Therefore I gave everybody a piece of paper and said, "Close your eyes and think of people around you -- your family, your neighbors, your relatives, your friends -- every person you know who is not a Christian. Write down their names." I gave them about 15 minutes to write down the names. Most people had 20, 30, 40 names. One person had over 80 names. So, everyone made a Name List of family, friends, neighbors and co-workers that didn't know Jesus or weren't walking with God.

Then I told them, "Look at your Name List and pray. God wants you to share with everyone and you need to know how to start. After praying choose five people that you want to immediately share the gospel with. Put them in the first group. Choose another five people for the second group. Then choose another five for the third group. Now you have a target group. You can pray for them, and ask the Holy Spirit to prepare them and give them a hungry heart, so that when you share the gospel, they will listen and accept Jesus Christ."

The third problem is that we don't know **how** to share. I told them, "You may not know *how* to share, but it's very easy. It starts with your own story." I gave everyone another piece of paper, and I gave them my example. I said, "Your story is very easy. There are only three parts. The first part is what your life was like before Christ. Before you were a Christian, what was your life like? Were you very troubled or angry? You can write down what your life was like before Christ. The second part is how you became a Christian. The third part is what has happened in your life since you became a Christian. Do you have a joyful life or peaceful life? Write only one page; don't make it too long. If it's too long, people won't have the patience to listen. And be sure to tell your story in an interesting manner."

I gave them 15 minutes to write it down. After they were finished, I said, "Everybody stand up and look at your testimony. Don't listen to other people. Read it out loud five times." Everybody can write, but not everybody can talk smoothly when they are talking to other people. So I told them, "Speak loud; it is very important. If you say your story out loud five times you'll have it memorized, so that you don't have to take your paper with you. You want to have it memorized, not just written down. If you just read it, it cannot move people's hearts."

Then the 30 people stood and read their testimonies out loud five times. After this, I said, "Now, split up into groups of two, and tell it to each other. When you listen, you have a responsibility to tell your partner which parts you don't understand. If there is a part that he can make more interesting, help him revise it. Talk to each other."

When we finished it, they were very excited. By that time it was already 10 p.m. I told them, "Your testimony can move people's hearts. When people hear your testimony, some will say, 'Oh, that's good. I want what you have.' Still, they may not understand the truth; they may not understand salvation. You must immediately teach them what the gospel is. Only this will give them real assurance of salvation." I said to them, "I have six lessons that are very easy. After you share your testimony, you need to immediately teach them lesson one. Lesson one is the gospel."

Since it was already 10 p.m., I asked them, "Do you want to continue, or come back tomorrow morning?"

They said, "No, we want to continue! We are very excited. Out here, we never have any outsiders come to teach us." So we pressed on.

I gave everybody lesson one. It was only two pages. The first part is to teach a lost person, very clearly, how to gain eternal life through Jesus. That's very important. If you only give your testimony, that's just a story. They need to hear the gospel so that they can make a decision.

So I taught them the first part of the lesson very slowly and said, "Write down every sentence that I teach you. Even if I teach you examples, write down every sentence. Write down everything, and then I want you to teach it to other people this week." I tried to teach them using a very simple method.

After I taught them, I asked them to practice teaching each other the lesson. After they practiced, I made sure that they could all teach it to other people. Then I gave everyone five copies of lesson one. I said, "This week, when you go back home, find the five people from group one on your Name List. You can approach them at home, in the field, under a tree, in a restaurant, anywhere. Just share your testimony with them. After you share your testimony, immediately give them a copy of lesson one [the gospel] and teach it to them." Then I said to them, "One thing is very important. When you want to share your testimony, don't ask people for permission. Just start telling your story." Why? I explained my experience to them.

One Egg or Two?

During my time in America and Hong Kong, I worked in a hospital as a chaplain for over 20 years. Every time I visited the patients, they lay on their beds. When I would visit each patient I would say, "How are you today? Are you feeling better?" I would say "I am the hospital chaplain. I want to introduce the gospel to you." Or I would ask, "Do you know Jesus?" I was very gentle.

Most of the people that I visited were very nice. But when I mentioned the gospel or Jesus, they would say, "No, I am very tired" or "No, I don't want to listen" and then I could not continue. Once outside I would stop and update my records. Out of every 15 beds, only one or two persons would listen to my testimony. The other ones just did not want to listen. I did not have a chance. If they did not listen, how would they have a chance to accept the gospel?

One time I went back to visit Taiwan. Normally, when I was there I would buy a bowl of soy milk with a Chinese doughnut for breakfast. They would always ask me "Do you want an egg in it?" But the egg was 10 Taiwan dollars, so I did not want it! I was very careful with my money.

One time, I went to a different restaurant. As I placed my order, the owner, who was very busy, asked me, "One egg or two?!"

I said "Just one."

When I brought my bowl of soy milk to the table, Grace asked, "Why did you get an egg today?"

I said, "Oh! Today he did not ask me 'yes' or 'no' but just 'one' or 'two.' "So I said 'one!'"

So I watched this man, and he always asked people "one or two eggs?" Nobody told him 'no!' He was very smart! Suddenly God opened my mind and I thought, "Yes, I am sharing the gospel and it is a good thing. Why do I need to ask their permission? I need to just give it to them."

Jesus taught about a shepherd who had 100 sheep and lost one. He left the 99 to look for the lost one. The lost one belonged to him, right? So when he found the lost sheep, what did he say? "Little sheep, do you want to go home? May I introduce myself? I am the shepherd." No! He thought, "It is my sheep. I will take him back home!" Afterward, he was very happy. There was a celebration.

But when we share the gospel, we stand outside the door and ask, "Do you want to hear?" or "May I introduce you to the gospel?" If they do not answer, then the door is closed. No! Just bring them in! God created them, but they are lost. When you talk to a person, just tell him your story. Tell him: "Hey you do

HEAVENLY FATHER'S HEART
A Vision-casting Vignette

When Ying Kai was a young student in Taiwan, he worked hard to pass an important exam that would enable him to get into a good middle school. He really wanted a new bicycle to ride 30 minutes to the new school, but doubted he would get it since his family was so poor. One day, however, as he passed his parents' bedroom, he heard his father comment to his mother that he would buy a new bicycle for Ying. Ying was overjoyed. That night before bed, he asked his father for a new bicycle. But his father said "no!" Ying was perplexed but did not give up because he knew his father's heart! As he persisted, his father finally said "yes." The next day he had a new bicycle.

Ying says: "Because I knew my father's heart, I never gave up. If I didn't know his heart, I probably would have given up. So if we know our heavenly Father's heart, we will have

Continued next page.

not know me, but I used to be a very bad person." Everybody loves to hear a bad person's story!

So when I went back to the hospital, I would tell the patients, "Oh, you don't know what I was like before. I used to fight with my wife every day." Very few people said, "Oh, no, I don't want to hear it." They loved to hear it. They loved hearing gossip and bad stories.

Then I told them about when Jesus changed my life and about the kind of life I had now. Then I immediately gave them the first lesson about how to have assurance of salvation through believing in Jesus. Fewer people turned me down. I began to keep track in my records that for every 15 patients, eight or nine of them listened to my complete testimony and lesson one. So more people became Christians!

I told the 30 farmers, "Don't ask people. Just give your story. Then give them lesson one. It gives people a chance to hear about Jesus' love. That's very important."

When we finished I told them, "Next week, I will come back, and you will report to me and to one another what happened."

The Second Week

The next week, at the end of November, Grace and I came back to the church. Thank God! All 30 people came back.

In the beginning of the meeting, we sang, and prayed together. Then I had them share testimonies (reports for accountability). I asked them, "How many of you shared the gospel last week?" Only 11 people said "yes". Percentage-wise, that was not bad. But, honestly, I was a bit sad, because for me it was a new teaching, a new experience. I thought that everyone would obey Jesus' Great Commission. They loved to receive my teaching, everyone was very excited, but only 11 people shared the gospel. The other 19 didn't share anything. That was one of my first CPM lessons: not everyone will pass the training on.

Next I asked how many people they had shared the gospel with, and how many had believed in Jesus afterwards. One person said that he had shared with three, and one became a believer. Someone else had shared with five, and none of them became believers.

more confidence to do what He wants us to do."

All throughout the Bible, God chooses a person to save him and his whole household... Noah, Lot, Rahab, the Gerasene demoniac, Cornelius, Lydia and the Philippian jailer. [As Ying has time, he explains each of these Bible stories in detail.]

God chooses you to save you and all those who belong to you. This is your heavenly Father's heart. If you know His heart, then you will not give up asking Him for what is on His heart. The responsibility is yours – to witness to your own. Don't give up! God will eventually save many of them.

One old farmer shared with a lot of people. I can't remember how many, but 11 people had become Christians that week through his witness! He gave his testimony. He said, "I became a Christian over 20 years ago, but nobody taught me how to share the gospel. But after last week's training, I was very excited. So in my village, I knocked on every door. I shared with everybody, and 11 people became Christians." That was very encouraging to everybody.

From him, I discovered a truth: the Holy Spirit chooses the person, not us. If I chose, I wouldn't have chosen him – I might not have even trained him. He was old and not very handsome. His language was very hard to understand. But God chose him. That was another CPM lesson for me: we must train everyone.

Later on in the movement, this same man gave another testimony. Every morning, he got up at 5 a.m. and read the Bible. He had a devotion time for 2 hours. From 7 a.m. to 5 p.m., he worked in his field. At 5 p.m. he would go home, take a shower, and cook to take care of his very old mother. From 7 p.m. to midnight, he would lead four different groups in his town on different nights of the week. Later, in 2001, in that one year alone, he started over 110 small groups, and he became the official church minister of this registered church. I was very happy. Eventually, he became one of my big trainers. So, God chooses the person. We never know. Don't choose. Train everyone! Then let God choose.

During the first third of this second training session, after having them give reports in the accountability time, I cast vision to them one more time. I took a few minutes to share with them a vision-casting vignette called "Heavenly Father's Heart." I told them, "If you know the Heavenly Father's heart, you will have more confidence to share the gospel."

Then, in the second third of our meeting, I taught them lesson two on prayer. After I taught them lesson two, I asked them to practice in the final third of our meeting and to teach each other. Then I gave them homework. I said, "If, last week, you led three people to become Christians, go back to teach them lesson two. I am also giving five copies of lesson one for each new believer. You can give them these copies to help them win other people. Ask them to write down their testimony and their Name List, and ask them to immediately find five other people to share the gospel with."

In the beginning, that was my way. But later, I changed it and just let them make their own copies – as many as they needed so there would be no time lag in them training the new believers in lesson one. Later, as I learned more, I just told my trainers, "When you share the gospel by teaching them lesson one, immediately give the new believers several copies of lesson one to teach other people. Don't wait. The same day that they believe it is very easy for them to learn how to share with others. Take many copies of lesson one so that you will be ready to witness and then train them to witness. Don't be restrained because you lack materials."

After practicing lesson two, the 30 farmers set goals for people they would witness to and/or train. Then I prayed for them and sent them out.

Aftermath: A Pattern is Set

We started the first group of 30 people, in November 2000, and after three months, they were leading 27 small groups, and over 200 people had come to believe in Jesus! This moved my heart.

I thought to myself, "Before, every year, Grace and I led 40-60 people to Jesus. But right now, after three months, through those 30 people we have already led 200 people to faith. 200 new believers!" I thanked God.

In total, in the year 2001, that group of 30 people alone catalyzed the beginning of 906 small groups. They took the gospel to 17 different towns. There were a total of over 10,000 new believers. That was just one initial T4T group. It moved my heart. So I thought, "If you have the Holy Spirit with you, you can see miracles."

This group served as a model for how to begin the training for trainers process. Each day Grace and I would return to our area looking for two types of people: lost and saved. If they were lost, Grace and I witnessed to them. If they were saved, we offered to train them (including the people we had just led to faith).

In the beginning, with my early T4T groups, I would go back every week. For farmers it was okay, but I found that for people who were busy year-round, it might not be okay. Farmers are especially busy two times during the year. For 3-4 months out of the year, they have less to do. It's very easy for them to go out to share the gospel. But later, in the cities and factories, people did not have enough time to finish their witnessing assignment in just one week. They were too busy. So I began a pattern of coming back every two weeks.

That also gave me more time to train more groups. As time went by I trained more and more groups. Every day Grace and I trained three or four; one day we trained seven groups. But in one week, seven days, if I am training five groups in one day, I can only train 20 or 30 groups. But if I train them in two-week intervals, I can double the number of groups I train.

Later I found that God had prepared many persons of peace in different towns and villages. As time went by, we heard a lot of remarkable testimonies. In that year, there was a lady who was 67 years old when she became a Christian. In that year, she led over 46 families to become Christians — families, not individual people!

In another town, there was a man who was 26 years old. In two months, he led over 20 families to become Christians.

In another district, there was a lady working in a factory. Someone shared the gospel with her, and she received Jesus. On the second day, we went back, but we could not find her. After three weeks, she came back. Grace asked her, "Where have you been?"

She said, "The night someone shared with me, I cried the whole night because I had received Jesus. I thought, 'Who can share the gospel with my family?'" So the next day, she borrowed money, bought a ticket, and flew back to a city in another area of the country that is seen as less receptive. In three weeks, she led 26 people to Christ.

There was a young medical doctor who became a Christian, and her husband was against her. One day, she put a *Jesus Film* on the table. That day, the husband watched the movie, and it moved his heart. She led her husband to Christ. Also, in three months, her whole family, over 20 people, became Christians.

In another city, there was a factory with over 2,000 workers. There was a Christian in the factory. I trained him, and in one week, he started 19 groups. I did not think he could do that good of a job. But God is much greater than us. It's not what we're doing, because the Holy Spirit can work. I thank God.

There are many of those testimonies. I found that Jesus has already put many persons of peace everywhere. But if we hadn't shared the gospel with everyone, we would have lost them, because we would never have chosen them. You never know who God's chosen person is.

Each day I wake up and have an extended time on my knees in prayer. Then I enter my area to witness to the lost and train the saved. I use this T4T method, and God has already opened my heart. I am still learning, but I want to share with you what I have learned. I am so thrilled!

From Steve: Word, Works and Wineskins

The chapters that follow give a clear model for how to do our part in initiating CPMs using the T4T process. The lessons that follow have been adapted from what Ying implemented and the T4T applications of many others around the world. These lessons are based first on principles from the **Word** of God which are timeless and authoritative.

> [7]*The works of His hands are truth and justice;*
>   *All His **precepts** are sure.*
> [8]*They are **upheld forever and ever**;*
>   *They are performed in truth and uprightness.*
> [9]*He has sent redemption to His people;*
>   *He has ordained His covenant forever;*
>   *Holy and awesome is His name.*
> [10]*The fear of the LORD is the beginning of wisdom;*
>   ***A good understanding have all those who do His commandments;***
>   *His praise endures forever.* (Ps. 111:7-10, NASB, emphasis mine)

Secondly, the lessons are informed by what we are learning in the various **works** of God around the world in CPMs. By looking at the example of multiple CPM case studies, we see how men and women of God are applying God's Word in their context and how He is fulfilling His promises for a harvest.

> [2] *Great are the works of the LORD;*
>   *They are **studied** by all who delight in them.*
> [3] *Splendid and majestic is His work,*
>   *And His righteousness endures forever.*
> [4] *He has made His wonders **to be remembered**;*
>   *The LORD is gracious and compassionate.* (Ps. 111:2-4,
>   NASB, emphasis mine)

God designed His works to be studied and remembered by those who delight in Him. There are deep principles and practices in these case studies about how God initiates church-planting movements that can be applied in any setting.

Finally, various adaptations are suggested based on the flexible **wineskins** (methods and structures) of how people are adapting T4T effectively in their contexts (Matt. 9:17). You will need to adapt these applications to your own ministry so that the people in your community can obey the Word in a genuine manner.

Walk with us through the following pages to find out how you can position yourself for a movement of God in your community.

Be a Doer, not just a Hearer!

Write down how God has spoken to you and what you need to obey as a result:

CHAPTER 4

Why It's Working

A Theological-Scriptural Basis for CPMs and the T4T Process

Church-planting movements are emerging in a growing number of places around the world. T4T, as a best practices process for pursuing CPMs, has been adapted effectively in a wide range of contexts – from Asia to Africa, from literate to non-literate peoples, from Animists to Western societies. What is the reason behind this rapid increase in Spirit-empowered movements?

The very foundation for these CPMs is a return to some basic biblical principles of how God works and how we must cooperate with Him. Before diving in to the methodology of T4T, it is critical that you understand the kingdom framework within which it operates. These principles that sometimes seem mysterious and novel to us were the atmosphere within which the first century church lived. It was their spiritual DNA that drove them to the actions they pursued and the things they expected to happen when God's kingdom comes. Let's take a second look at the words of the King and His disciples.

Kingdom Kernels

Jesus' entire ministry was focused on initiating the kingdom of God. He used the word "kingdom" over 100 times, while He used the word "church" only twice. His first words in Mark were about the kingdom:

> The time is fulfilled, and the kingdom of God is at hand; repent and believe in the gospel. (Mark 1:15, NASB)

The word "repent" means to change your whole way of thinking.

Jesus was launching a kingdom so radical in nature that we must realign our whole concept of what God wants to do in and through us, especially in *how* He will do it.

Jesus' central prayer was about the kingdom:

> [9]Pray, then, in this way:
> "Our Father who is in heaven,
> Hallowed be Your name.
> [10]'Your kingdom come
> Your will be done,
> On earth as it is in heaven." (Matt. 6:9-10, NASB)

Jesus taught us to pray that our city, neighborhood, nation or people group will so reflect his glory and reign that it is like heaven on earth. **Does Jesus ask us to pray for something that He doesn't intend to fulfill?** God is not satisfied with a handful of believers, small groups or churches in a people group. *His* vision is a multitude of people worshipping Him from every people group.

His central mission was about the kingdom:

> This gospel of the kingdom shall be preached in the whole world as a testimony to all the nations, and then the end will come. (Matt. 24:14, NASB)

Everything in history is moving toward this final destination.

His final teaching in Acts was about the kingdom:

> To these He also presented Himself alive after His suffering, by many convincing proofs, appearing to them over a period of forty days and speaking of the things concerning the kingdom of God. (Acts 1:3, NASB)

Jesus' first and last words were about the reign of the King. They summed up His life mission.

The mission of the disciples in Acts was about the kingdom:

> But when they believed Philip preaching the good news about the kingdom of God and the name of Jesus Christ, they were being baptized, men and women alike. (Acts 8:12, NASB)

> After they had preached the gospel to that city and had made many disciples, they returned to Lystra and to Iconium and to Antioch, strengthening the souls of the disciples, encouraging them to continue in the faith, and saying, "Through many tribulations we must enter the kingdom of God." (Acts 14:21-22, NASB)

> And he entered the synagogue and continued speaking out boldly for three months, reasoning and persuading them about the kingdom of God. (Acts 19:8, NASB)

The closing words of Acts were about the kingdom:

> And he stayed two full years in his own rented quarters and was welcoming all who came to him, preaching the kingdom of God and teaching concerning the Lord Jesus Christ with all openness, unhindered. (Acts 28:30-31, NASB)

From the beginning to the end of Jesus' ministry His focus, both personally and through His disciples, was on the King's reign.

Jesus knew that if we could get the kingdom (King's reign) right, we would get church right. He taught us in the Lord's Prayer to plead with the Father that the kingdom would come so fully in our cities, neighborhoods and people groups that it would be just like heaven (Matt. 6:9-10).

But the King's ways are not intuitive, not what we naturally default to. *They are counter-intuitive.* That is, they are not naturally or intuitively understood by us because they are *spiritual* principles, not natural ones. We must be very purposeful if we would see the King's reign, not just the church's or the pastor's reign.

This was a startling discovery that Ying Kai had to come to in order for God to launch a movement through him. He came to the realization that his past "successful" ministry was

Jesus knew that if we could get the kingdom (King's reign) right, we would get church right. But the King's ways are not what we naturally default to. They are counter-intuitive. We must be very purposeful if we would see the King's reign, not just the church's or pastor's reign

inadequate to reach the masses of lost people in his area. He surrendered to learning a different way of cooperating with the Spirit of God to see Acts repeated in his context. All along the way he was surprised by how this would unfold and had to continually adapt himself to God's leading.

> If we do not understand the ways of the King's reign, we will not welcome it when it starts, nor fan its flames – and, we may even find ourselves opposing it!

The same thing occurred with me among the Ina. In the rapid movement of the kingdom there I found myself often questioning if we were on the right track biblically. Only by frequently reviewing the New Testament, especially the kingdom parables and Acts was I able to recognize the leading of the Spirit and cooperate with Him rather than quench His work.

If we do not understand the ways of the King's reign, we will not welcome it when it starts, nor fan its flames – and, we may even find ourselves opposing it!

Knowing that the ways of the King are counter-intuitive, Jesus painted many word pictures of the kingdom in the form of parables, starting most of them with "the kingdom of God is like...." Each is a *kernel* of truth about the overall mystery of the King's reign.

The good news is that God delights in revealing the truth of His kingdom to His followers when we come with open hearts and minds – like little babes:

> Jesus answered [His disciples], "To you it has been granted to know the **mysteries of the kingdom of heaven**, but to them it has not been granted . . . . But blessed are your eyes, because they see; and your ears, because they hear. (Matt. 13:11, 16, NASB, emphasis added)

Parables are a mystery to those outside, but to those who come like little children, God will disclose the mysterious nature of the kingdom. Surrender your pre-conceived ideas to Him and ask Him to speak afresh to you.

The Ways of the King's Reign from the Kingdom Kernels

In these few examples of the kingdom parables, ponder the counter-intuitive nature of kingdom movements.

Sower and the Soils

> [3]And He spoke many things to them in parables, saying, "Behold, the sower went out to sow; [4]and as he sowed, some seeds fell beside the road, and the birds came and ate them up. [5]Others fell on the rocky places, where they did not have much soil; and immediately they sprang up, because they had no depth of soil. [6]But when the sun had risen, they were scorched; and because they had no root, they withered away. [7]Others fell among the thorns, and the thorns came up and choked them out. [8]And others fell on the good soil and yielded a crop, some a hundredfold, some sixty, and some thirty. [9]He who has ears, let him hear."
>
> [18]Hear then the parable of the sower. [19]When anyone hears the word of the kingdom and does not understand it, the evil one comes and snatches away what has been sown in his heart. This is the one on whom seed was sown beside the road. [20]The one on whom seed was sown on the rocky places, this is the man who hears the word and immediately receives it with joy; [21]yet he has no firm root in himself, but is only temporary, and when affliction or persecution arises because of the word, immediately he falls away. [22]And the one on whom seed was sown among the thorns, this is the man who hears the word, and the worry of the world and the deceitfulness of wealth choke the word, and it becomes unfruitful. [23]And the one on whom seed was sown on the good soil, this is the man who hears the word and understands it; who indeed bears fruit and brings forth, some a hundredfold, some sixty, and some thirty. (Matt. 13:3-9, 18-23, NASB)

No matter how well you cast the seed of the gospel, there will be four types of responses. Though other responses initially look promising, only one type of soil is good and bears fruit. If we expect better results than Jesus, we are deluding ourselves. We must be prepared for both fruitful and non-fruitful responses.

That is normal.

It is impossible to predict where the good soil will be – only God knows. We only discover the good soil by sowing the gospel message to a lot of people! By contrast, the human way we intuitively use is to try to pre-determine who will be receptive and then focus all our energies there. The result is that we are often disappointed in the end. However when we find good-soil people, we will see their lives multiplied 30, 60 or even 100 times.

What application does this have for CPMs?

CPMs are birthed in the good-soil persons. We need methods that enable us to sow the gospel to a great number people, not pre-judging who will respond, so that we find the fruitful ones. We must not be distracted by the many who will respond but prove unfruitful.

Instead, in CPMs we need to spend most of our time discipling the fruitful obedient disciples. Only by investing in the small percentage of good-soil people will a multiplying movement emerge. Unfortunately, the intuitive way we often default to is to pre-judge who will respond (thus not sowing enough) and then spend most of our time with people who walk in disobedience and prove unfruitful. Such "intuitive" ways actually prevent us from cooperating with the King's work in the lives of people around us.

The Treasure Hidden in the Field and Pearl of Great Price

> [44]The kingdom of heaven is like a treasure hidden in the field, which a man found and hid again; and from joy over it he goes and sells all that he has and buys that field. [45]Again, the kingdom of heaven is like a merchant seeking fine pearls, [46]and upon finding one pearl of great value, he went and sold all that he had and bought it. (Matt. 13:44-46, NASB)

If we help non-believers discover the value of the King, not simply try to get them to make a decision, we will help them become fervent followers of Jesus. People often will joyfully give up all if we hold up the King appropriately. Kingdom movements are built on the shoulders of men and women who radically turn from their old ways and fervently follow Jesus because of their vision of Who He is. That's why CPMs can be a mile wide and a mile deep as we present the value of the King and help believers make a joy-filled radical commitment to Him. Such people will endure whatever persecution comes because they value the King even more than the loss of earthly life.

In CPMs, we must present the true value of the King and His claims, and then call people to total commitment to Him and His kingdom. Only by elevating the King can a movement start. We must press for *disciples* not simply *decisions*. That's what T4T attempts to do.

The Tares or Weeds

[24]Jesus presented another parable to them, saying, "The kingdom of heaven may be compared to a man who sowed good seed in his field. [25]But while his men were sleeping, his enemy came and sowed tares among the wheat, and went away. [26]But when the wheat sprouted and bore grain, then the tares became evident also. [27]The slaves of the landowner came and said to him, 'Sir, did you not sow good seed in your field? How then does it have tares?' [28]And he said to them, 'An enemy has done this!' The slaves said to him, 'Do you want us, then, to go and gather them up?' [29]But he said, 'No; for while you are gathering up the tares, you may uproot the wheat with them. [30]Allow both to grow together until the harvest; and in the time of the harvest I will say to the reapers, "First gather up the tares and bind them in bundles to burn them up; but gather the wheat into my barn."'"

[36]Then He left the crowds and went into the house And His disciples came to Him and said, "Explain to us the parable of the tares of the field." [37]And He said, "The one who sows the good seed is the Son of Man, [38]and the field is the world; and as for the good seed, these are the sons of the kingdom; and the tares are the sons of the evil one; [39]and the enemy who sowed them is the devil, and the harvest is the end of the age; and the reapers are angels. [40]So just as the tares are gathered up and burned with fire, so shall it be at the end of the age. [41]The Son of Man will send forth His angels, and they will gather out

of His kingdom all stumbling blocks, and those who commit lawlessness, [42]and will throw them into the furnace of fire; in that place there will be weeping and gnashing of teeth. [43]Then THE RIGHTEOUS WILL SHINE FORTH AS THE SUN in the kingdom of their Father. He who has ears, let him hear." (Matt. 13:24-30, 36-43, NASB)

No matter how well we sow, the enemy is fighting against us. Counterfeit followers will arise in any kingdom movement. That is normal (e.g. Judas). We should not be surprised when some fall away. There will be problems. But the fact that there will be problems should not distract us from planting and harvesting the good seed!

> Where no oxen are, the manger is clean,
> But much revenue comes by the strength of the ox.
> (Prov. 14:4, NASB)

T4T helps adjust our expectations of the problems that might develop when the kingdom of God begins to explode. It helps us not be blindsided when problems arise and second-guess ourselves.

The Seed Growing Quietly and the Mustard Seed / Leaven

[26]And He was saying, "The kingdom of God is like a man who casts seed upon the soil; [27]and he goes to bed at night and gets up by day, and the seed sprouts and grows--how, he himself does not know. [28]The soil produces crops by itself; first the blade, then the head, then the mature grain in the head. [29]But when the crop permits, he immediately puts in the sickle, because the harvest has come." (Mark 4:26-29, NASB)

[31]He presented another parable to them, saying, "The kingdom of heaven is like a mustard seed, which a man took and sowed in his field; [32]and this is smaller than all other seeds, but when it is full grown, it is larger than the garden plants and becomes a tree, so that THE BIRDS OF THE AIR come and NEST IN ITS BRANCHES." [33]He spoke another parable to them, "The kingdom of heaven is like leaven, which a woman took and hid in three pecks of flour until it was all leavened." (Matt. 13:31-33, NASB)

Large movements start from small beginnings. If we plant the right DNA of the kingdom, the growth of the kingdom is inevitable. It is critical that we get the beginnings right! This is why T4T focuses so heavily on the initial expectations for the new disciple.

For example, a common practice in the first few moments after a person comes to faith is to help him think through the implications of being a follower of Jesus and a fisher of men. Within minutes he receives encouragement to think about his lost family and friends and learn a way to witness to them (and eventually train them). From the moment of his salvation he is receiving a vision to be the mustard seed of a movement.

As T4T is implemented, it looks small in the beginning, but the exponential nature of the process means that before long it grows far beyond our human efforts.

The Two Sons

> [28]But what do you think? A man had two sons, and he came to the first and said, "Son, go work today in the vineyard." [29]And he answered, "I will not"; but afterward he regretted it and went. [30]The man came to the second and said the same thing; and he answered, "I will, sir"; but he did not go. [31]Which of the two did the will of his father? They said, "The first." Jesus said to them, "Truly I say to you that the tax collectors and prostitutes will get into the kingdom of God before you. [32]For John came to you in the way of righteousness and you did not believe him; but the tax collectors and prostitutes did believe him; and you, seeing this, did not even feel remorse afterward so as to believe him." (Matt. 21:28-32, NASB)

Obedience is the mark of true discipleship. Obedient disciples are not those who give verbal assent only, but actually obey what the Father commands. Ideally we want people who both "say" yes and "do" yes. But bottom-line, we are looking for people who "do" yes!

T4T is built on an obedience-based discipleship model. Disciples move on as they obey each lesson from Scripture. As they do "yes" at each stage, they move on to the next – from salvation to baptism to early discipleship to forming a church to leadership development and training others. Loving and mutual accountability is a foundational expectation in the T4T process.

The Scribe in the Kingdom

> And Jesus said to them, "Therefore every scribe who has become a disciple of the kingdom of heaven is like a head of a household, who brings out of his treasure things new and old." (Matt. 13:52, NASB)

A significant number of kingdom multipliers in the gospels and Acts were "religious" people who already knew the Scriptures but previously either didn't know Jesus or didn't understand the radical nature of the kingdom. Often the scribes and the Pharisees in the gospels were Jesus' main detractors. However, some understood the kingdom and became great allies in the kingdom advance.

> The word of God kept on spreading; and the number of the disciples continued to increase greatly in Jerusalem, and a great many of the priests were becoming obedient to the faith. (Acts 6:7, NASB)

When people like this come to understand the true nature of the King and his kingdom, they have a huge storehouse of Scripture that they can view through a new lens. Out of this storehouse they are able to mature rapidly and offer great resources.

T4T helps us not only start from scratch in winning new believers, but gives a practical process to mobilize existing believers with lots of Bible knowledge to live out the counter-intuitive ways of the kingdom. When they do, they can be great force-multipliers. Mobilizing and training existing Christians is a high value in CPMs all over the world.[6]

A number of the most fruitful people that Ying and Grace have trained in the T4T story were existing believers with a lot of Bible

---

[6] Virtually every CPM that I have studied has included significant mobilization and training of existing national believers – same culture as or near culture to the target people group.

knowledge but very little kingdom obedience. As the Kais lovingly challenged their biblical worldview, these believers have grown in fruitfulness. A great example is the old farmer from Ying's first group that had been a Christian for 20 years but became a CPM catalyst in his 21st year to lead many people to faith. Through his personal efforts and the new believers he trained, 110 new groups were started (he didn't start them all himself!).

This small sampling of kingdom kernels helps us re-think why and how we disciple followers of Jesus. In CPMs it is essential to splice into our discipleship the kind of New Testament DNA that will transform us into true kingdom organisms.

The Spirit as Attacker and Teacher

An important principle behind why CPM methods such as T4T are working is that they cooperate with the work of the Holy Spirit as *Attacker* and *Teacher*. Any ministry process is effective and lasting only as it helps a person abide in and cooperate with the Spirit of Jesus.

Abide in Me, and I in you. As the branch cannot bear fruit of itself unless it abides in the vine, so neither can you unless you abide in Me. . . . You did not choose Me but I chose you, and appointed you that you would go and bear fruit, and that your fruit would remain, so that whatever you ask of the Father in My name He may give to you. (John 15:4, 16, NASB)

> The Spirit of God is blowing throughout the world! He waits for us to align ourselves to move with Him. A key to seeing CPMs emerge is understanding and cooperating with two roles of the Spirit as Attacker and Teacher.

In the old days of sailing ships, when no wind was blowing, ships went nowhere. One thing sailors did in times of calm was to take every square inch of sailcloth and hang it from as many yardarms as possible. *They could not make the wind blow, but they could be ready for the wind when it did blow.* Failing to put up the sails would mean they were going nowhere even when the wind did blow.

John 3 describes the Spirit of God as a wind. We cannot make Him blow; He blows where He wills. We cannot create movements, only the Spirit of God can. But we *can* align ourselves, raise the sails of kingdom-oriented ministry, so that when the Spirit does blow, we are ready to move forward. T4T is a process that raises the types of ministry sails that can move with the blowing of God's Spirit.

The Spirit of God is blowing throughout the world! He waits for us to align ourselves to move with Him. A key to seeing CPMs emerge is understanding and cooperating with two roles of the Spirit.

Attacker – John 16:8

And He [the Holy Spirit], when He comes, will convict the world concerning sin and righteousness and judgment. (John 16:8, NASB)

Jesus makes it clear that one role of the Spirit is to convict.

The word for "convict" literally means to accuse, interrogate, harass or even attack. It is used to describe a lawyer attacking a person on the witness stand until he or she confesses guilt.

While you read these words, the Holy Spirit is out there all around your neighborhood, city or people group *attacking* lost people. He is doing three things:

1. He is showing them their *sin*.

2. He is creating a desire for a different kind of *righteousness*.

3. He is creating a longing to avoid the fear of death which is eternal *judgment*.

He is the attacker, not we. He is tearing down the objections of their minds and hearts.

Many of us go about evangelism assuming that we are the first to witness to someone. We aren't. The Spirit was there before us. Many of us assume we must pick up rocks before we can witness. We're wrong. We're never commanded to pick up rocks. That's the job of the Spirit – removing the obstacles of the hearts of people. Many of us assume it is our job to convict. It's not. There is only one Convictor. God Himself says . . .

> And I will give them one heart, and put a new spirit within them and I will take the heart of stone out of their flesh and give them a heart of flesh. (Ezek. 11:19, NASB)

coming New Year, I must go home to share with them."

As she was waiting for the train that would take her home, she suddenly felt something stir in her heart. She could not wait. She picked up her cell phone and called her parents. Once again, her father answered the phone. She said, "Dad, I still want to talk to you."

The dad said, "What do you want to talk to me about? About God?"

She said, "Yes."

Her father said, "Okay. I'm listening." The Holy Spirit had already prepared her father's heart. That day, she led her father to Christ. Her father was waiting for her when she arrived. He wanted her to share with the whole family. It's the Heavenly Father's heart. He is preparing people all around you!

Our job is not to attack, pick up rocks or convict. Too many evangelism methods major on helping us do what only God can do! When our evangelism focuses on that, we end up frustrated. Our job is to find the people the Spirit is already attacking![7] How much easier!

---

[7] I am in debt to my colleague Kevin Greeson for helping me understand this better. Kevin does a phenomenal job of sniffing out prepared people!

Have you ever been strolling along and smelled a coffee shop (while craving a cup of coffee) and then began sniffing out the smell until you found the shop? In the same way, our job is not to tear down the obstacles of people's hearts, but rather to *sniff out* those that the Spirit is attacking. We find them through witnessing to them. And when we find these prepared people ("persons of peace" Luke 10:6), they will eventually believe – usually sooner rather than later.

In every society the Spirit of God is preparing persons of peace. A person of peace is literally a "son of peace" like James and John were "sons of thunder" and Barnabas was a "son of encouragement". "Son of" indicates the characteristic of this person. Because the Spirit is preparing his heart, a person of peace is peaceful toward you and the kingdom. From the testimony of Matthew 10, Luke 10 and the book of Acts, a person of peace is a lost person who accepts you and your gospel message. He becomes a channel of evangelism to his network of relationships (family, friends, neighbors, co-workers). He may not accept your message immediately, but he does not reject it and is open to learning more and more. Within a reasonable time period, he does believe.[8]

T4T helps us sniff out these prepared people. Through training believers to witness to **many** family, friends, neighbors and even strangers, we find those God is preparing. We don't build relationships with just a few lost people and then months or years later finally reveal to them that we are believers and begin to share the gospel. If we do, we may find that the few people we've invested so much time in really aren't open to the gospel.

Rather we *use a gospel witness to filter our relationships,* looking for the people whom the Holy Spirit is *already* attacking. *Then* we build relationships with them as we guide them into the kingdom. We follow the path of least resistance that the Spirit has *already created* in the society we work in.

---

[8] Much of the interpretation of the person of peace and *oikos* passages in this book was first popularized by Dr. Thom Wolf. e.g. Thomas A. Wolf, "Oikos Evangelism: The Biblical Pattern", 110-117. In Win Arn (editor), *The Pastor's Church Growth Handbook.* Pasadena: Church Growth Press, 1979.

Teacher – John 14:26

> The Helper, the Holy Spirit, whom the Father will send in My name, He will teach you all things, and bring to your remembrance all that I said to you. (John 14:26, NASB)

> As for you, the anointing which you received from Him abides in you, and you have no need for anyone to teach you; but as His anointing teaches you about all things, and is true and is not a lie, and just as it has taught you, you abide in Him. (1 Jn. 2:27, NASB)

A second role of the Spirit is that of Helper or Teacher. Unfortunately, much of the discipleship methodology people use depends heavily on them being the teacher, discipler or trainer. They assume this pattern from looking at the life of Christ who spent so much time with the twelve apostles. This model of discipleship is elevated over Paul's model of discipleship. *Unfortunately, this means that many people are using a **pre**-Pentecost rather than a **post**-Pentecost model.*

Jesus' discipleship depended on his own *physical* presence with the disciples because they had not yet received the Spirit! Many of our current discipleship models *overly* depend on our frequent and continued physical presence with our new disciples. When we are not there or when we finally exit the group, they struggle and sometimes stop meeting.

But this neglects a critical teaching about the Spirit. After the Spirit has come, our physical presence is not nearly as essential. Personal involvement is *not unimportant.* But we need a discipleship process more akin to post-Pentecost that depends less on human intervention. It is a model that takes the great risk of depending on the presence of the Spirit in the life of the new believer. This is the essential nature of the priesthood of the believer.

Paul the apostle provides a good example of a post-Pentecost discipleship model. Jesus intensely discipled only 12, probably because the Spirit had not been given yet. However, post-Pentecost, because every new believer had the indwelling Spirit, disciples could mature much more rapidly and pass on this discipleship to others more quickly. Paul gives us a clear example of moving from place to place – sometimes staying in a place for only days or weeks. Yet he left behind maturing, spreading, multiplying groups of believers. How? He trusted the Spirit to be their Teacher, not Paul (or Cephas or Apollos – 1 Cor. 1:12; 3:4-7).

This does not mean that Paul did not teach. But he taught new believers how to *listen* to the Spirit of God, apply the Scripture and grow in faith without Paul's continued presence. Paul re-visited, wrote letters and sent colleagues to help. Nevertheless, they grew rapidly in his absence because they had learned to rely on the presence of the Spirit.

Any discipleship program that creates a dependence on the human teacher rather than the ever-present Teacher of the Spirit is doomed to plodding human-dependent growth. In contrast CPMs are centered on enabling all believers to rely on the Spirit of God in fulfilling God's purposes and His calling on their life. Specifically T4T is a process of helping disciples depend on the Spirit as their Teacher. When you do that, you will find that they can mature more rapidly than you thought, and minister sooner than you expected. In fact, most fruitful-soil disciples will begin witnessing and serving within hours and days rather than months or years.

As you read the T4T story in the previous chapter, it becomes apparent that the Kais' daily practice of witnessing to the lost and training the saved aligned them with kingdom realities. By seeing the world in a clear spiritual dichotomy – lost and saved – the Kais cooperated with these twin roles of the Spirit: 1) Finding those whom the Spirit is attacking by witnessing to many and 2) training the saved to rely on the Spirit as Teacher so that they can obey all they learn and pass it on to others.

Turning Discipleship Maturity on its Head

[11]And He gave some as apostles, and some as prophets, and some as evangelists, and some as pastors and teachers, [12]for the equipping of the saints for the work of service, to the building up of the body of Christ; [13]until we all attain to the unity of the faith, and of the knowledge of the Son of God, to a mature man,

to the measure of the stature which belongs to the fullness of Christ. [14]As a result, we are no longer to be children, tossed here and there by waves and carried about by every wind of doctrine, by the trickery of men, by craftiness in deceitful scheming; [15]but speaking the truth in love, we are to grow up in all aspects into Him who is the head, even Christ, [16]from whom the whole body, being fitted and held together by what every joint supplies, according to the proper working of each individual part, causes the growth of the body for the building up of itself in love. (Eph. 4:11-16, NASB)

Obedience-based versus Knowledge-based Maturity

Eph. 4:11-16 turns our understanding of how disciples mature on its head and explains one aspect of why CPMs work. In some Christian ministry, we assess how mature a believer is based on *how much he knows*. But the New Testament assesses the maturity of a believer based on *how much he obeys* (e.g. John 14:15; James 1:22-25)

Think about every sermon, Bible study and Bible passage you have heard or read (knowledge). Estimate what percentage of that you *consistently obey*. It can be a bit embarrassing. You may say, "I consistently obey about 30% of all I know." In a knowledge-based assessment of maturity, can we be comfortable with disobeying 70% of all we know. Is that really biblical maturity?

> *In some Christian ministry, we assess how mature a believer is based on **how much he knows**. But the New Testament assesses the maturity of a believer based on **how much he obeys!***

If one has been a believer a long time he may have lots of knowledge, but may also have a low obedience factor. Despite his knowledge-based "maturity," his disobedience factor is high!

In contrast, a newer believer in a CPM may not know as much of the Bible as the knowledge-based disciple, yet his value is to obey everything he knows. He consistently obeys 90% of all he hears from God's Word. His disobedience factor is only 10%.

Which one is really more mature? CPMs emphasize a process of helping believers obey all they know, and therein is true maturity.

The Maturing Progression – Believe-Serve-Mature

In knowledge-based discipleship, we *delay* how quickly a new believer can serve or lead based on how much he *knows.* Knowledge-based maturity follows a progression of "believe – mature – serve." In this knowledge-based model, when people come to faith, they are put through discipleship classes and generally not entrusted with much responsibility. Their basic maturation process often extends over years. Many churches and ministries don't let them take responsibility until they have "matured" to a certain point.

Ephesians 4:11-16 teaches a radically different order. In verse 11 leaders are given to the church. In verse 12 they equip God's people (to know Christ, serve, etc.). In verse 12, God's people serve or do the work of ministry. In verses 12-13, the result is that they and the body mature through this process. The biblical progression of maturity is . . .

- NOT "believe – mature – serve"

- BUT RATHER "believe – serve – mature"

In the New Testament, believers matured *BY* serving. T4T follows this same New Testament pattern. Instead of holding new believers back from serving and leading until they mature, we help them mature BY serving in appropriate ways and eventually leading as they prove faithful! It is obedience-based discipleship. In CPMs, the basic maturation process is much faster than a knowledge-based model.

As you will see in the following pages, the Kais have seen a rapid maturing process at work in new believers because they train them to love and serve God immediately. Those of us close to this movement have been amazed at how quickly solid leaders have developed in such a young movement. It's because they follow the believe-serve-mature progression of Scripture.

Can T4T Work Where I Am?

Still lingering in your mind may be this question: "But can this happen where I am? My situation is different."

If T4T were only bearing fruit in a few similar contexts, we might be tempted to say "no." But all over the world, CPMs are emerging, and T4T is playing a huge role in many of them. We can no longer use the uniqueness of our situation as an excuse that T4T (adapted to be culturally appropriate) cannot work where we are.

There is a theological reason behind this: **the harvest is ready!**

In John 4, Jesus chided His disciples for missing a harvestable person (the woman at the well). They, too, had an excuse:

> Do you not say, 'There are yet four months, and then comes the harvest'? Behold, I say to you, lift up your eyes and look on the fields, that they are white for harvest. (John 4:35, NASB)

Perhaps, the wheat fields that Jesus was pointing to were *green*. Each of the disciples knew it would take four more months of maturing before they would be ready to harvest. But Jesus used that agricultural analogy to describe a heart attitude of the disciples. While Jesus sat at the well, tired from traveling, whom did the disciples pass on the road to the Samaritan village? In all likelihood, they passed the woman coming to the well. They missed her, while Jesus found her. Their circumstances were identical. Twelve found a field that was not yet ripe, while One found a field ready for harvest.

Today, many people approach their fields of ministry *assuming* that it will take a certain number of months or years before people are ready to believe. Others, however, believe that their fields are ready now. Their eyes have been opened to realize that the Spirit has *already* prepared some people in these fields for harvest.

Does this mean that all fields will yield the same harvest? Absolutely not! There is no doubt that the conditions of the field in which Ying Kai has seen over 1.7 million come to faith are incredibly ripe. However, another person without harvest-eyes might have missed even this fruitful field.

All fields do not yield the same harvest, but all *are* harvestable. You must believe this not because of the nature of your context, but rather because of the nature of your God! Your field may not yield 1.7 million believers but it will bear fruit as you labor in kingdom ways, and this will be fruit that multiplies.

Does this mean that there are no hard, resistant people groups or contexts? Absolutely not! There are many highly resistant groups, be they Hindu, Muslim, Buddhist, atheist, post-modern, post-Christian, etc. Do we belittle the difficulty of these places when we say the harvest is ready?

All fields do not yield the same harvest, but all are harvestable. You must believe that not because of the nature of your context, but rather because of the nature of your God! Hardened nations still contain harvestable individuals!

As Jesus went about proclaiming the gospel, he made a radical statement:

[35]Jesus was going through all the cities and villages, teaching in their synagogues and **proclaiming the gospel of the kingdom**, and healing every kind of disease and every kind of sickness. [36]Seeing the people, He felt compassion for them, because they were distressed and dispirited like sheep without a shepherd. [37]Then He said to His disciples, "**The harvest is plentiful,** but the workers are few. [38]Therefore beseech the Lord of the harvest to send out workers into His harvest." (John 4:35-38, NASB, emphasis added)

The harvest is not only ready, but it is also plentiful! In light of this situation, Jesus sent out the twelve on their first mission. What people group was Jesus describing when He made this statement? Jews.

But what did Paul say about his beloved Jews?

For I do not want you, brethren, to be uninformed of this mystery–so that you will not be wise in your own estimation–

that a partial **hardening** has happened to Israel until the fullness of the Gentiles has come in. (Rom. 11:25, NASB, emphasis added)

The very same people group is described in two ways: harvestable and hardened! Do you serve in a tough nation, city, neighborhood or people group? That does not negate the fact that there is still a *plentiful* harvest waiting for you *now* (as opposed to a generation from now).

Hard nations contain harvestable individuals! There may be hardened people groups, but in every one there are harvestable individuals! You may have to work harder to find the harvest, but it is there. In some contexts, perhaps one out of every ten or twenty lost people is a prepared person of peace (Luke 10:6), while in other contexts it could be one out of a hundred or thousand. You just have to work harder to find the first persons of peace.

But after you have found the Spirit-prepared person of peace, the movement can be just as explosive! Don't forget the movement we described in the Middle East in chapter two – a hardened people if ever there was one, and yet they are now seeing a harvest.

T4T helps you operate under kingdom expectations that the harvest is ready now. T4T helps you find the harvest.

Just a Tool

These are just a few of the spiritual principles behind why CPMs develop and how T4T as a model works. Many more will be uncovered in coming chapters. T4T is a spiritual PROCESS of training disciples to train others to train others.

Even so, it is still only a practical application of a spiritual process. Therefore, it is not sacred. The spiritual principles it tries to follow are.

This book seeks to help you understand the kingdom principles and then give you a practical way to implement them. We encourage you to *adapt* the tool, but not to *violate* the kingdom principles. We pray that implementing a culturally appropriate model of training trainers will be liberating for you and result in a movement of God's kingdom around you!

The pages that follow give you a detailed idea of how to start down the T4T journey adapting it for your own context. Come discover the mysterious ways of the King! Become a disciple-making *re*-revolutionary!

Be a Doer, not just a Hearer!

Write down how God has spoken to you and what you need to obey as a result:

Part Two
THE PROCESS OF T4T

CHAPTER 5

How to Begin — Session One

How T4T works and what to do in Session One

T4T is a Process

Say it out loud with me three times: "T4T is a process, not a set of lessons!"

As Training for Trainers has spread around the world, we have found that this is the most misunderstood aspect of T4T. Many people think that T4T is a six-lesson discipleship program that will somehow result in CPMs – or that is how they hear it presented. They say: "I finished T4T [meaning six lessons]. Now what?"

T4T is an on-going disciple-making process that we don't just "finish" in a few weeks. It cascades generation by generation, and the challenges we have at each new stage are still a part of the T4T process. It includes good biblical content but is wrapped up in a dynamic, life-on-life, loving process of following Jesus and fishing for men.

Part of the misconception about T4T probably developed over time as those of us close to Ying's movement learned about what he was doing. When we asked Ying about the phenomenal growth in his region, a few things began to emerge.

One of the first things to emerge was that he had six basic lessons for discipleship. In the beginning, some people tried to implement T4T by only teaching six lessons and failed to see much fruit.

As more time went by we learned that Ying encourages every new believer to witness five times a week. So now T4T was "witness to five people a week and pass on the six lessons." This got varying degrees of results by early adopters of T4T.

As more time went by, we saw that Ying also had frequent training retreats for leaders. Some people tried to incorporate the leadership training events with varying levels of success.

Then it became apparent that Ying had a long-term discipleship aspect to training, using inductive studies in Mark after he finished the basic discipleship lessons. So many T4T adopters began to do Mark studies.

In fact, T4T is an all-in-one process that God uses to take a person from lostness to maturing disciple who can start new groups and train others to reproduce the process.

God's heart is for bringing in a harvest. He is looking for workers who are willing.

> Then He said to His disciples, "The harvest is plentiful, but the workers are few. Therefore beseech the Lord of the harvest to send out workers into His harvest." (Matt. 9:37-38, NASB)

The problem throughout history has never been with God — He is willing, passionate for His people to be reached. The problem is not the harvest — the Spirit is doing His part to prepare a harvest even among hard peoples. The problem is with us.

The problem throughout history has never been with God – He is willing, passionate for His people to be reached. The problem is not with the harvest—the Spirit is doing His part to prepare a harvest even among hard peoples. The problem is with us—we need to recapture the first-century discipleship revolution that turned the world upside down. We need a discipleship *re*-revolution.

God desires to spark CPMs all over the world. CPMs are His work. But He waits for cooperating servants. We don't have to convince God that we want a harvest. He has to convince us. The T4T process is a very effective way to help God's servants cooperate with *the way His Spirit works.*

The All-in-One CPM Process of T4T

But what do you think? A man had two sons, and he came to the first and said, "Son, go work today in the vineyard." And he answered, "I will not"; but afterward he regretted it and went. The man came to the second and said the same thing; and he answered, "I will, sir"; but he did not go. Which of the two did the will of his father? They said, "The first." (Matt. 21:28-31, NASB)

Prior to 2003, many CPM practitioners tried to accomplish the basic elements of a CPM plan through an assortment of means. We all had a method for evangelism, a different method for discipleship, a different one for planting churches, a different one for leadership development, etc. We often tried to piece them all together, but new believers didn't naturally know how to flow from one stage to the next. It took a lot of coaching to move the CPM from one stage to the next.

As T4T reports began to surface in 2004 and 2005, we originally thought it was just an evangelism tool. But we couldn't understand why it was seeing such growth in new believers and churches. Then we realized that it was also a discipleship tool. As we examined it further, we realized it was also a church-planting tool and a leadership development tool. In fact, T4T was accomplishing all the basic parts of a CPM plan well, developing new believers from one stage to the next as they were being discipled/trained and gathered into reproducing churches.

Gradually we came to understand that T4T was more than just a multi-purpose tool, like a Swiss Army knife. Rather, it was a *process* that moves the disciple from saying "yes" to doing "yes." The T4T process gives these disciples confidence and competence to move from one stage to the next.

What T4T has done for many CPM practitioners is to tie together all the basic parts of a CPM plan well, and **enable believers to naturally progress from one stage to the next as they are trained: evangelism, discipleship, church planting,** *leadership development -- repeating the process generation by generation.* When the results consistently generate 4th+ generation disciples and new churches in several places in a short period of time, then a sustained church-planting movement has emerged.[9]

As you read in Chapter 1, in one CPM assessment done of Ying's work, we discovered 18 generations of believers represented in one survey of church leaders! The training and patterns at the 18th generation were still strong and clear.

T4T is a **process** of how to disciple and train believers who are willing to truly mean "yes" at each stage. The **content** of lessons that you will need in your context will vary depending on many factors. The content is the most adaptable part of T4T.

When people ask me to "send them T4T," I cringe. What they are looking for is content, but they may completely miss the **process** of training trainers. The process must take people from lostness to 4th+ generation believers and churches. It's not simple discipleship. It's a discipleship *re*-revolution that leads to church-planting movements!

T4T's Goal: Build Multiplying Generations of Trainers

True disciples are followers of Jesus AND fishers of men (Mark 1:17). Jesus wants disciples who love God with all their being and others as much as themselves, passionately pursuing the Great Commission. As we have seen, the best term for this type of disciple is "trainer" because it carries with it the idea of passing on what one receives (Matt. 10:8).

As you implement T4T, many questions will arise in the week-by-week craziness of a budding movement. Nothing will go exactly according to plan because we are dealing with real, fallen human beings, because we have an enemy fighting against

---

[9] For a thorough explanation of how T4T fulfills the basic parts of a CPM plan, see "The Basic CPM Plan and T4T" in the "T4T Supplemental Materials" on the website www.T4TOnline.org.

us (remember the parable of the tares), and because we are subject to the sovereignty of God.

Most of the questions you face can be answered by remembering the goal: **To build multiplying generations of trainers.**

- Question: "How long should I continue training a group?"

  » Answer: "How long do you need to stay to initiate multiple generations of trainers?

- Question: "What should I do if someone I am training brings a new believer to my group rather than starting his own?"

  » Answer: "What will it take to help him have confidence to start his own group and become a trainer of trainers?"

- Question: "Should I repeat a lesson on sharing the gospel?"

  » Answer: "What is necessary for them to become effective witnesses and eventually trainers of trainers?"

- Question: "How much time do I need to give the group to practice the lesson each week?"

  » Answer: "How much time is required for your trainees to become **confident** and **competent** trainers of others?"

Keep the goal in mind and it will help you answer most questions. *You are trying to build a movement of confident and competent trainers who can pass on the DNA from generation to generation.*

Most of your questions can be answered by remembering the goal: *To build multiplying generations of trainers.*

2 Timothy 2:2 Process

And the things you have heard me say in the presence of many witnesses entrust to reliable men who will also be qualified to teach others. (2 Tim. 2:2, NASB)

2 Timothy 2:2 encourages multi-generational growth of trainers. The Great Commission itself commands us to teach others to obey all that Jesus commanded (which includes the Great Commission). Every generation is to be a training generation.

The T4T process is the expectation that every person trained will in turn witness to others and train them in all he has been trained in, who will in turn witness to others and train them in what they have been trained in, etc. To begin that process, trainees are taught to witness regularly, mainly to their *oikos* (Greek word for "household" meaning your circle of influence). Your *oikos* is composed of family, friends, neighbors and co-workers. After people believe, trainees then begin to form training groups (whether just two people or 20 people) in which they pass on to the new trainees what they have learned. They train this next generation to become trainers by witnessing regularly to their own *oikos* and forming other training groups in which they pass on what they have learned, in order to help the next generation become trainers.

> Your *oikos* is composed of family, friends, neighbors and co-workers.

What I describe in this chapter is T4T "Classic." It is T4T as originally developed by Ying Kai and most often applied. In later chapters, I will explain how others have taken the T4T process and adapted the content for their own contexts

What to do in the First Session

How does the T4T process start? T4T training is always about training **believers** to witness, make disciples and start churches. But finding believers to train happens in two ways:

- Sometimes it starts when you win one person or a group of people to faith. At that point, three things are very important for them to know – why, whom, how. You do that in the first session of T4T training. With a new believer, this most often happens as soon as he believes.

- Sometimes T4T starts when you find existing believers and cast vision to them. They agree to be trained. In that first session, they also need to know three things – why, whom, how.

You can start with new believers or existing Christians, but the way you begin the T4T process is essentially the same. In the first session of T4T, whether with new believers or existing believers, you have to deal with three reasons Christians don't witness just like Ying did with his first group of farmers.

Session One: WHY-WHOM-HOW

With every group of believers, there are three common reasons why they don't witness.

WHY? Cast Vision

Especially with existing Christians, there can be a motivation problem: "Why should I begin witnessing, or become bolder?" To overcome this, you have to *cast vision* of the life God has created for them – to be followers of Jesus and fishers of men. As an example of this, you remember the vision-casting vignette called the "Great Commission" that Ying shared in Chapter 3.

- **Review**: the Great Commission teaches all believers three things:

  » Go, not come

  » Share with everybody, not just some

  » Make trainers, not simply church members

You begin to give them a vision for their circle of influence and beyond: "What has God saved you for? Do you realize that He not only wants to reach you, but also to reach your whole

JESUS' GREAT COMMISSION

A Vision-casting Vignette

The section here called "Jesus' Great Commission" is not only what God used to change Ying's approach to ministry. It is also the first vignette he uses to cast vision to a new group of believers in his first training session.

You, too, can use this to cast vision. Here is a short outline of the vignette:

Jesus' Great Commission commands us to do three things...

1. Go, not come – we must go where the lost people are.

2. Everybody, not just some – share with everyone because you never know whom God will choose.

3. Make trainers, not just church members – train every believer to obey what he learns AND pass it on (be a trainer).

Continued next page.

household through you?" In Session One, you must cast vision for why the disciples should walk down this revolutionary path.

In the early days of trying to reach the remote Ina, I traveled many places trying to mobilize national believers to go into distant valleys to plant the first "seed" churches. One day, I discovered that a small tribe within the Ina had been reached by missionaries 60 years earlier. With great expectation, I took an Asian brother with me who was fluent in the trade language, to help me with my limited language, and off we trekked to find these few small churches.

Hidden in a mountain valley, surrounded by lush bamboo forests and waterfalls, we found a small church. The 80 believers in this place were actually a sub-group of the Ina. I was so thrilled to discover them!

In my limited language, I poured out my heart about the Great Commission, teaching from Matt. 28:18-20. I helped them come to the realization that their valley held the only known Ina churches, and it was their responsibility to take the gospel to other Ina valleys – to win and train others. They were shocked. Living in their isolated world, they had assumed all Ina villages were Christian. Then, my Asian brother preached a much longer sermon from Acts 1:8 about the command to go to all places.

When we finished, the group was visibly shaken. The conviction of the Spirit had fallen on them. The leader of the group stood up before the congregation and said with tears to the group: "For 60 years we have been disobedient to this call. Today, God has called us to obey!"

My friend and I were ecstatic. We spent time praying with the group before we left. We had cast vision, and they had heard God speak.

> If we will change our approach to follow Jesus' Great Commission, His Spirit will empower us to see results far beyond what we have experienced previously.
>
> [For a fuller version, see Chapter 3 "The T4T Story"]

A month or two later, I returned to make concrete plans with them about when we would begin to train them and how they would go to new villages with the gospel. But what I didn't know was that after we left them, they began to count the cost. They realized that if they began to reach out, it could well result in persecution. On this second visit, the group that earlier had come under God's conviction now said "no." I was heart-broken.

It was then that I realized that **conviction does not equal obedience.** I was seeing a living example of the parable of the two sons – where one son said "yes" but did not go work in the field.

Not every group you cast vision to will both "do" and "say" yes, but no group will commit if you fail to cast vision. **Successful CPM initiators cast vision to many groups to find the few that will both say and do "yes."** There were later groups of national believers that I cast vision to who eventually said and did "yes" and were used by God to start that CPM.

This leads naturally to the second question we must deal with.

WHOM? Name List

Once God does convict an individual or group and they agree to move forward, you have to give them something to commit to. Only this tests their commitment. Many Christians do not witness because they do not know whom to talk to.

In T4T, during the first session, take the mystery out of whom to talk to by having new trainers make a **Name List**. Explain to them the idea of *oikos* – their circle of relationships including their family, friends, neighbors and co-workers. Have the

FAMILY SAVED AT MIDNIGHT

By Ying Kai

Would you wake up your whole family at midnight and share the gospel with them? In Acts 16, the Philippian jailor could not wait. Perhaps his family thought, "It's midnight, why are you waking us up?" Perhaps he said, "If it had not been for these men, I might be dead right now. These two gentlemen saved us." He could not wait. He asked Paul and Silas to come to his house. At midnight, the jailer and his whole family came to Christ. God loves you, chooses you, and works through you to save your whole family.

I have a friend who is a Chinese-American medical doctor. When he was very young, his family emigrated from Hong Kong to the States. When he went to the States he decided, "I will become a medical doctor and make a lot of money and have a good reputation." He became a doctor but was not satisfied. He thought, "I want to be the head of my department." So

Continued next page.

participants take out a sheet of paper and pray: "God, bring to my mind people in my *oikos* who don't follow Jesus." Then have them write down all the names of people in their *oikos*. It takes time. Take the time to look at their Name Lists and find ways to encourage and help them with it. Sometimes, you may have to prompt them to think about people they meet regularly in various circles – work, class, market, neighborhood, club, organization, family, etc. Sometimes they don't know a name, but write down a description: "the lady who sells me bread."

Once everyone has made their lists, have them pray again. They should call out to God asking Him whom they should share their story with first. As they finish praying, encourage them to circle five names of these people God put on their hearts. It may help to encourage them to start with those they think would be most receptive to hearing, but don't limit them to that. Sometimes they choose a family member who lives across the country. Perhaps they will send them an email or make a phone call or visit. During this time, God convicts the trainees whom to share with first in their endeavor to bring the gospel to everybody.

Then take time to pray that God will open up the hearts of these people in the coming days as they go to witness to them. The witnessing will go a lot better if the Attacker has already prepared the way (see Chapter 4 for this term)! If the group is large, they may pray in small groups for these specific individuals on their list and for boldness to open their mouths to talk.

HOW? A simple bridge plus a gospel presentation

A third reason that Christians do not witness is because they don't know how to start and share the complete gospel. Once the group has received the vision and made a Name List, teach them how to actually share the gospel. The trainee must learn two things in this area: 1) a bridge to share the gospel and 2) a gospel presentation.

A **bridge** is simply a way to transition a conversation to spiritual matters, especially the gospel. Many Christians don't start a gospel presentation because they have no easy way to start. Many of us have found that if we can just get started, going through the gospel itself is not that difficult.

A short one to three-minute testimony can be an excellent bridge (other types of bridges will be referenced later). The testimony does not include the gospel. The trainees will share that afterward. The testimony needs to be just a short bridge to the gospel.

To teach the trainers their testimony, use the simple progression of 1) my life before Christ, 2) how I came to Christ, and 3) my life since Christ came in. Or for non-salvation testimonies, use an example of 1) a problem, 2) how God changed the problem, and 3) victory

---

he studied and got a PhD.

After this he landed a job at a very famous hospital in Los Angeles as the head of the department. He was only 40 years old. There were many very well known doctors working under him. At this hospital he became very rich. He had everything. He had three daughters and was very happy. He was really pleased with his life.

But one day, he received a report after his annual check-up. He was told: "You have a tumor in your liver that is the size of a golf ball. You need to prepare to die. Even with an operation, there is not much chance. You will not live longer than six months, but you could die much sooner." That night he could not sleep. He thought to himself, "What can I give to my family after I die? My oldest daughter is only 16 years old and hasn't even finished high school. I can't even go to her high school graduation." He decided to make recordings of birthday and graduation greetings for his daughters but

Continued next page.

felt that no one would listen to them after he was gone. As he thought about his death, he could not sleep.

Then he remembered, "When I was a teenager in Hong Kong, I joined a church." After he came to the States, he never went to church. Now he thought again about Jesus, but he didn't know how to pray. Finally he found the telephone number of the pastor in Hong Kong, and tried to call him. He got through to the pastor and told him his whole story.

The pastor led him to read Psalm 103:1-5 and told him, "Only if you repent and turn will God help you and perhaps heal you." So, in the middle of the night, he asked Jesus to help him. He knelt down and prayed with the pastor on the phone. When he hung up, he felt very peaceful, because he had eternal life. Now he could face his own problems!

He had received salvation, and thought to himself, "I cannot wait." So, at midnight, he woke up his wife. His wife said,

Continued next page.

since then (e.g. freedom from alcoholism, overcoming a bad temper, finding a way to forgive someone, etc.).

Have the trainers take out a sheet of paper, or a half sheet of paper to keep it short, and write down their testimony. Have them simultaneously read it out loud several times. This helps them say their testimony in a more natural way as well as memorize it.

Then have the group divide into pairs to practice telling their story to each other. Encourage them to help each other remove words that are too "churchy" or with concepts that wouldn't make sense to a non-Christian. Encourage them to give each other feedback on how moving the testimony is and suggestions for sharing it better.

Only when the trainers are confident to share their testimonies should you move on to the gospel presentation. If you have run out of time, then stop there and encourage them to simply share their stories this week.

But one thing is very important to remember: a testimony is designed to move someone's heart to listen to the gospel, but it is not the gospel itself! *The goal of the testimony is simply to help us bridge to the gospel.*

Therefore, your first training session should include a **gospel presentation** that must be very simple to learn and pass on. Ying does this with his Lesson

One on "How to have Assurance of Salvation." (This is one of the most adapted parts of T4T since some ways of presenting the gospel are more appropriate in one context than another. A number of gospel presentations are presented in the supplementary materials.) At this point in the first T4T session, you need to introduce a very simple gospel presentation that will be effective in your context and easy to pass on.

When you have effectively taught this gospel presentation, divide the group up into pairs to practice re-teaching the presentation to each other. This is not a time to relax as a trainer. Instead, walk around the group listening to them, answering questions, encouraging and praising them, and correcting as needed. Give them plenty of time to practice to make sure they have the confidence and competence to present the gospel accurately.

Once the trainees are confident to share it, make sure that they are ready to share the gospel in the coming week. If you have used a gospel tract or handout, make sure they have extra copies to give to people they witness to. It is also important to encourage them to pray for the needs of people they witness to because often God works miracles to demonstrate His love to the lost as they hear this witness.

> Heal the sick who are there and tell them, "The kingdom of God has come near to you." (Luke 10:9, NIV)

"Why are you waking me up?" He said, "I have given you everything, but I haven't given you eternal life. Tonight, I received eternal life. I want to share this with you." Right there in his bedroom, he led his wife to follow Jesus.

They both thought, "We can't wait." So, at midnight, they woke up their three daughters. The mother said, "Dad has given you everything. You go to a very good private school. He has given you everything. But he has not given you something very important: eternal life."

The father said, "I will lose my life very soon. But I have received eternal life, so I can face my problems. I know where I will go when I die. I want to share the gift of eternal life with you." So in that night, the whole family became Christians. They held hands, knelt down in the living room, and prayed together. They were very happy.

When they stood up, the second daughter, who was only 12 years old, said, "Dad? Jesus loves us, is that right?" He

Continued next page.

said, "Yes." So she said, "I think Jesus loves you, too. Make an appointment for surgery. We will pray for you and ask Jesus to heal you." So they all knelt down again and prayed for the father.

The next day, the doctor made an appointment for surgery. After five days, several doctors operated on him. When they performed the surgery, they could not find a tumor. There was only an indention in the liver the size of a golf ball. So they closed the incision and told him, "You're healthy. Jesus has already removed the tumor for you."

Hallelujah! He resigned as the department head and went to Vancouver to study at Regent College. He is still in that seminary serving as the head of the Department of Chinese Studies Program. He has sent a lot of missionaries back to Asia. So God, through you, can save your whole family. There is a sense of urgency!

Remind the trainers to train their new believers

Before ending the first session, encourage the trainees not only to witness, but also to repeat the entire Session One with those who believe. If you are using a tract or photocopies, they need to have enough copies to give the new believer to use with his own *oikos*. Remind them that if someone says "yes" to the gospel, they need to *immediately* take time to train him in three things: 1) why, 2) whom and 3) how – bridge and gospel. This should happen within minutes or hours after the person believes.

In T4T encourage the trainees to set up separate times to meet with these new believers, not to bring them back to the original training group. Remember, the goal is to multiply generations of trainers. Even if it is a group of two (the new trainer and the new believer), it is usually best for them to meet separately rather than try to cluster them together or bring them back to a 'parent' group. This will build up the new trainer more quickly.

Commission them and remind the trainees: Don't ask, just tell!

Remember Ying's story of one egg or two in Chapter 3? It's a great story to tell at this point before the training session ends.

Then challenge the trainees to obey what God has put on their heart. They do not need to ask permission to share, or earn the right to share. *On the cross Jesus earned the right for them to share.* That's all they need. Don't ask, just tell!

Before adjourning, have the trainees **set goals** to share with the names circled on their Names Lists. Then have them pray for one another to go out in God's anointing. This is a great time to lay hands on each person and pray for them. In essence, every week, you are re-commissioning one another to live as followers of Jesus and fishers of men. Everyone commits to this, including the one leading the group! You must be an example of what you are teaching.

Session Two: When They Return

Loving Accountability & Pastoral Care

The following week (or two weeks later) when the trainees return is the moment of truth. As the session begins, spend time asking them how they are doing and ministering to their needs. Also take time to praise God in a time of worship. Then, move to loving mutual accountability: Did they actually do what God told them to do (include yourself in this)? *The fastest way to keep this group from becoming a movement is by failing to ask them about the assignment God gave them!*

Accountability is difficult for any of us, but the Scripture is filled with exhortations to accountability:

> And let us consider how we may **spur one another on** toward love and good deeds. ²⁵Let us not give up meeting together, as some are in the habit of doing, but let us **encourage one another**—and all the more as you see the Day approaching. (Heb. 10:24-25, NIV, emphasis added)

All of the "one anothers" of Scripture are exhortations to live in accountability with one another. We can't ignore this, for the Day of Christ is drawing nearer. Time is running out. We must help each other love Jesus better and love others more fully – including sharing the gospel.

Even though it may not feel natural, we must develop *loving accountability* in our training groups. This is the fastest way to change habits and lifestyles. Therefore, in Session Two, introduce loving accountability...

- "How did it go sharing with the names you circled?"

- "How did they respond?"

- "With those who believed, what happened when you trained them in Session One (Why, Whom, How)?"

As you go around the group sharing what happened, take time to celebrate each successful witnessing venture and each new salvation. Have a mini-party or pep rally right there!

Also take time to encourage those who are fainthearted or were rejected in their witness. Take time to pray for people they witnessed to who have not yet believed. Help troubleshoot for and encourage people who did not share at all. Make it *loving,* not legalistic, accountability.

Take them to the next step

After some time of pastoral care, worship and loving account-ability, cast vision to your group again of how God wants to use them. Some will be discouraged and need this word of encouragement. This is a great time to use the "Heavenly Father's Heart" vignette (see Chapter 3). Ying uses this vignette to encourage his trainees in their Second Session. Many of them have just begun witnessing and experience rejection. He wants to reassure them that their Heavenly Father will give them many in their household who believe, even though it may take time.

After casting vision then teach the group lesson two of your discipleship program. Lesson two is usually on devotional life or prayer.

Afterward, have them practice teaching lesson two in pairs while you monitor and encourage them in gaining competence and confidence. They need to do this because they will train their new believers in lesson two in the following days.

Before you finish, help them think through what goals they should set for that week:

- Since they will witness to five people a week, have them look at their Name List again and circle the names of people they will witness to. Some will be new names, some will be the same.

- Since some of the trainees will have seen new salvations, help them make plans to meet with these new believers and train them. Encourage them to repeat the process with their new group: pastoral care, worship, loving accountability (including making a Name List), casting vision, teaching them how to witness (testimony and gospel), giving them time to practice, and finally setting goals and praying with them for the third generation that they will win.

- Help them set goals that move one step closer to multiplying generations of trainers

As they set these goals, once again pray for one another and re-commission each other. Make sure each person is prepared for the next step.

If you master these simple things, you will have started the process of T4T. You have learned how to help believers begin returning to the original discipleship revolution.

Summary of Session One (WHY-WHOM-HOW)

In Session One with believers (whether they are new believers you won or existing believers) help them work through the WHY-WHOM-HOW of becoming a trainer. Remember, your goal is **to build multiplying generations of trainers**.

- Why? Cast vision to them.

- Whom? Make a Name List of their oikos and prayerfully prioritize it.

- How? Give them a gospel bridge (e.g. testimony) and a gospel presentation. Give them adequate time to practice it and then set goals with prayer as they live out their assignment from God.

In Session Two, you begin setting a pattern for the weekly three-part T4T meeting. These three parts (or three thirds) are integral to helping to develop trainers, not just church members or witnesses:

First Third:

- Pastoral Care

- Worship

- Loving Accountability

- Vision Casting

Second Third:

- New Lesson

Final Third:

- Practice the Lesson

- Set Goals and Pray for each other

Minutes and Hours

One of the most critical aspects of the T4T process that must be established in Session One is to immediately instill kingdom DNA in the identity of a new believer when he first comes to faith. **A brand new believer needs to walk through this WHY-WHOM-HOW session within minutes or hours of his salvation – even if it is an abbreviated version.** This positions the new believer to be used by God immediately.

Suppose you have just led a person to faith. What are some of the first words out of your mouth? Some of the first should be Session One. You immediately help him learn the three things above: Why, Whom and How.[10] This is what happened in the book of Acts when a person was given a vision for his household sometimes

---

[10] As you will see later, you will also put in a lesson on baptism very quickly.

prior to salvation (e.g. Acts 2:39, 11:14, 16:31). **Within minutes** you coach the new believer to reach his *oikos*. If you wait a week or two, you may miss the opportunity to set kingdom DNA.

> *A brand new believer needs to walk through this WHY-WHOM-HOW session within minutes or hours of his salvation — even if it is an abbreviated version.* **This instills the kingdom DNA identity into the new believer and positions him to be used by God immediately.**

- WHY (Vision) – "What has God saved you for? Do you realize that He not only wants to reach you, but also to reach your whole household through you?" (If you have time, share the Great Commission vignette, see above.)

- WHOM – "Make a Name List of every person you know who is not walking with God." Then coach him on whom to talk to first this week (usually five people each week). Have him circle these names on his list and re-visit the list each week in his weekly witnessing. You can use questions like these:

  » "Let's pray through this list. Whom do you think God wants you to tell first?"

  » "Who are the people who would be excited about the change God has brought to your life?" [In oppressive contexts help him find safe people when possible.]

  » "Who most needs to hear this right now?"

- HOW – "Share the story of what God has done in your life (testimony)." This is *very simple* for a new believer because of the miracle that has just occurred (Titus 3:3-7). All he has to do is tell people the story of what has just happened in his life. Depending on the situation, you will want to coach him on how to share this news in a way that will be best understood by people in his *oikos*. Jesus did this very thing with the Gerasene demoniac: "Just tell them the great things God just did for you!" (Mark 5:19). He didn't have much training but could tell his story. If time allows, do your best to help the new believer learn an effective gospel presentation to go with it – preferably the one you just shared to lead him to faith. Have him practice it with you before he goes home to his family.

You should do the WHY-WHOM-HOW of Session One within minutes or hours. If you can't do it immediately upon his salvation, schedule it with him within hours. By doing this you set the DNA for him to become a follower of Jesus and fisher of men. The longer you wait, the harder it is to build into a believer the DNA of a kingdom disciple-maker.

Be a Doer, not just a Hearer!

Write down how God has spoken to you and what you need to obey as a result:

CHAPTER 6

Building a Movement Through the 20%

In the T4T story, the very first group that Ying trained demonstrated an important truth of kingdom movements:

> *Not everyone we train will become a fruitful person or a trainer of trainers. We have to look for the small percentage that will bear spiritual fruit 30, 60 or 100 times and invest more attention in these for a CPM to emerge.*

When Ying's trainees returned to their second T4T meeting, and he asked if they had obeyed the previous things God had told them, their responses varied. Some had not witnessed at all. Some had witnessed but seen no decision. Some had witnessed and seen people believe.

As Ying met with this group and many others over the weeks to come, he encouraged them to continue to witness, to meet with people they had led to faith and to train them in discipleship including reaching out to others. Four types of trainees began to emerge in his T4T groups in relation to becoming a trainer of trainers.

- **Attendees:** some trainees did not witness and only attended the meetings.

- **Witnesses:** some trainees began to witness and led people to faith, but never started new groups.

- **Starters:** some trainees led people to faith and started new groups. However, they didn't train their new group members to reproduce the process.

- **Trainers:** some trainees led others to faith, started groups AND trained these new believers to witness to and train others. They truly became trainers not just trainees, but their numbers rarely exceeded 15-20%.

This percentage has held true not only for Ying but for T4T groups around the world.

In T4T, each person is encouraged and trained **to witness**.

Each person is encouraged and trained **to train trainers.**

But not all do.

The same will be true as your trainees return to your T4T groups. It is one of the foundational dynamics of a kingdom movement.

Jesus told the parable of the four soils to illustrate the truth that there will be varying responses to the gospel, and *only one* is the type we are hoping for: fruitful people. The main application of this parable is in relation to people hearing the gospel and responding wholeheartedly to the life of the kingdom. Jesus doesn't want us to be blindsided by the three unfruitful types of soil. He wants us to be realistic. Some people will simply reject the gospel. But many others will profess faith without ever producing much fruit. Only a percentage will accept the gospel and bear fruit 30, 60 and 100 fold. These are *normal* kingdom dynamics. Bearing fruit can be the spiritual fruit of life transformation as well as the spiritual fruit of new disciples we make.

Understanding the four-soils principle of the kingdom is critical in relation to the witnessing and training others aspect of CPMs. The parable does not hold an exact parallel to the four types of responses mentioned above: attendees, witnesses, starters and trainers. But the principle of only a few bearing multiplying fruit is absolutely critical for you to understand in a CPM.

In a church-planting movement, only a small percentage of believers will multiply their lives 30, 60 and 100 fold. This is called CPM reproduction. While all of the people in your training group may be faithful to obey the Scriptures they study (e.g. "husbands love your wives," "children obey your parents," etc.), not all will be fruitful in relation to reproducing, i.e. training trainers.

Unless you recognize this principle and are willing to invest more of your time in the fruitful soil people, the budding ministry will fail to become a movement.

Session Two Onwards: Finding the Fruitful Soil

If in Session One the trainees have heard from God and made commitments to witness and train, then when they return for Session Two onwards, you should see four types of trainees develop through the training and accountability process. Your goal is multiplying generations of trainers, so it is indispensible to discern where the fruitful-soil persons are who will pass the kingdom DNA on to the next generation.

Let's unpack the four types of responses we see in relation to the trainees witnessing to and training others.

Attendees: Attend the group, but do not witness
Some people will never witness consistently. In the beginning, the percentage may be high. As time goes by, however, with good coaching and loving mutual accountability, some of these move out of this category and begin to witness. In the beginning many of them are fearful of setting new patterns as a witness. Some never begin to witness, but many eventually do.

Witnesses: Witness, but do not start groups
In your T4T groups, others *do* witness and many of them actually lead the lost to faith in Jesus. Some of these people even become "super-spreaders."

During the SARS epidemic a few highly contagious individuals spread the disease to an unusually large number of other people. Medical experts called these individuals "super spreaders." In many CPMs today a small percentage of new believers actually

Continued next page.

WITNESSING IN DEATH

By Ying Kai

Through you, God can save your whole family. When I worked as a chaplain in a hospital, one afternoon, when I had just left the hospital, my pager rang. I answered. It was the children's ICU. A nurse said, "Are you a pastor?" I said, "Yes." She said, "We have a girl here. She is five years old, and she just passed away. Her father asked me to find a chaplain to pray for them. So I said, "Okay, I'm coming."

When I got there, I found the girl's father. He said, "Are you the pastor?" I said, "Yes." He said, "Please, pray for us, because my daughter just passed away." I looked at his beautiful daughter lying there. I said, "Yes, I will pray for you. Please tell me which church you belong to." He looked at me and said, "I am not a Christian." I said, "If you are a non-Christian, why did you ask for a pastor to pray for you?"

He pointed at his daughter and said, "She loved Jesus, and she asked me, if she died, to ask for a pastor

become super spreaders who are able to evangelize an extraordinarily large number of people.

Whether your T4T members are normal witnesses or super spreaders, there's a celebration in heaven over every lost person who repents.

However, there is just one limiting issue with "witnesses" from a T4T perspective. These dear people may not become group starters. They may not become trainers. They sometimes only feel confident or qualified leading people to faith but not starting a group on their own. That's fine. Continue to encourage them. Some of their new converts will join other new groups, or occasionally come back to the original group. This happens all the time. But for a movement to grow, new believers must be gathered into new groups and trained to become trainers. The good news is that, like the "attendees" above, with proper training and coaching, witnesses may later become group starters and trainers.

Starters: Witness and start new groups, but do not train their groups members to reproduce the process

Some of the people in the group will not only become effective witnesses, but they will start groups of their own. Is that good or bad? It's good.

However, there is one issue with "starters." Remember, the goal is *multiplying generations of trainers.* Starters do not have a vision (or possibly confidence) beyond starting the next generation of groups. They are effective witnesses and start new groups. Many of these new groups become churches. In effect, starters are church planters, but they *fail to see that their role is to train people in their groups to witness to and train others.*

Ying refers to them as "workers" rather than "trainers." They work hard to start new groups, but may still be following a traditional model of group starting or church planting. If they don't go beyond that, they will not be the ones through whom a multi-generational movement flows.

Starters are great! We need them. But planting new churches is not enough because our end-vision demands more. We must develop trainers of trainers.

Trainers: Witness, start groups and train their members to reproduce the process

If we train our trainers effectively, using the approach we will discuss in the next chapter, it is very likely that real trainers will emerge. Trainers are the "good soil" of CPMs that lead to multi-generational reproduction. Just like the fruitful soil of Jesus' parable was only one out of four types of responses, we also find that the percentage of trainees who become fruitful trainers is only around 20%. This kingdom percentage is almost impossible to increase much.

to pray for our whole family." Even though she died, she could still witness in her death! It moved my heart, so I knelt down and held the daughter's hand, and I began to pray. "God, because you are merciful, you love us. Today we lost a daughter. We are very sad, but we also have faith, because we know she belongs to you. Once again, if we are in your family, we know we can meet in heaven." I continued to pray for about 15 minutes.

The father knelt down at my side, and he held my hand. When I finished praying, he said, "Pastor, teach me. I want to be a Christian. I want to meet my daughter in heaven." I asked him to sit down beside me, and I shared the gospel. Immediately, he believed in Jesus. That afternoon, he led his wife and his two sons to believe in Jesus. So this five-year-old daughter, because she had faith, led her whole family to become Christians, even in her death.

An important principle of CPMs is this: *Go with the good fruitful soil!*

Therefore an important principle of CPMs is this:

Go with the good <u>fruitful</u> soil!

Whether it relates to the few persons of peace who believe out of the many we have witnessed to, or the few trainers of trainers who emerge out of the many we train, we must give extra attention to the fruitful people. Unfortunately, it is easy to allow the unfruitful people to monopolize our time, and movements never emerge.

Trainers 1) *witness* effectively, 2) *start* a group or multiple groups, *and* 3) *train* the new believers in their groups *to become trainers of others*. While the **starter's** goal is to start a group, the **trainer's** goal is to start a movement. He realizes that the new group he starts will also have four types of people – attendees, witnesses, starters and trainers. He realizes that if he trains them effectively, God convicts them and they obey what they learn from the Word, some will begin another generation of groups that have the same potential to keep the discipleship revolution multiplying generation by generation.

I learned the importance of helping people change from being starters to being trainers from personal experience. In my prior training sessions, I had encouraged my partners to witness to persons of peace and their households, and then to start churches with them. In my mind I was hoping that these new churches would multiply into new generations, but it wasn't happening. I discovered that the problem was not my partners, but me! I had trained them to become good church starters, but not trainers of trainers, not CPM catalysts.

In the next training session I challenged the group to start no more churches, but rather to help the groups they had already started to witness to others and start new groups. To my amazement, a number of them did that very thing: they turned from starters into trainers. When I adjusted my expectations and loving accountability, God birthed new generations through these dear co-laborers.

Living out the 20% Principle

Around the world, even in the best of situations, we find that *only about 20% of those we train will become trainers of trainers.* These are normal kingdom dynamics and it rarely rises higher than this. There are also times that we get no trainers out of our groups. Typically the longer a group of people have been believers the smaller percentage of them will become trainers of trainers (because they have few non-Christian relationships or are too busy with other ministry responsibilities).

- In your context, how many genuine trainers of trainers do you feel you need for a movement to start?

- If only 20% become trainers of trainers, how many do you probably have to start training to find this many trainers?

- If only 20% become trainers of trainers, and you only train three to four people, what is the likelihood that you will see a movement start?

Don't Predict: Just Train

Trainers are the 30, 60, 100-fold people of the four soils parable. A careful examination of CPM case studies around the world and personal interviews with the CPM practitioners reveal an interesting phenomenon in almost all of them. The first breakthrough people of peace usually resulted in 100 people coming to faith (in their *oikos*), and occasionally 60 or 30. Perhaps this is why Luke's Gospel doesn't even mention the 30 and 60 times. He only mentions the 100 times.

> Other seed fell into the good soil, and grew up, and produced a crop a hundred times as great. (Luke 8:8, NASB)

Perhaps 100 times was the biblical norm for fruitful people. It often holds true in CPMs.

The true potential of trainers, however, is not the number of people they personally lead to faith, even if they are super-spreaders, but the **disciple-making process** that begins through them to build a movement through the people they have led to faith. They see the power of reproduction and, empowered by the Holy Spirit, press hard into making this a reality.

Remember Ying's story of the old farmer who in one year alone, started over 110 small groups. He is an example of a trainer of trainers. Though he was probably a super-spreader, too, more importantly he was a trainer who trained his new believers to repeat the process for many generations. There are "old farmers" out there in every city and people group.

It is impossible to predict who these breakthrough trainers will be. Many CPM practitioners admit that the people we think will be the most fruitful usually are not and the people that we think may never succeed at all are often the most fruitful. Perhaps this is the delight God has in exercising His sovereignty.

You cannot predict which kind of lost people will prove to be people of peace. So, you just sow the gospel a lot to find them.

In the same way, you cannot predict who will become a trainer. You just have to train a lot of people to find them. And most often, the trainers will be people you would not have naturally chosen!

- Who would have chosen the Gerasene demoniac? Yet, he proclaimed the gospel to ten cities (Mark 5:20).

- Who would have chosen fishermen for apostles? Yet, they rocked the Roman world and changed history.

- Who would have chosen a hardened jailer or a possible widow or single woman, Lydia? Yet, the movement that began through them reached the city of Philippi (Acts 16).

When you try to predict the people you think will become CPM breakthrough persons, and invest only in them, you will usually fail. **Don't choose. Train everybody.**

As I worked with 33 national partners who were trying to start a CPM among the Ina, two of them whom I predicted to have great potential became quite bogged down in the remote county-seat town in which they worked. I say "worked" but in actuality fear had set in, and they refused to even leave their small one-room flat except to buy rice and vegetables. Something had to change.

At one of the next quarterly trainings of the 33, a newcomer showed up to join the 33. His name was Little Moe, and he was only 14 years old. Little Moe paid attention diligently to everything we shared in training. He was eager to go out and try what he was learning about TRT, our oral version of T4T, among the Ina. He longed to see a movement start, and believed that God could use him. Though he was just a studious 14-year old, I would never have picked him as someone God would use to build a movement.

For some reason, we sent him to join the two brothers who were bound in fear. The three of them returned to the little one-room flat hours away down the mountain road. Little Moe was shocked at the paralysis of fear the other two men displayed. Little Moe shamed them: "How dare you stay in this room when God has sent us here to share the gospel with the Ina!"

He grabbed the two of them, and took them to a nearby village. When the villagers asked the three of them why they were there, Little Moe said, "We represent the Most High God, and He wants you all to hear this message!"

A few people began to gather around the trio, but Little Moe told them they would not begin sharing until the whole village gathered. Soon a hundred people were gathered to hear the news. Little Moe shared the Creation to Christ gospel story, and the **entire village** believed! It was the first time this had ever happened among the Ina.

It didn't end there. A few days later, Little Moe encouraged the trio to go to another village. The same scenario played itself out and the whole village believed. All through the bold obedience of a 14-year old that I would **never** have picked. As Little Moe and the other two brothers began to disciple and train these new believers, it was the breakthrough needed for a movement in that county.

Fear is contagious, but so is faith. Little Moe's faith transformed the situation from fear to a movement of God.

> *Fear is contagious, but so is faith.*

This is the power of trainers. God uses them to transform humble beginnings into a movement.

Building a Movement

Trainers are the tools God uses to build a CPM. Through their lives, the kingdom spreads into multiple people, groups, and streams of multiplying churches.

This is not to be unappreciative of or to disparage "witnesses" and "starters." Even though trainers may be the trainers of a movement, witnesses and starters are bearing fruit themselves. God uses them to start churches and bring in many new believers. You should be thrilled to have them in your T4T groups. But remember that if you only encourage your trainees to be witnesses or starters, no movement will result; their fruit will not usually become a CPM.

As you consistently train with the T4T process and trainers rise up, a multi-generational movement starts. The power of 20% reproducing generation by generation is truly exponential.

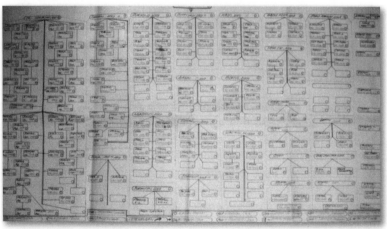

Nine Generations of Muslim-Background Churches

About a year prior to writing this book, some colleagues and I consulted with one of the team leaders we supervise in Southeast Asia. He was leading an emerging CPM that was demonstrating a lot of first and second generation church planting, with some third generation churches starting occasionally. It wasn't a CPM yet, but was getting close. As we listened, it was apparent that some elements of the T4T process were missing. We counseled him to incorporate the lessons from the next chapter into his training meetings, to see if multiplication could be accelerated.

When the team leader returned to his ministry, he began to train his Muslim-background believers in these principles. A year later, he showed me a chart (see previous page) that just *one* of the key trainers in his CPM network drew. It was a chart of all of the groups and churches that have been spawned through the training of one trainer. On the chart, I could make out two groups marked as 8th generation and recently they just got a 9th generation! This growth from 3rd to 9th generation occurred in the span of 18 months as the believers better understood and cooperated with God in the T4T process.

Fill Your Schedule with Training

If about 20% will become trainers, then you have to train *many people* in order to find God-prepared trainers.

How do you build a movement through T4T? You have to train a lot of people trying to find those the Spirit is raising up as CPM-breakthrough people – trainers of trainers. *Do whatever it takes to fill your schedule with training groups*. This is the highest value activity of CPMs. If there are a lot of existing Christians in your environment, then all you may need to do is cast vision to them (see chapter 11 on vision casting) and begin meeting with groups of them at various times.

How do you build a movement through T4T? You have to train a lot of people trying to find those the Spirit is raising up as CPM-breakthrough people – trainers of trainers.

Do whatever it takes to fill your schedule with training groups.

If however, you have very few Christians in your context, you will have to do several things to get your first T4T groups:

- You and your team must sow the gospel broadly to win the first believers to train.

- Mobilize lots of short-term teams – be they outsiders or national partners – that will hunt for your first persons of peace to win and train.

There are numerous ways to get to your first training groups, but the bottom line is you have to train a lot of people for a CPM to start. You must train scores and even hundreds of people for a CPM to take off.

When Ying and Grace began their work, they just did two things other than pray: witness to the lost and train the saved. As the weeks went by, they began to fill up their personal calendar with training appointments. On average, these training appointments took two hours. Ying and Grace are empty nesters, so they had a lot of time on their hands. They figured they could train one group in the morning (e.g. housewives), another group in the afternoon (e.g. students) and 1-2 groups in the evening (e.g. factory workers, farmers or professionals). They worked six days a week, sometimes seven—though Grace cajoled Ying to take off a Sabbath.

These groups ranged in size from two, Ying and one new believer, to a whole church of several hundred. But usually they were small – no more than 20 people.

Do the math. As they won people to the Lord or recruited existing Christians, Ying and Grace were personally training 20-30 groups a week. If the average size of the groups was ten, then they were training 200-300 believers every week. What's 20% of this? 40 to 60 trainers began to emerge through each week's training groups.

But Ying and Grace didn't stop witnessing or casting vision to new groups of believers. Eventually they had too many groups to fit into one week. So, they told their original groups that they would only meet every two weeks. On the off week, they encouraged every trainer to start new groups. On the off weeks, Ying and Grace now had an open weekly calendar to add new groups. In this way, they were able to double the number of groups they trained.

As time passed they added more groups than this, so Ying would train some and Grace would train others at the same time. Through training hundreds of people in a reproducible process they found the CPM-breakthrough people the Spirit had prepared.

The principle is this: *you must fill your weekly (or bi-weekly) schedule with as many training groups as possible.* Do what you can to move other commitments off your calendar to free time up to train trainers.

One young missionary couple frequently hired the same taxi driver to take them to the airport an hour away to pick up visitors to their city. After much witnessing to her, and a miracle in her life, she accepted Christ. As a taxi driver, she was extremely busy, usually working 12-hour shifts. The young couple never seemed to be able to nail down a time to meet with the woman to train her in T4T. Eventually they hit upon an ingenious solution. They decided to train her an hour on the way to the airport, while waiting for their guests and the hour on the way back home. Since they used her services very frequently, this became their regular T4T training time for her.

If you're like most people, you're a busy person. But take a hard look at your weekly schedule. How many two-three hour T4T time slots could you really free up if you tried? Most of us can find several time slots each week. Suppose you find that you can give three time slots. Now you have a target to shoot for. Win the lost. Cast vision to the saved. Do whatever it takes to fill up those time slots with three T4T groups and start the T4T process. If you meet with your groups every other week, you now have the potential to train *six* groups.

What better way to spend your time than to initiate a movement in your community? Like a mustard seed, even through six small groups, God can launch a movement.

The Power of Two (Groups)

In the beginning, as a new believer witnesses, he may start only one new T4T group. But as time progresses, and he keeps witnessing, we always encourage him to start at least one more group. This is because the reproduction effect of where the movement goes is so much greater when he does. This is not unrealistic since the new trainers will witness to dozens, even hundreds of people as the months go by.

The difference between starting one group or two groups is so great that many good ministries fail to become movements just because they fail to do this. We often illustrate this point by using a simple T4T spreadsheet. When each new generation trainer only starts one new group, the numbers in the spreadsheet remain relatively small (incremental addition growth). But when each new generation trainer starts two groups, even with just three or four people in each group, the numbers of new believers and groups skyrocket.

That's the power of two – encouraging trainers to start at least two groups. One of the most effective trainers I know came to a CPM training Ying and I led. He was already implementing T4T but just not seeing much more than addition growth. After we did this spreadsheet, his eyes were opened. He exclaimed, "This is what I've been doing wrong! I've only encouraged my trainers to start one group each, and we are not seeing a CPM yet. We need to change this one expectation."

Little tweaks like that can make the difference between good church planting and a church-planting movement. Don't just work hard; work smart! Raise the right sails that can move with the wind of the Spirit. Release future generations to let the Spirit be their Teacher so that a discipleship revolution starts.

The principles of this chapter are the counter-intuitive ways of the kingdom – the 20% rule, investing in the fruitful soil, training a lot to find the trainers, the power of two, etc. It *will be* hard work – it has to be. You'll be exhausted at times. But it must be *kingdom* work. Work counter-intuitively: don't do things the way you expect them to work naturally, but rather look for the very different ways God's kingdom operates.

The Two-Week Cycle

Still, all of us are busy people. Perhaps you want to lead four groups, but discover you only have time to lead two groups a week. Take heart. You can *double* the number of groups by meeting with them, like Ying did, every other week instead of every week.

It also gives your new trainees *time* to lead their own groups. Suppose that a new trainee only has one spot free in his week (especially in the early days of his discipleship). If he is already committed to being trained by you each week during that time slot, he might feel like he has no time to lead his own group (that's probably not reality, but it could feel that way). If you free him up on the 2nd week of the training cycle, then suddenly he has an open time slot. It gives him time to witness and start a new group before he returns to give an account to your group. Lack of time is no longer an excuse.

Although we want to encourage each trainer to *eventually* start two new groups, training them every other week can help them get their *first* group started. This is a long-term pattern that can also increase your margin, giving you more capacity for starting and training new groups.

In the beginning, however, meeting weekly will probably be best so that you can set the DNA of a CPM well. Use your own judgment as you look at the amount of discretionary time your trainees have. In special circumstances, you may want to meet with brand new believers more than once a week for the first week or two simply to help them get firm in their faith and walk with the Lord.

But remember your goal: *multiplying generations of trainers.* Do what you need to do to help them grow into followers of Jesus and fishers of men.

The real question is: ***What do we need to do in our weekly (or bi-weekly) meetings that enables our trainees to really become trainers?***

That's the next chapter.

Be a Doer, not just a Hearer!

Write down how God has spoken to you and what you need to obey as a result:

CHAPTER 7

The Three-Thirds Process

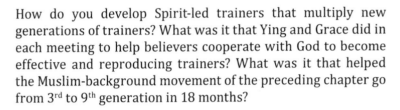

How do you develop Spirit-led trainers that multiply new generations of trainers? What was it that Ying and Grace did in each meeting to help believers cooperate with God to become effective and reproducing trainers? What was it that helped the Muslim-background movement of the preceding chapter go from 3rd to 9th generation in 18 months?

The core T4T process that enables believers to gain confidence and competence to be used by God as trainers is the three-thirds process. It is the way we interact in each training meeting. This is one of the least understood aspects of T4T. If you miss this, you may only end up giving people good evangelism training and good discipleship training. You might end up with a few groups or even churches. That's not bad. That's good. But it is not the best.

Church-planting movements require generational new church multiplication.

The Three-Thirds Training Process

Remember, T4T is a process of how we interact with our trainers. It is a process of building trainers who are both lovers of God and lovers of others who fulfill the Great Commission. It is a process of building trainers who follow Jesus and fish for men.

The three-thirds process enables us to move people from trainees to trainers.

A T4T session, especially in the early sessions, includes three basic sections. The sections emphasize the *trainer* nature of the meeting. We help the participants move beyond the mentality of a discipleship meeting or Bible study in which they only receive. The three sections help them look beyond their own lives and initiate a process to invest in other people.

Generally, a T4T session lasts about two to three hours. That seems to be sufficient time to do these three sections well. Each of the thirds is roughly the same length of time. So if you have a 120-minute meeting, your aim is for the each third to take about 40 minutes.[11]

Each culture and context will vary. In some extreme cases, you may only have a lunch hour to hold a T4T session with workmates. In that case, each third might take only 20 minutes. It is rather difficult to do it all in one hour, but it is better to get all three thirds in than to leave out major parts of the training session.

Three Thirds with Seven Parts

There are seven parts within the three-thirds meeting. In other words, there are seven things you are trying to accomplish in the three thirds of the meeting: four parts in the first third, one in the second third, and two in the last third. Three-thirds (sections) with seven smaller parts. In the three sections, we are 1) looking back, 2) looking up and 3) looking forward.

- **First Third: Looking Back** – the goal of this time is to evaluate how the trainers did while apart, celebrate together and encourage them that God can build a movement through them.

- **Second Third: Looking Up** – the goal of this time is to look up to God for new direction by studying a new lesson or Bible study.

- **Final Third: Looking Ahead** – the goal of this time is to prepare the trainers to implement the things God has

---

[11] As the T4T group becomes a church, often the last third (practice) is shortened and the three-thirds process is merged into the weekly church meeting.

been teaching them – evangelism, discipleship, training others, starting a group, etc.

LOOK BACK	LOOK UP	LOOK AHEAD
First Third	**Second Third**	**Final Third**
1. Pastoral Care	5. New Lesson	6. Practice the Lesson
How are you doing?	» Short-term reproducible discipleship lessons	7. Set Goals & Pray for each other
2. Worship		
3. Accountability	» Then, long-term self-feeding inductive Bible studies	
» Follow Jesus How are you obeying the Word?		
» Fish for men Witness, training, training trainers		
4. Vision Casting For what they can be and do		

First Third: Looking Back

In the first third, you are trying to evaluate how the trainers did while apart, celebrate together and encourage them that God can build a movement through them.

There are four parts, or activities, aimed at doing that. The order is not sacred, but generally these four fit best in the first third of the meeting. Occasionally, people might move one of the seven parts to a different third, but this order generally works best.

Part 1: Pastoral Care

(Each of these parts can eventually be led by the trainees. They can practice how to lead them in the last third.)

In T4T take time to genuinely ask the question: "How are you doing?" This is a time of pastoral care or personal care in which there is ministry to the needs of the trainees. The needs range over the whole spectrum from problems in their prayer life to concerns about their marriage; from frustrations about witnessing to excitement about a victory over a troubling habit; from concerns about getting their first group started to questions about how to deal with an errant leader of a third generation group.

Take time to ask, "How are you doing?" and then listen. This is a time to encourage the whole group to exercise the principle of 1 Cor. 14:26 and for spiritual gifts to emerge:

> When you assemble, each one has a psalm, has a teaching, has a revelation, has a tongue, has an interpretation. Let all things be done for edification. (1 Cor. 14:26, NASB)

Sometimes someone shares an insight from the Scripture related to a concern that someone raises. At other times the group encourages the person who has shared and prays for the need he has expressed. Sometimes you share an answer based on your experience with the same type of issue.

This is a time to minister to the needs of the group and troubleshoot problems. It is easy for such a time to take over the whole meeting. To prevent that, there are a number of ways to make it meaningful, yet not take up the whole meeting:

- Break up into smaller groups. If the group is large, taking the time to hear the main concerns can take a lengthy amount of time. Breaking the group into pairs or triplets can facilitate more sharing and ministry. If there are major questions that arise in the triplets, they can bring the question to the whole group.

- Stop after the allotted time. Not everyone needs to share a concern. If you've allotted ten minutes for this part, then generally the main issues will arise and you can care for those needs. Then you move on. Remember, a lot of personal ministry goes on before, after and outside the meeting, so not everything must be dealt with now.

- Save counseling of major issues for a later time. Some issues will arise that are so huge that they would dominate the entire two to three hours. Instead, listen to the concern, pray for the situation and find a time after or outside the meeting to address that issue in a deeper way.

- Move the pastoral care to the final third. Though not the preferred option, one trainer found that by moving pastoral care to the very end of the meeting, he could stay as long as necessary to deal with the issues.

Part 2: Worship

This is fairly straightforward – time to praise God together in a culturally appropriate, reproducible way. It could be with a guitar, a cappella, with an MP3 player, etc. Some groups read Psalms out loud. It is amazing how authentic, heartfelt worship in spirit and truth can bring healing to people as they encounter their Father through the Spirit (John 4:23-24). We were created for the praise of God's glory (Eph. 1:12). God longs to descend upon His people as they re-orient their hearts to Him.

A number of groups mix the first two parts together. They take time for worship and minister to one another (pastoral care) in twos and threes during this time. One of your goals is to do this in a way these new believers can eventually lead themselves.

Part 3: Accountability[12]

One of the most critical parts is one we often neglect: loving accountability. If the command from Jesus is to 1) follow Him (love Him) and 2) fish for men (love others), then we ought to hold each other accountable to actually do this! As mentioned in a prior chapter, mutual accountability is the "one anothers" of Scripture helping us grow in Christlikeness. In part three, we live out Heb. 10:24-25 to spur one another on as the Day of Christ draws nearer. On two specific occasions, Jesus' own disciples gave an account when they came back from a mission for Him (Mark 6:30; Luke 10:17).

---

[12] Some people combine the Pastoral Care and Accountability sections.

The apostles gathered together with Jesus; and they reported to Him all that they had done and taught. (Mark 6:30, NASB)

What do we hold people accountable for? Definitely NOT for obeying US! This approach would move us into cult-like patterns. Instead, we hold one another accountable for obeying GOD through His Word.

During this part of the first third, we ask *appropriate* questions to help the trainers live out the vision of 1) following Jesus and 2) fishing for men. In the Mark 6 passage above, the apostles reported what they had done (following Jesus' command) and taught (fishing for men). In T4T groups, we help trainees fulfill the "kingdom come" vision one step at a time. To do this we ask a progressive set of accountability questions that *move them forward*, not set them back in defeat and despair.

> Although you will give your trainers a vision to train trainers from the beginning, you have to ask questions that move them a step forward toward a movement each time you are together.

For example, what if you ask your T4T group in the second session: "How many of you witnessed, led people to faith, started a group and then helped that group start a new one?" What will the result be? Besides sheer confusion, the group will become frustrated and perhaps give up. They are not ready for a question like that. It's not appropriate for their stage of growth.

T4T accountability questions fall into two areas:

1) Following Jesus questions. You don't want to build a "movement" of trainers who slavishly share the gospel. You want people who are growing in their love for Jesus and godly character. Therefore, you can ask questions like this:

- How did you obey the lesson from last week?

- What is God doing in your life related to our Bible study on [prayer, marriage, etc.]?

- Guys, how did you do loving your wife, since that was our lesson from last week?

2) Fishing for men questions. Since this is the hardest area for many people, it is usually helpful to ask more questions in this area to enable the trainers to move step-by-step toward training trainers. You ask questions from week to week that build upon the progression from witness to starter to trainer.

- WITNESS: Who are you witnessing to? Who has believed?

- STARTER: When are you training them in the same process?

- TRAINER: How are these new believers doing witnessing to and winning others?

- TRAINER OF TRAINERS: When are they training their groups?

*If you want real obedience-based discipleship, avoid one of the chief traps: **Never give an assignment or goal unless you plan to ask about it at the next meeting.** Failing to ask about it is the fastest way to kill obedience-based discipleship.*

- **TRAINER OF TRAINERS WHO TRAINS TRAINERS: How are the trainers, that you are training, doing in training their new groups?**

Do you see how these questions naturally lead from one stage to another? Do you see that the last question is the CPM question?

- *You* – the generation 1 group

- *Trainers* – the generation 2 group

- *New groups* – the generation 3 group.

When you add that to yourself as the trainer, there are four generations of believers involved. It's 2 Timothy 2:2 all over again.

Notice how the questions are open-ended questions, rather than yes-no questions. Yes-no questions typically are not very helpful. *"Did you witness this week?"* often results in heads nodding "yes," but no real accountability. Great! You move on to the next question none the wiser that they may not be witnessing.

An open-ended version of the same question is *"Who are you witnessing to? Who has believed? Tell us about it."* These questions invite people to open up and don't make it easy to answer "yes" and move on.

The accountability time is not a judgmental time or harsh time. **Rather it is a loving, encouraging time.** Essentially what you are saying is this:

> *Brothers and sisters, God wants us to love Him better and reach the nations. How are we doing at loving Him better? How are we doing being people through whom God would spark a movement?*
>
> *What? We stumbled this week. That's okay! God can still use us this week. Let's help each other. Let's pray for each other. Let's go together this week to witness to our first people. God's Spirit will help us!*
>
> *We're a band of brothers and sisters on this journey. We can walk this road together.*

Said in love, often with tears, sometimes with laughter and joy, the accountability time becomes a source of encouragement rather than an occasion of fear because it is built on mutual trust. It becomes a real troubleshooting time to help the trainees become trainers.

If you want real obedience-based discipleship, avoid one of the chief traps: **Never give an assignment or goal unless you plan to ask about it at the next meeting.** Failing to ask about it is the fastest way to kill obedience-based discipleship. The trainees realize very soon that no one will really ask them about their personal walk or witness, so they make little progress in either. Remember: **conviction does not equal obedience.** We must help each other obey through the one-another encounter time of accountability. We don't want to look in the mirror at our face, but walk away forgetting how to change!

Anyone who listens to the word but does not do what it says is like a man who looks at his face in a mirror, and, after looking at himself, goes away and immediately forgets what he looks like. (James 1:23-24, NIV)

We all need accountability. It is too easy to get into patterns of attending worship and even having quiet times, but not making deep heart changes. Let's not rest until we follow Jesus' words to "obey everything I have commanded." This loving accountability is followed in the same verse with Jesus' loving promise, "And surely I am with you always, to the very end of the age." (Matthew 28:20, NASB)

Part 4: Vision Casting

One of the most forgotten elements of T4T is the importance of casting vision to our trainees of what they can become in Christ and what the Spirit can do through them. This doesn't require much time, but it is indispensable for a movement.

Vision casting is a way of life – continually helping brothers and sisters see the potential of who they are in Christ, what God wants to do in them and what God wants to do through them. Since we live in such a fallen world, it is easy for each of us to forget the spiritual reality and destiny God has prepared and walk by sight only. To change that we must spur one another on to walk by faith, not sight.

To walk in this lifestyle, each week in the meeting we take a few minutes – often five minutes or less – to share a short word of encouragement for the trainees not to give up in the journey toward Christlikeness and the Great Commission.

Discouragement can quickly creep into any group, especially one with as lofty a vision as a T4T group. Your role as trainer is to remind them one more time of a heavenly reality. You need to take time for a holy pep rally.

The easiest way to do this is through short, frequent vision-casting vignettes. These vignettes need only take a few minutes but serve as vivid reminders of who they are in Christ and the destiny God has for them. Though short, these words hold the ability to bring encouragement to the fainthearted (1 Thess. 5:14).

Many of the vision-casting vignettes that Ying and others use are about reaching the lost:

- In Session One, Ying uses the vignette "Great Commission" (see Chapters 3 and 5)

- In Session Two, Ying used the vignette "Heavenly Father's Heart" (see Chapter 3)

In Session Three, however, Ying casts vision for who the disciples can become in Christ during this first third. He uses a vignette called "Holy Spirit's Power."

In the supplementary materials on the website, www.T4TOnline.org you will find many examples of vision-casting vignettes that you can use each week in your training. Most vision-casting vignettes come from the many Scripture verses that call us to obedience to Christ and His mission. They also come from testimonies of what is happening in your work, a nearby work, or other stories of what God is doing around the world.

Second Third: Looking Up

The second third is very straightforward. It's something we are generally familiar with. It includes one main part.

Part 5: New Lesson (or Bible study)

This is the time we especially look up to God by gathering around His Word to hear what He has for us this week. In this portion of the meeting, we reinforce the authority of the Word and our commitment to obey whatever it says.

That's radically different from Bible study. Some Christians emphasize Bible study, but not **obedience** to the Word. When that happens, the unspoken value is the *truth* of the Word, but not the *authority* of the Word to act upon in everyday life.

Obedient Christians are a radical breed. They are not trying to be innovative, but just biblically obedient in a culturally appropriate way (though this sometimes appears innovative).

The goal of the middle third is to give the trainees **enough biblical content to obey and pass on**. You don't want to give them so much that they can't obey. Nor do you want to give them so much that they can't pass it on. It mustn't be overly complicated and difficult to reproduce. In the first 6-10 sessions, most T4T curricula use simple reproducible discipleship lessons for their initial short-term discipleship. After those 6-10 sessions they introduce inductive study of Scripture using simple inductive questions for long-term discipleship.

The most common inductive questions in T4T are "**SOS**":

- **Say**: What is this passage saying?

- **Obey**: What should we obey from this passage?

- **Share**: Who is someone we can share this message with?

Because the goal of the middle third is to give the trainees reproducible biblical content to obey and pass on, this is the *most flexible and adapted part* of T4T. For example, in non-literate contexts, you have to use extremely simple Bible stories, mnemonic devices and applications, or they can't obey them and pass/teach them to other new believers. Photocopies of lessons won't work in a context like that.

In educated contexts, you don't need the extra work of teaching oral Bible stories and having trainees memorize them. All they need is a simple sheet of paper and a Bible. Any of them can photocopy the sheet or open the Bible and pass this on to another new believer.

One successful missionary in the Middle East wrote completely new Bible lessons that would address the Muslim context. Another wrote lessons to fit a Hindu context. Another wrote lessons to fit an American post-modern context.

The bottom line is this:

- Your discipleship lessons must be **biblical.**

- The first few lessons must deal with the most important **basics of spiritual life** in a culturally appropriate application.

- They must be **simple enough** that the average new believer can train someone else with them.

Most people find that it is easiest to start with a set of T4T lessons that were written for a context similar to their own, use them as is, and then adapt them when they run into difficulties. In the supplementary resources of this book and on the T4T website, a number of different curricula are given as examples of this in multiple languages.

One of the biggest mistakes trainers make in this area is giving *too much content* because we are often such content-driven people. This is not to minimize the importance of content. It is critical. But it is the volume necessary that we overestimate. Remember the goal: multiplying generations of trainers. Give them enough to obey and pass on, but not so much that they get overwhelmed. If they get overwhelmed, it will be hard for them to have the confidence to go teach others what they have learned.

The goal is to develop a trainer, not simply get through content.

Another common mistake is spending so much time on the lesson that you leave out the time for practice at the end. When you do that, you have just violated the basic goal. You were trying to get through content, not build a trainer! **The goal is to develop a trainer, not simply get through content.**

Final Third: Looking Ahead

During the final third of the meeting, you move into preparation mode: preparing the trainers to really live out what God is speaking to them about growing in Christlikeness and becoming a trainer of others. If your goal is to build multiplying generations of trainers, then **you must give them time to prepare for the coming week.** Every good coach walks a team through *multiple* practice sessions before entering each week's game. But why do we think that our trainers can hear a lesson one time, then immediately go out and train someone else in it without lots of practice?

Your goal in the last third, as the trainees look ahead, is to give them **confidence and competence** to fulfill God's plans.

> Such **confidence** as this is ours through Christ before God. Not that we are competent in ourselves to claim anything for ourselves, but our **competence** comes from God. He has made us competent as ministers of a new covenant—not of the letter but of the Spirit; for the letter kills, but the Spirit gives life. (2 Cor. 3:4-6, NIV, emphasis added)

Part 6: Practice

What do we want our trainers to do beyond obeying the lesson personally? We want them to witness in the subsequent week, start groups and then begin training their groups in the three-thirds process. We want them to emulate everything they just received – all three thirds. Therefore, we must take a significant amount of time to let them practice as we wander around them coaching, correcting, praising and encouraging – just like a

ONE-LEGGED DUCK

By Ying Kai

There was a husband who very much enjoyed his wife's cooking. He really enjoyed roast duck and so his wife often cooked this for him. He especially enjoyed the legs. After she cooked roast duck for him two or three times the man noticed that the duck always had only one leg. The husband said, "Where's the other leg? Why is there only one duck leg?"

The wife answered "Oh, all the ducks in our backyard only have one leg."

"No, that's impossible! Show me."

"Okay," said the wife, and they went to the backyard. It was about 7:30 at night and all the ducks were asleep. All ducks sleep on one leg, right?

The husband said, "Hey, this is easy!" and he clapped his hands. When he clapped all the ducks woke up and put two legs down. He said, "See! Don't cheat me! They have two legs!"

Continued next page.

> But the wife said "Yes, but at our dinner table nobody claps so there is only one leg!"
>
> Affirmation and appreciation are important qualities in a trainer. When you are in the practice time with your trainees, hover over them, listen to them, correct them, but especially praise their good efforts. They will gain the confidence to train others.

good coach helping his team prepare for a game.

The most obvious thing that the trainees must practice is the lesson. If you just studied lesson four, then they practice lesson four. In an ideal world, your trainees would lag just one week behind your group with the group they are leading. However, this assumes that they led people to faith the very first week of training and then began to train them immediately. But what if there is a time lag of several weeks. Your group is on lesson four, and their groups are on lesson two?

How can you best prepare them to lead *their* group? Remember your goal of developing a trainer. Even though you might practice lesson four first, you probably want to take time to review and practice lesson two again.

> *The goal of the practice time is to give them competence and confidence to train others in the three-thirds process.*

The goal of the practice time is to give them **competence and confidence** to train others in the three-thirds process.

Competence: You want them to pass on the content of the Scripture lesson and the *process* of T4T accurately. Coaching them during the practice and gently correcting mistakes helps to reinforce this. As I mentioned earlier, in one assessment of Ying's CPM, 18 generations of believers were identified. What was being taught at the 18th generation was the same as the first. There are a number of ways to help this become a reality, but practice with coaching helps greatly.

Confidence: Very few people are going to lead their own group and teach them a new lesson if they don't have the confidence to practice it in the safety of the original group. As you take time to practice, they become more comfortable with the lesson and the three thirds, and can repeat it with confidence. In the final third, you help them think through how they will do this with their own group.

An important part of practice is actually doing a talk-through, and even role play at times, of what will likely happen with the person they will witness to or the group they will lead. What will happen first? If they say this, what will you do? If they say that, what will you do? What will you do in the first third with your group (e.g. what songs will you sing, what questions will you ask and what vision casting will you share)? How will you teach the lesson in the second third? How will you prepare them in the final third? This is essentially what Jesus did in giving His instructions to the 72 disciples in Luke 10.

Be sure to help them practice more than just the lesson. Help them practice all three thirds including the vision-casting vignette and the accountability questions. Remind them of a song or two they can sing with the group. You don't have to save all your practice time for the end. In fact with oral learners, you may need to stop every 10-15 minutes to practice something: vision casting, a song, a memory verse, re-telling a story, etc.

One important rule of thumb to remember is this: **the less educated or literate a group is, or the less familiar with the three-thirds process, the more time they need to practice**. Even if you have to cut the lesson short in the middle third, *always* allow enough time to practice. Always encourage the trainers to share the lesson they learned with someone else, even a non-believer, just to reinforce the learning and training process. Only with practice will you build a trainer.

Part 7: Set Goals and Pray

Never end your meeting without setting goals for the coming week (or two weeks) and praying for God's guidance and power to obey the lesson, witness to others and train trainers. After the practice time, encourage the participants to cry out to the Spirit to give them clarity on what goals they should set. Some goals will be carry-overs from previous weeks: things like "witness to five people this week" because that is a built-in expectation of the group. But the Lord may give them specific names of people to witness to this week.

Their goals will also relate to gathering new believers into a training group, or helping the group(s) to move to the next stage (helping them witness to their *oikos* or start their own training groups). Their goals may relate to troubleshooting an emerging problem in a group they lead and in confronting a brother.

Whatever their goals, have them write them down. If desired, you can ask them to give you a copy of their goals, so you can pray for them during the week. You can also ask for a copy of their Name List so that you can pray for their *oikos* with them.

Once they've taken time in prayer to write down some goals, have them share these with the group. If the group is large, they may have to break into smaller groups.

The T4T session ends by taking time to pray for each person, often gathering around and laying hands on the person. It is a time to pray for God's anointing for the coming week and for God to open the hearts of people the trainee will encounter.

In essence, every meeting is a commissioning service!

Summary: The Three-Thirds Process

LOOK BACK	LOOK UP	LOOK AHEAD
First Third	Second Third	Final Third
1. Pastoral Care	5. New Lesson	6. Practice the Lesson
How are you doing?	» Short-term reproducible discipleship lessons	7. Set Goals & Pray for each other
2. Worship		
3. Accountability	» Then, long-term self-feeding inductive Bible studies	
» Follow Jesus How are you obeying the Word?		
» Fish for men Witness, training, training trainers		
4. Vision Casting For what they can be and do		

The three-thirds process is a key principle God uses to build CPMs through the T4T process. To help trainees become trainers the meeting is divided into three thirds with seven parts.

Three thirds, seven parts. Each part is critical. But a few parts are more important than others in helping to develop and move a person from trainee to trainer. If you leave them out, you rarely get to a movement. Do you know which ones they are?

That's the next chapter.

Be a Doer, not just a Hearer!

Write down how God has spoken to you and what you need to obey as a result:

CHAPTER 8

The BOLD Parts

I was leading a T4T overview session for missionaries and church leaders. I had just finished explaining the three thirds of the T4T process with their seven parts (previous chapter). I had just written on a white poster paper something like this:

LOOK BACK	LOOK UP	LOOK AHEAD
First Third	*Second Third*	*Final Third*
1. Pastoral Care How are you doing?	5. New Lesson	6. Practice the Lesson
2. Worship	» Short-term reproducible discipleship lessons	7. Set Goals & Pray for each other
3. Accountability » Follow Jesus How are you obeying the Word?	» Then, long-term self-feeding inductive Bible studies	
» Fish for men Witness, training, training trainers		
4. Vision Casting For what they can be and do		

My co-trainer, Allen James,[13] walked up to the poster and asked the group: "Which parts get you to reproduction?" A look of confusion spread over the group. You could see it in their faces: "What do you mean? They're all important."

Allen persisted: "I want each small group to vote on two of the seven parts that you think *most* help trainees start a new generation – get to reproduction – train trainers. All seven parts are important. That's why they're in there. But which ones are most important to build trainers of trainers?"

The small groups in our class of 30 people began working on this assignment.

> **Exercise:** Right now, do the same thing. **Write down all seven parts.**

1. Pastoral Care

2. Worship

3. Accountability

4. Vision casting

5. New Lesson / Bible study

6. Practice

7. Set Goals and Pray

> **Now put a check next to the two parts out of the seven that are most important to get to reproduction – to help a trainee become a trainer.** Which are the most important to help the participants go out, lead people to faith, start a new group and then train them to repeat the process?

When our group came back together, Allen began to put check marks next to each of the seven parts as the groups voted on them. In this particular instance, the group actually

<hr/>

[13] I am indebted to my colleague Allen James for the concept of the "red or BOLD parts" and this method of emphasizing the parts of T4T that get to reproduction – help trainees become trainers.

voted correctly – the majority guessed the most important reproduction elements. Allen was a little surprised; this was the first time a group had correctly guessed all of them. There are actually FOUR parts, not two, that are most important to get to reproduction.

Allen circled them with a red marker. As he looked at the poster, with four parts circled in red, he announced, "Don't leave out the red parts! They are the most important parts of the T4T process."

Ever since then, we have called the parts that get to reproduction: the red parts. For the sake of ease in this black and white book, we will call them the **BOLD parts**.

The BOLD Parts

Each of the seven parts are important. Remember, there are four parts in the first third of each meeting, one part in the second third and two parts in the last third. All of them are important in the discipleship process or they wouldn't be in there.

The question, however, is which parts are most important for *reproduction*? Some parts are more important for biblical conviction, caring for needs or encountering God. So, all are important. But the goal is to build multiplying generations of trainers. So which parts most help you do that? Which parts most help trainees become trainers? Which parts help to launch a discipleship *re*-revolution?

There are four: **accountability, vision casting, practice,** and **set goals & pray**. These are the **BOLD parts**.

LOOK BACK	LOOK UP	LOOK AHEAD
First Third	*Second Third*	*Final Third*
1. Pastoral Care	5. New Lesson	6. Practice the Lesson
2. Worship		7. Set Goals & Pray
3. Accountability		
4. Vision Casting		

THE FOUR CALLS

*A Vision-casting Vignette
By Ying Kai*

Every believer should hear four calls (voices) calling him to witness.

Call from Above: In Isaiah 6, the King sits on His throne calling out for someone to go for him to the lost. Isaiah couldn't be quiet but jumped up and volunteered. Jesus said, "Go into all the world and proclaim the gospel to the whole creation." (Mark 16:15) The King commands us all to tell others how to come back to Him.

Do you hear the voice from heaven above?

Call from Below: In Luke 16, a rich man died and went to hell. He was in so much pain that he cried out to heaven, begging them to send someone to warn his living family members not to go to hell. The lost people who have died and gone to hell still call out for someone to warn their family to repent.

What do you think the dead relatives of the people around you would say to you if they could stand here?

Continued next page.

ACCOUNTABILITY is a key component for multiplication *if you do it right.* As mentioned in the previous chapter, loving accountability can help you move the group forward one step at a time toward training trainers. Your accountability questions must progressively become more CPM-focused as the weeks go by, from witnessing questions to CPM questions:

- *WITNESS: Who are you witnessing to? Who has believed?*

- *STARTER: When are you training them in the same process?*

- *TRAINER: How are these new believers doing witnessing to and winning others?*

- *TRAINER OF TRAINERS: When are they training their groups?*

- ***TRAINER OF TRAINERS WHO TRAINS TRAINERS: How are the trainers, that you are training, doing in training their new groups?***

VISION CASTING for who trainees can be in Christ and what God can accomplish through them is critical for reproduction. Many of us never think about casting vision, but all of the men and women who initiate movements understand the importance of keeping God's vision before the people.

In T4T, vision casting is not trying to get someone to buy into the program.

It is not a multi-level marketing sell. Vision casting is simply trying to keep God's heart in front of the trainees to encourage their faith. Therefore, keep it biblically focused.

PRACTICE has already been emphasized in the previous chapter. It is very rare for a trainee to become a trainer without enough time to practice in the training session. Practice gives him the confidence and competence to train someone else. The practice time enables you as the trainer to make sure they are passing on the content and expectations faithfully to the next generation.

SET GOALS AND PRAY is the fourth part that most leads to reproduction. Taking time for people to hear what *God (not the trainer)* is saying is important for the next week, writing it down, and then being prayed for by others is an act of commitment not unlike taking a vow. There is a sense of holy reverence and anticipation about what God is going to do. Although the trainees will make commitments to obey the Bible lesson during the middle third, goals in this final third are usually in two areas related to fishing for men: 1) Whom will you witness to? 2) Whom will you train and how?

In a very closed country, I was asked to do an intensive two-day training for a group of national believers. On the first day, I sent them out with the assignment to share in the evening

Do you hear the lost in hell below crying out for you to tell their families about the gospel?

Call from outside: In Acts 16, Paul had a vision of a man from Macedonia calling to him. He said, "Come over and help us!" Paul realized that God was telling him to go there to tell people about Jesus.

All around us, lost people are calling out for us to help them. When you see people each day, you should not hear the words from their mouth (e.g. "Help me in my field."; "Those groceries cost 25 dollars."), but the cry from their heart ("I am lost and need saving.").

Do you hear the call from lost people outside calling you to tell them the Good News?

Call from inside: In 1 Corinthians 9, Paul said "Woe is me if I don't share; I am under compulsion." His own spirit spoke to him from inside telling him that this was what he was created to be and do. He couldn't avoid sharing; this was his identity.

There is something inside all of us believers that

Continued next page.

reminds us that we must be witnesses. We were called to be fishers of men. This is who we are.

Do you hear the call from inside your own heart telling you to speak!

(This vignette can be shared with hand motions pointing UP, DOWN, OUT, IN.)

a gospel presentation they had just learned and report back the next morning. The next day, one young man [call him "D"] walked into the room with a young lady in tow. She bashfully smiled at me while he proudly announced in broken English:

"Steve, this is 'L' She was born in 1993.

Last night, she believed in the Most High God.

Today she is here for training."

Think about what he told me: 1) her physical birthday; 2) her spiritual birthday; 3) her destiny ("she is here for training")! All through the second day of training (we were doing an intensive 2-day training), I would refer to "D" as the first generation and "L" as the second generation. As we discussed plans for "L" to witness to her *oikos*, we began to call them the 3rd generation.[14]

Do you see what can happen with good accountability and healthy goal setting with prayer? In the course of 24 hours, a plan for three generations was set into motion!

Pressed for Time

Before reading this book and understanding the bold parts, think about how you would have dealt with this scenario:

Your T4T group was supposed to meet from 7 p.m. to 9 p.m. Unfortunately, people have arrived late, and you're not getting started until 7:45. You would like to let the meeting take a full two hours, but some of the members of the group have to leave at 9 p.m. Now you've only got 1 hour and 15 minutes for a two-hour meeting. Which of the seven parts would you be tempted to leave out to save some time?

---

[14] In T4T, we don't normally encourage trainees to bring their new believers back to the original group. If I were in an on-going T4T relationship with "D," I would have encouraged him to begin training "L" at another time in the week.

Remember, how would you have answered PRIOR to reading this book?

1. Pastoral Care

2. Worship

3. Accountability

4. Vision casting

5. New Lesson / Bible study

6. Practice

7. Set Goals and Pray

Many of us would leave out **vision casting** first, simply because it is something we're least familiar with.

The second part that gets left out when we are pressed for time is **accountability.** Most of us aren't too comfortable with accountability, so it is easy to leave it out, or do "superficial accountability." In superficial accountability, you nod your head and say something like this: "Did you all do what we learned in the last lesson?" Heads nod in response. "Great, let's go on to the next lesson!"

The third part to get left out is usually **practice.** The scenario runs like this. You spend 40 minutes on the first third although you were trying to shorten it. But the sharing in the pastoral care time and the worship time were just "too good" to cut short. You hurry to the Bible study which takes up most of the remaining 35 minutes. You look at your watch and it is almost 9 p.m. Wow! You remark: "Well, we've run out of time! We'll practice next week. Let's close in prayer." You've just left out the practice.

And you just left out the fourth part: **goal setting with prayer.** Yes, you prayed at the end, but it wasn't really a commissioning.

When pressed for time, which parts do we tend to leave out? **The BOLD parts!** Perhaps this is because we're uncomfortable with them, but usually it's because we unconsciously have a different goal. Our goal is to get through content, or have a great encounter with each other, or have awesome worship, NOT to develop multiplying generations of trainers.

What are you left with?

When you take out the bold parts, **what are you left with?**

1. Pastoral Care

2. Worship

3. ~~Accountability~~

4. ~~Vision Casting~~

5. New Lesson / Bible study

6. ~~Practice~~

7. ~~Set Goals and Pray~~

A **traditional Bible study**, cell group or Sunday school group! **And you RARELY get to reproduction of trainers.** We default to what we know best (intuitive), and what we know best does not usually spark a CPM (counter-intuitive).

Don't leave out the BOLD parts!

How do you avoid the pitfall of leaving out the bold parts?

-   Simply **remembering** that in **every training** you must include all seven parts in a three-thirds format will solve a lot of the problems.

-   If you are pressed for time, instead of leaving out parts, **shorten each part** and keep the same three-thirds proportions of a meeting.

    »   For example, you find that you only have 1 hour and 15 minutes, divide that into three-thirds – roughly 25 minutes for each third. That will mean you need to shorten the lesson, or *just do half a lesson* in order to keep the goal of building a trainer. (Though it is usually better to meet for at least two hours and just run over-time!)

» In recent trainings, we have experimented with 60-minute "lunch hour" T4T trainings. We've been very pleased that we can still get in all three-thirds in a meaningful manner. We just lower our expectations on how much content we can get through. This should not be your norm unless you have no other way to meet for more than an hour.

- Remember that the three-thirds are approximate time divisions in your meeting. Some weeks, some thirds may take longer. When in doubt, leave **extra time for practice** as it usually takes longer than you think to help people become confident and competent.

> *When pressed for time, which parts do we tend to leave out?* **The BOLD parts which get to reproduction!** *If you do, what are you left with? A traditional small group! And you rarely get to reproduction.*

- A rule of thumb is to **cut down the amount of content** before cutting down anything else. You are just trying to give them enough to obey and pass on.

- **Schedule more time for the meeting than you actually need.** If you need two hours, then schedule a 2 ½ hour meeting – say 7:00-9:30.

An American Example

In Chapter 2, I referred to a dynamic church in Waco, Texas being used by God to birth a movement worldwide. Antioch Community Church has planted many churches in the USA and supports over 200 missionaries and church planters around the world through their ministry: Antioch Ministries International (AMI).

Yet, AMI became aware that the many good things could easily lull them into missing what is most critical in finishing the task of world evangelization. Over the last three years, AMI has been re-tooling teams overseas and the church at home to become more CPM-oriented as we've implemented a training program for home and field workers. They have worked hard to develop a T4T model in the US and abroad that will implement all three-thirds effectively.

After the trainings, they worked out a basic model for their church as they reached out to the lost in fresh ways. The first year of re-tooling after the training they saw over 300 salvations in Waco alone. They started targeting areas of town and going to sow the gospel very broadly. They saw upwards of 70 salvations in one neighborhood over a two-week time span. The teams were trained to follow up with T4T. Out of this one evangelistic push, they started a few budding groups and won some 3rd generation believers.

But implementing T4T in new contexts with newly saved people was not enough. Antioch Community Church has a very strong emphasis on the church meeting in homes through their "life groups." After the CPM training, they began incorporating the T4T process into that small group structure. When they realized that the life group structure was leaving out some of the bold parts, they introduced them back into the expectations for a life group meeting. In addition, some groups have started meeting every other week in order to give their members time to start their own new groups. They have made a fundamental shift in their focus: from multiplying when groups get large to planting new groups among the *oikos* of group members by emphasizing the BOLD parts.

The number of conversions, baptisms and new group starts have taken off. Just making a few important adjustments can have an incredible impact. AMI is learning even better how to cooperate with the Spirit in the kingdom of God. They are returning to the original discipleship revolution of Acts!

AMI is an example of a radical shift taking place around the world as to how we envision starting new groups and churches.

To understand that shift, read the next chapter.

Be a Doer, not just a Hearer!

Write down how God has spoken to you and what you need to obey as a result:

CHAPTER 9

Starting New Generations, Not Just Multiplying Groups

By now, it is probably obvious that T4T is different from traditional small group multiplication. In typical small group (or Sunday school) multiplication, we bring new people into our current group, whether they are new believers or just older Christians. As the group gets to a certain size, it divides into two or three groups with new leaders. The idea is **grow, then multiply.**

T4T is fundamentally different. T4T is NOT grow, then multiply. The design is not to bring new believers into existing groups. Instead, T4T is **launch and repeat:** as trainees lead people to faith, empower them to launch new groups and then to repeat the process with their new trainees. Multiply trainers. In T4T you don't wait for a group to grow before launching new groups out of it.

These new groups become their own house churches or sometimes new small groups in an existing church. The goal is to initiate a movement of new groups starting under the Lordship of Christ.

New Generations of Groups or Churches

In T4T every new believer is *potentially* a new group. Not every believer will launch new groups, but T4T encourages and empowers trainees to start new groups, not bring their new believers or Christian friends into existing groups. Every believer is empowered to start a new group or church as the Spirit guides him under the mentorship of a trainer and existing group. It's explosive!

As the trainee leads friends to faith, he does not fold them into the original group where he is trained. In the beginning his new group may be small, so naturally he will want to reach some friends and family for Jesus so their group can become larger.

> T4T is fundamentally different from growing and then dividing a group. T4T empowers trainees to lead people to faith, launch new groups with them and then to repeat the process with their new trainees.
> **Launch and repeat. Multiply trainers.**

Even though it is starting to sound like "grow, then multiply," it's not. Every T4T group grows in size simply because it's just unnatural for a husband to win his wife and not to bring her into his own group! Existing T4T groups also grow in size because not all of the participants will start new groups (remember: attendees, witnesses, starters and trainers). But the spirit of "launch and repeat" continues in the group. The trainee may lead his family and friends to faith and incorporate them into his new group. **At the same time** he is training them to witness to their *oikos* and launch new groups with them. For example, even though a trainee includes his wife in his own group, he may encourage her to start a second group with ladies in her neighborhood. At this point, the wife would be a part of two groups: her husband's and her new group of ladies.

If we only emphasize **grow, then multiply**, we lose a lot of potential for growth. Members of grow-then-multiply groups have little incentive to win new people or bring them into the group. They enjoy the size and intimacy of the existing group.

Instead, the T4T process continually casts vision that God can birth a movement through each member! Although members may sometimes bring their new converts back to the original training group, they are gently coached to start new groups with these believers in the weeks that follow.

We structure T4T meetings in three thirds precisely because we want our trainers to start new generations of groups, not simply grow a group and multiply it in a tightly-controlled process.

Why do trainees bring new converts to the original group?

SCENARIO: You just had your first T4T session with your new trainees. They go out and witness. At the second meeting, Frank brings Joe and Harold to the training session. Joe and Harold are new believers that Frank led to faith. Your goal is to make Frank a trainer of others, but he has just brought them back to you. Why did he do this?

- Perhaps it is the way things have always been done, and he is not catching the new paradigm.

- Perhaps he missed the vision of starting his own training group.

- Perhaps he doesn't have time to train them on a separate night of the week.

- Perhaps he thinks you're the trainer, and he wants to bring them to the expert.

- Perhaps he lacks confidence to start his own group.

All of these can be true, but usually it is because he lacks confidence or vision to start a new group.

So what do you do? You remember your goal: multiplying generations of trainers. What is your course of action to help Frank become a trainer who forms Joe and Harold into a new group of three?

First, what do you NOT do? You don't scold him for bringing them! He was faithful! You don't belittle him, chide him or embarrass him. He was a faithful witness.

Instead, you praise him in the accountability time. "Frank, this is awesome! You faithfully led Joe and Harold to faith. Let's stop as a group and give God praise for this."

But, if you don't do some correction, this will become the new pattern for others who lead people to faith. You will only end up with witnesses, not trainers.

Therefore, you can do something like this: "Frank, this is awesome that you have brought Joe and Harold to faith. But you know, our group is on session two and they need to learn session one [WHY-WHOM-HOW]. Joe and Harold, if you don't mind, we'll go through lesson two as a group, but afterwards, you two, Frank and I will stay late to review session one."

You don't hold the entire group back and start over on session one. If you do, the group will never move forward. You keep the plan as is. But after the three thirds are over (or during the final third), you pull Frank, Joe and Harold aside. You say something like this: "Frank, you remember session one that we did last week. Why don't you walk Joe and Harold through it, while I sit here and help out. Remember it answered three questions about why Christians don't witness: WHY-WHOM-HOW."

By doing this, you are reinforcing that Frank is a **trainer,** not just a **trainee.** You help him lead the two new believers through the session. Before you all leave, you pull Frank aside. "Frank, there's no need for you to bring these two guys to this meeting. We're already pretty large, and are ahead of them in the lessons. When would be a good time that you could meet with them as a group of three? Each week during our training time, I'll coach you on what to do when you train them."

This one little act, based on your goal, can make all the difference between growing-then-multiplying and launching-and-repeating, thereby starting a movement of new multiplying trainers.

Generations of Groups

Your hope is to get consistent 4th+ generation believers and groups for a CPM to emerge. Not every participant in our group will start a new group. In fact not everyone will witness (attendees). Some will witness and bring people back to the original group (witnesses). Some people (starters) will start new groups but fail to catch the vision to train them to repeat the process. They start one group but not a movement. But some people (trainers) will catch the concept to train trainers. They will launch new groups, often more than one as time goes by, and train those new believers to witness, disciple people and train them to launch new groups of trainers.

Messiness: Groups or Churches?

Where no oxen are, the manger is clean,
But much revenue comes by the strength of the ox.
(Prov. 14:4, NASB)

Solomon made it very clear. If you want a stable with no mess, don't get an ox in the first place. But if you want to plant and harvest, you need several oxen and plan to clean up a lot.

Which would you rather have: a clean, orderly system with few results OR hundreds of people coming to faith and groups starting, but with it lots of problems? You can't have growth without mess. It's a kingdom dynamic. (Remember the parable of the tares.)

A large number of Paul's epistles were written to address problems. That's the nature of ministry. We don't enjoy the problems, but they are often a sign of growth.

I used to have this verse (Prov. 14:4) taped to the inside of my desk in my office where only I could see it. When we worked with the Ina, team members often came into the office to discuss strategy. Inevitably we were putting out fires and solving problems: persecution, leadership development, dissension, false teaching, lack of access, etc. As each new problem would come up, as difficult as it was, I would look down at the verse and smile inside. I would say a prayer of thanks: "Thank you, Father. We would not be having this problem if people weren't coming to faith, being discipled and starting new churches!"

T4T *never* follows a neat exact progression. CPMs are much messier than neat, orderly organizational charts, and much more exciting! Launch and repeat!

Thrive in the messiness of movement

Keep the vision of multiplying generations of trainers before you, and keep pushing the movement that direction through the power of the Holy Spirit. You'll have lots of exceptions, surprises and morphs along the way, but the direction of the movement will continue to track toward new generations of groups. Here are some examples of how it doesn't always follow this progression exactly:

- Frank starts a new group with Joe and Harold. His wife leads Joe's and Harold's wives to the Lord. Instead of starting a new group with them, she brings them into Frank's group. Not two groups but one.

- Joe leads a group at the office to faith, and another couple of sports buddies to faith. He starts a 3rd generation group at work, but brings his sports buddies to Frank's group.

- Later on, Frank's wife launches a new group with some ladies she led to faith in the neighborhood. Now, she is attending three groups. She attends your training group, a group her husband Frank leads, *and* she leads a group with the neighborhood ladies.

- Several months later, Frank starts two new groups. Now he is attending your group to be trained, and leading three groups personally. As time goes by, the first group he led decides to free him up to lead these two new groups. Harold takes over leadership of that group.

Getting confused yet? Don't you love it? This is the messiness of a movement, but it's all moving in the same direction – toward multiple generations of trainers and groups. This is the power of the King's reign over the lives of disciples who love Jesus. It's out of your control, but in God's control just like God intended. It's a discipleship revolution!

Don't get distracted by the messiness. Keep pushing toward a CPM.

Groups or churches?

In the messiness, the question often comes up: "Does each new group become a church (e.g. house church) or just a discipleship group?" The answer is "yes." Both happen.

Ideally, in T4T, the design is for each new T4T group to become a house church. And this *often* happens.

In reality, that doesn't always happen. Sometimes, two or three groups meet for T4T, but because they're all connected, they decide to meet at another time for a larger worship and preaching time ("church").

Sometimes, the context is not appropriate for house churches. For example, one time Ying and Grace were teaching T4T in a large government-registered church in a closed country. Ying and Grace were teaching the 1000+ church members to win friends and start T4T groups. Grace inadvertently told them to start new "house churches." When the session was over, the pastor told Grace: "We can't tell them to start house churches, or we will have trouble! Tell them they can start 'official home Bible studies' but not house churches." As soon as the break was over, Grace corrected herself. The group began to do exactly what T4T teaches, but instead of making independent house churches, they all became official home Bible studies of the church.

In some contexts, a hybrid will work best. In one city in a limited-access nation, underground churches have adopted T4T. Instead of starting new house churches immediately, their T4T groups come together on Sundays to worship and listen to Bible teaching. When the Sunday group gets too large for their context and would invite government reprisal (usually 300-400 people) they launch a new Sunday celebration in another part of the city with some of the T4T groups.

In some contexts, the T4T groups *function* as churches though they are not called churches. In a very large mega-church in America, Ying was teaching T4T. The well-known pastor listened to Ying teach, then announced: "We are implementing T4T in our church."

Ying asked him: "Are you willing to let the groups become house churches?"

The pastor replied: "Yes, we are going to let them baptize in their groups, do the Lord's Supper and give offerings. If they want to come to the larger church meeting on the weekend, great! But we want them to function as churches. If they want to function as new churches by not coming to our Sunday celebrations, that is also okay."

This was an amazing step for this influential church.

Don't get overly concerned about what you call the T4T groups. In 90% of the situations I know of, they generally become house churches that find ways to fellowship with each other beyond the home meeting. In other situations, the groups become small group meetings of a larger church.

One word of caution about the latter: If you use T4T simply as a way to launch new cell groups for your church, the potential for CPM is greatly limited. All cell churches have an inherent size limit built in depending on the gifts and skills of the senior leadership, as well as the size of their facilities.

Giving groups the freedom, even the empowerment, to become new churches takes the limit off the budding movement. You could view yourself as the pastor of a large church. If you are a pastor, how much better to view yourself as a **pastor**

PRAY FOR WHAT YOU NEED AND TAKE A RISK

By Ying Kai

The Holy Spirit has all the gifts, and He can give you what you need. For instance, if you feel that you cannot speak very well, the Holy Spirit can help you. If you feel that you are very weak in faith, the Holy Spirit can give you faith.

From 2000 to 2002, I worked with the very first group of farmers I trained where our first CPM broke out. I finally stopped going there because they could run everything by themselves. But until then, I trained them frequently. Then in 2004, a CPM assessment team came in to assess our CPM. They wanted to see the first place where the CPM began. I called the original group and set up a time for a visit. When we met together with the farmers I found that I could not understand what they were saying, and they could not understand me! They said, "We are all from a different people group and speak

Continued next page.

of pastors and your church as a **training base for a movement!**

Take the shackles off. This is what we mean by the counter-intuitive ways of the kingdom!

Taking a Risk

Is this risky? Absolutely! Every CPM experiences a myriad of challenges. But every dead church experiences a whole other set of problems. The challenges of CPMs are much preferred over the alternative.

Perhaps the biggest concern about a CPM is that it feels out of control. It IS out of control – out of *your* control. But instead, you have commended it to the *King's* control. The King's reign!

> a dialect different from the trade language."
>
> I said, "No, before you could all speak the trade language."
>
> They said, "No, we speak only our dialect." They said, "Before, **you** could speak our dialect."
>
> I said, "No, I only spoke the trade language to you." For months the Holy Spirit translated. It was a miracle.
>
> When you pray, ask God to help you. The Holy Spirit can give you any gift. In your city, your area, your people – whatever you need -- talk to the Holy Spirit and he will help you.

> After they had preached the gospel to that city and had made many disciples, they returned to Lystra and to Iconium and to Antioch, strengthening the souls of the disciples, encouraging them to continue in the faith, and saying, "Through many tribulations we must enter the kingdom of God." When they had appointed elders for them in every church, having prayed with fasting, they **commended them to the Lord** in whom they had believed. (Acts 14:21-23, NASB, emphasis added)

Paul's first missionary journey lasted 9-12 months. Toward the end of this journey, Paul and Barnabas began to backtrack to the churches they had started. This meant they returned to the most recently planted churches first. These churches were just a few weeks and months old in the faith. Paul explained to them that it was going to get very messy because of the tribulations ahead.[15] Then, with weeks-old and months-old believers, Paul and Barnabas appointed some of them as elders or overseers in each church.

What is significant here is the phrase "commended them to the Lord." Knowing that they didn't have long with each of these new churches, Paul and Barnabas took a risk to commend them to the Spirit of God rather than stay on and commend these leaders to themselves. They lived out the counter-intuitive ways of the kingdom. They took a risk to trust that the Spirit would remain on as Teacher, and He would do a much better job of controlling the movement than Paul and Barnabas.

When Paul returned a year or so later, he found a movement continuing to grow.

> So the churches were being strengthened in the faith, and were increasing in number daily. (Acts 16:5, NASB)

He continued to coach them and guide them, but he didn't babysit them. He let the Spirit be their Teacher. It was worth the risk.

Giving up personal control and management of all the believers and groups is an important step for any leader who longs to see a church-planting movement develop. This is the only way to launch new generations of churches rather than gradually grow and multiply groups in an orderly system. Spirit-control **is** the discipleship revolution.

Biblical Precedent: Life-on-Life Fluidity

T4T is not a revolution. It is a *re*-revolution. The discipleship revolution has been played out all through history, starting in the pages of Acts. The precedent has already been set, and T4T's goal is to help us live out the New Testament expectations for disciples and churches.

---

[15] In fact, one of the first controversies to face the first century church was whether or not to allow people who had recanted their faith under threat of persecution to re-enter the church when they repented.

Paul's work in Ephesus is a good example of the biblical precedent for a CPM. In Acts 19:1-7, Paul entered Ephesus and found some "disciples" who really were not fully in the kingdom yet. They had not heard the whole message of the gospel. Paul led them to faith, and the men were filled with the Spirit. The evangelism phase had begun.

Paul then entered the synagogue and for three months boldly proclaimed the gospel of the kingdom (Acts 19:8). He argued from the Old Testament scriptures that Jesus was the Christ. Some believed. The evangelism phase continued.

With the group of believers from these two incidents, we come to two of the most significant verses in Acts:

> **But** when some were becoming hardened and disobedient, speaking evil of the Way before the people, he **withdrew** from them and took away the disciples, reasoning daily in the school of Tyrannus. This took place for two years, so that **all** who lived in Asia heard the word of the Lord, both Jews and Greeks. (Acts 19:9-10, NASB, emphasis added)

In the growing messiness of the Ephesian work, Paul began to meet resistance by the non-believing Jews. What often happened at this point in previous journeys was something like this: "Then the Jews dragged him out of the city, stoned him and left him for dead" (Acts 14:19). Perhaps the most significant words of this passage are **"but . . . he withdrew."** Paul perceptively realized that the growing opposition threatened to derail his ability to stay in Ephesus. When he realized this, he changed his *modus operandi.* He moved from primarily "evangelism mode" to "training mode." (Remember the dichotomy: win the lost, train the saved.)

He took his disciples, which must have been a significant number, and led them to a lecture hall – the school of Tyrannus – where he met **daily** with his disciples. In all likelihood, this scenario played out something like this:

> Several hundred people have come to faith in the great commercial center of Ephesus. Paul needs to give them more attention. He and his team hunt out a place to meet with them

safely outside the watchful eyes of the synagogue officials. They find a room that they can afford to rent or that is donated to their use. Paul moves his base of operations to this classroom. Each day, various groups of disciples come in to be trained by Paul and Silas and their team. One group meets on Monday mornings, while another group meets on Monday nights, while another group meets during the afternoon siesta on Tuesdays. Some groups are fairly organized, while some disciples come in each day whenever they have free time. It is a place of spiritual energy and development. The vision is huge: let's reach the whole area of Asia! Evangelism, discipleship and church planting become a lifestyle expectation of each new believer.

One new disciple, Epaphras from Colossae, in Ephesus on business, hears the gospel and returns home where he starts a new church in Colossae (Col. 1:7, 4:12), and then helps them start churches in nearby Laodicea and Hierapolis (Col. 4:13-16).

Other young disciples travel back to their hometowns in the province or on business and take the message of the kingdom with them, leaving churches in their wake. They pass on the pattern they received from Paul (Philip. 3:17, 1 Cor. 4:17).

The Roman roads are well developed, and the disciples return to Ephesus periodically, some more often than others, to receive instruction, advice and more content. Others return to share news of breakthroughs. Others return defeated and need encouragement from the band of disciples.

Soon this pattern of evangelism, discipleship and church planting is an expectation spreading like a virus all over the busy commercial roads and small country lanes of the Roman province of Asia. Thousands of people are coming to faith. Miracles amaze many (Acts 19:11). It's pretty messy as believers still holding onto sin come under increasing conviction and clean out deeply rooted demonic strongholds (19:19).

Scores, perhaps hundreds of churches begin during this time at the hands of ordinary believers, some meeting in homes, others in lecture halls, some in synagogues (at least for a while). Some groups become one church, but still meet in homes. Other groups become separate churches meeting in homes. It's very confusing and fluid. Seven famous churches in Asia Minor arise during this time and will later receive special words from Jesus in Revelation.[16]

The pattern is so well set and the expectation to follow Jesus and fish for men so strong that **in two years' time, every** Jew and Gentile living in the Roman province hears the word of the Lord (19:10). Not all believe, but there is a province-wide buzz about this kingdom movement.

The movement is messy as hundreds of disciples (trainers) come and go in that legendary lecture hall of Tyrannus. Paul stays in one place; they come and go. Leaders are gradually developed in every place. Whether they return with news of victory, defeat, encouragement or discouragement, "night and day for a period of three years [Paul does] not cease to admonish each one with tears." (Acts 20:31, NASB).

TRAINING. The *life-on-life fluidity* of tearful, heart-felt interaction, challenge and encouragement toward a movement of God. *Training* with *tears*. This is no sterile classroom training. This is real life, real joy, real tears. Open hearts shared honestly. More like a sports locker room than a classroom! As generations of believers develop, it is out of Paul's personal control, but still greatly influenced by him.

After three years Paul physically leaves the epicenter of the greatest movement in Acts. Hundreds of churches started. Thousands and thousands of believers. All of this in perhaps the most pagan, demon-controlled city in the empire. A place filled with black magic and demonic possession (Acts 19:11-20). The center of the province-wide cult of Artemis, so strong that it would provoke a riot against the Way (Acts 19:23).

No one in his right mind would call this a receptive place of harvest! A place known as the stronghold of Satan. A place filled with adversaries. It's just not intuitive. Human thinking says: "Find a more receptive place. It will be many more months or years before a harvest is ready."

---

[16] Most NT scholars believe the seven churches of Revelation, all within a day or two journey on Roman roads, were started during this period of time.

Really? What was Paul's view? Perhaps adversaries are a sign that the kingdom is being felt in many circles!

> But I will remain in Ephesus until Pentecost; for a **wide door** for effective service has opened to me, and there are **many adversaries**. (1 Cor. 16:8-9 NIV; emphasis added)

COUNTER-INTUITIVE. That's what kingdom movements are. That's what T4T should do: help you counter-intuitively align yourself to work with the King. Lead people to faith; **launch** new groups and **repeat. Multiply trainers.** CPMs are about launching new generations of trainers and churches, not controlled growth and multiplication. It's a discipleship *re*-revolution. The King's reign, not your reign.

CPMs are about launching new generations of trainers and churches, not controlled growth and multiplication.

Launch doesn't mean *drop*. Even though they are out of your direct control, there is a way to continue to guide and shape the movement. Find out how in the next chapter.

Be a Doer, not just a Hearer!

Write down how God has spoken to you and what you need to obey as a result:

CHAPTER 10

Mentoring a Movement

The risk of launching groups can be scary. That's why we don't just *drop* them.

As a spacecraft is launched, it moves from the control of the home base (mission control) to control by the astronauts. The launching process moves it to the leadership of the astronauts. Mission control doesn't drop the astronauts. Instead it monitors, gives feedback and sometimes clear instructions to change a course all the way through the journey.

In the eight to ten years of Paul's three missionary journeys, it appears from Acts and the Pauline epistles that six to seven church-planting movements developed in the eastern half of the Roman Empire through the power of the Spirit. Those CPMs were based in the following provinces in the following chronological order: 1) Cyprus, 2) Phrygia, 3) Galatia, 4) Macedonia, 5) Achaia, 6) Asia and possibly 7) Illyricum.[17]

In the Asia Minor CPM launched from Ephesus that we discussed in the previous chapter, Paul stayed with his leaders for three years (Acts 20:31). He stayed long enough to see a movement birthed around him (Acts 19:10). Paul was in mission control launching new work all over the province.

In Corinth, Paul stayed with the movement that emerged there for about 18 months:

---

[17] When Paul or his disciples reached Illyricum is uncertain. It happened somewhere in the three journeys because in Romans 15:19 he references laying a foundation there as a part of his three journeys.

And he settled there a year and six months, teaching the word of God among them. (Acts 18:11, NASB)

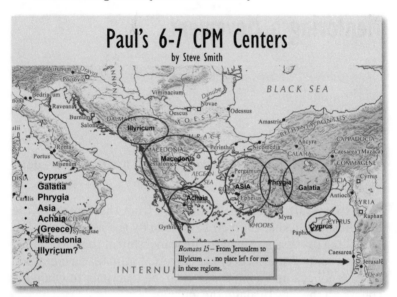

Again, Paul stayed long enough for a movement to be birthed around him. He was in mission control launching new work that spread all over that province of Achaia (Greece):

> Paul, an apostle of Christ Jesus by the will of God, and Timothy our brother, to the church of God which is at Corinth with **all the saints who are throughout Achaia**. (2 Cor. 1:1, NASB, emphasis added)

In other provinces (Galatia, Phrygia, and Macedonia), Paul was run out within weeks or months. Nevertheless, he returned often, sent emissaries, received emissaries and/or sent letters in a process of encouraging and training these young believers. The results were still similar – movements blossoming in various provinces (Acts 13:49; 16:5).

Paul had a purpose he was trying to accomplish, whether his visits were in short spurts, in months, or in years. He helped to guide a movement after it was launched, by monitoring it in a mentoring relationship in the months and years that followed.

How long should I stay with a group?

By establishing a long-term mentoring relationship with the emerging trainers and churches, you can help to guide, without controlling or quenching, a movement. The health of the long-term movement is shaped by how you establish on-going contact after the initial launch of new believers and churches.

> *By establishing a long-term mentoring relationship with the emerging trainers and churches, you can help to guide, without controlling or quenching, a movement.*

The question often arises: "How long should I stay with a group I am training?"

The answer is: "What's your goal?" If you remember the goal, you will find the answer.

- **T4T GOAL: Multiplying generations of trainers and churches – at least four generations and beyond.**

Church-planting movements are characterized by consistent 4th generation churches and beyond in *multiple* contexts. Almost every sustained CPM demonstrates many generations beyond this. Fourth generation simply marks the beginning of a CPM.

How long do you need to stay with a T4T group to accomplish that? The answer varies widely, but it is ALWAYS longer than the initial set of discipleship lessons you use, whether six lessons or ten!

Generally, to accomplish this goal and help the believers entrust themselves to the Holy Spirit, you must stay with your initial T4T groups 9 to 18 months. This assumes that the believers you are training are willing to keep implementing what you are teaching them. This assumes they are not stubborn, refusing to live in loving accountability.

There are two reasons to stay with them this long:

REASON 1: Consistent G4 Success

If your goal is to build a movement in which multiple generations of trainers and churches begin, then you need to stay with the group long enough (or return often enough) to mentor them through this process and set up healthy patterns of discipleship. Consider the charted scenario below. We will call your training group generation zero (GØ) simply because you are training existing Christians to start the first generation of believers in your people group[18]. You start the group at the beginning of January and leave the group after six weeks because you have "finished T4T" -- by which you mean the six lessons you are using for short-term discipleship. But generation zero doesn't start a new generation (generation 1 – G1) until sometime in February. In this scenario, how many **new generations** of groups would you have after your initial six sessions? ONE. You're at G1 only.

	Jan.	**Feb.**	Mar.	Apr.	May	June	July	Aug.	Sept.	Oct.	Nov.	Dec.	Jan.	Feb.	Mar.	Apr.	May	June	New Groups
Your Group	X																		1
Gen 1		X																	1
Gen 2																			
Gen 3																			
Gen 4																			
																			2

Some T4T groups begin new generations of T4T groups every few months, some every few weeks. In a few rare examples, they may start even more quickly . It all depends on how well you train the trainers, how effective they are in their witness, how long it takes for their *oikos* to put their faith in Christ, etc. Every situation is different.

In this scenario, by the time you get to the end of February, you are finished with short-term discipleship. But you still only

---

[18] If you had led the people in your first training group to faith, then they would be Generation G1.

have one new generation. You want at least FOUR new generations to be sure a movement is underway. The group is responsive to the concept of T4T and is catching on. So you press on with long-term discipleship using inductive Bible study in the middle third. In the practice times, you may review the first few discipleship lessons that they will cover with their new training groups. You spend time role-playing how they will start another generation, or how they can help their G1 groups start G2 groups, doing your part under the Lordship of Christ to help this become a movement.

> Generally, to get to consistent 4th+ generations trainers and churches, you must stay with your initial T4T group 9 to 18 months to guide them through the process.

Six months go by. They're having difficulty getting their G1 groups (several by now) to start G2 groups. But finally in June the first ones emerge. Party time! You're on your way to a movement. You've crossed a major hurdle to CPM – new believers starting groups with other people in their community. But if you exit now, you're still only at G2. So you stay on.

	Jan.	Feb.	Mar.	Apr.	May	**June**	July	Aug.	Sept.	Oct.	Nov.	Dec.	Jan.	Feb.	Mar.	Apr.	May	June	New Groups
Your Group	X																		1
Gen 1		X																	4
Gen 2					X														3
Gen 3																			
Gen 4																			
																			8

Now you have a bigger challenge. You've got to help GØ (your original group of trainees) train G1 to train G2 to start a new generation. Fortunately, G2 knows what it looks like for young believers to do effective evangelism and discipleship because that is who is training them! They take heart and win their *oikos*. Three months later in September, the first G3 groups start! Party time again. It's obvious the DNA is catching on.

You're excited. But if you leave now, you're still only at G3, and you know it takes consistent 4th generation and beyond for a ministry to become a sustained movement.

	Jan.	Feb.	Mar.	Apr.	May	June	July	Aug.	**Sept.**	Oct.	Nov.	Dec.	Jan.	Feb.	Mar.	Apr.	May	June	New Groups
Your Group	X																		1
Gen 1		X																	6
Gen 2					X														10
Gen 3									X										5
Gen 4																			
																			22

For some reason, G3 is having difficulty getting G4 started, but six months later the first G4 groups start. Now it's time for a major celebration. The work is spreading out through multiple streams of relationships, many of them completely unrelated to each other now. It's now February, over a year later. You could leave now, but only the first G4 group has started. You want to stay on long enough to make sure this is a pattern. During this time you are helping them establish healthy long-term Bible study and obedience patterns (more on this later in the chapter).

	Jan.	Feb.	Mar.	Apr.	May	June	July	Aug.	Sept.	Oct.	Nov.	Dec.	Jan.	**Feb.**	Mar.	Apr.	May	June	New Groups
Your Group	X																		1
Gen 1		X																	6
Gen 2					X														17
Gen 3								X											15
Gen 4													X						4
																			43

During this 18-month mentorship, prior generations continue to start new groups (not to mention that you are also starting new GØ groups).

GØ continues to start new groups: 6 by the time the 18 months are over.

G1 continues to start new groups: 17 by the time the 18 months are over.

G2 continues to start new groups: 30 by the time the 18 months are over.

G3 continues to start new groups: 10 by the time the 18 months are over (they haven't had much time to get things going yet in this scenario). G4 is almost ready to launch its first groups.

	Jan.	Feb.	Mar.	Apr.	May	June	July	Aug.	Sept.	Oct.	Nov.	Dec.	Jan.	**Feb.**	Mar.	Apr.	May	June	New Groups
Your Group	X																		1
Gen 1		X																	6
Gen 2				X															17
Gen 3						X													30
Gen 4														X					10
																			64

Why do you stay with a group 18 months? In this scenario, that's what it took to get 64 groups started with consistent 4th generation results.

In another scenario, this could take nine months. In another, three years.

The duration of your stay with a group is not dictated by how much content you are trying to get to them, but how many reproducing generations you want to develop.

> The duration of your stay with a group is not dictated by how much content you are trying to get to them, but how deep a movement you hope to initiate as you develop them as leaders.

Monitoring G4

A year ago, a colleague shared with me the marvelous work that God is doing among his Muslim people group. Miracle after miracle is occurring in which the Bridegroom is wooing His bride to Himself. I marveled!

He showed me a chart showing how many new churches had started and how many believers had been baptized. I praised the Lord with Him.

About this time, I asked him a diagnostic question to determine if this was a CPM yet or not. I asked, "How many of these churches are 1st, 2nd, 3rd and 4th+ generation?"

The colleague looked at me with puzzlement. "I don't know. I've never been asked!" A few weeks later, I received a great email from him in which he had polled the leaders from the new churches and sent me a breakdown of churches by generation. At this time, it wasn't a CPM yet, but it was getting close. It could very well be an emerging CPM.

What shocked me was his statement: "I don't know. I've never been asked." One of the reasons we don't get to CPM is because we aren't tracking our results by CPM indicators. CPM indicators are consistent 4th+ generation believers, baptisms, groups and churches. **Until you track it to 4th+ generation consistently, you don't have a church-planting movement.**

REASON 2: Stay with them long enough to develop solid leaders

The first reason you develop an 18-month mentorship is to help initiate 4th+ generation growth.

The second reason to stay with a T4T group at least 9 to 18 months is to build solid leaders at each generation. You are trying to set in place a leadership development system that will grow with the movement. Church-planting movements can also be called leadership-multiplication movements. Leadership development is the engine the Spirit uses to drive a lasting movement.

How are leaders developed during this period of time? See Chapter 17 for a fuller explanation. But let's look at one aspect of leadership development right now.

Recall that every training session involves three thirds. In the first third, the first part is pastoral care. In the pastoral care time, you ask the question: "How are you doing?"

	Jan.	Feb.	Mar.	Apr.	May	June	July	Aug.	Sept.	Oct.	Nov.	Dec.	Jan.	**Feb.**	Mar.	Apr.	May	June	New Groups
Your Group	X																		1
Gen 1		X																	6
Gen 2					X														17
Gen 3								X											30
Gen 4														X					10
																			64

Look at the generational chart above. What kinds of questions do you think your GØ groups will have in the pastoral care component in the first few weeks?

- How can I find time to pray consistently?

- How can I overcome this sin?

- How can I get my spouse to believe?

- I'm thinking about moving out of my boyfriend's apartment, pray for me.

- I'm still feeling attacked by demons; pray for protection for me.

- I'm getting ridiculed at work and may lose my job. What should I do?

Most of the questions will deal with basic discipleship and relationships.

What kinds of questions do you think the GØ members will have after six months?

- When can I find a time to meet with my new group?

- How long should we meet?

- How do I get them to obey the Word?

- They're not witnessing, what do I do?

- I'm leading two groups, plus coming to this group. I'm tired. Help!

After nine to ten months, what concerns will they have when you ask "How are you doing?"

- One of the guys leading a G2 group has fallen into sin. How do I help the G1 leader help him?

- One of my G2 groups has not started any G3 groups. How do I help them?

- I need to get some of the down-line leaders together for some encouragement. What would you suggest?

- Some false teachers are trying to lead some of our groups astray. What do we do?

- One of the G2 leaders has a question concerning a point of theology: divorce. The G1 leader didn't know how to answer, nor did I. What does the Bible say about this?

- I'm so busy overseeing these flocks and leaders, but my soul is getting dry. Help me get some time away with the Lord to be refreshed.

Do you see what is happening? As long as you keep asking these trainers how they are doing, you will not only deal with personal issues, you will **do good leadership development.** It is an excellent pattern of on-the-job leadership development. You are giving real-time feedback and intervention to a whole host of issues. You are helping them establish solid patterns of understanding and obeying the Word. This process is similar to what Paul did when he wrote Timothy and Titus their letters. He was helping them as they helped a host of new leaders (Titus 1:5).

There are other forums in which you will develop these leaders in a more systematic way. However, the most important way to develop them in the beginning is through the three-thirds process. If you stay with them long enough, and they stay with their groups long enough and so on generation by generation, then each new layer of leadership has the opportunity to share problems, needs, frustrations and other questions, and then receive immediate help.

Building a Movement of Leaders

Such a rapid growth of leaders need not be a shallow movement. On the contrary, as you remember from Eph. 4:11-16, believers mature much more rapidly when they are serving immediately (see Chapter 4). Prior to T4T, some CPMs were short lived. There were a few "super-spreaders" who led many people to faith and started many churches. But new leaders were not being developed widely. Over time, the number of new churches far exceeded the number of leaders. The result was ***leadership overload***.[19]

> ***Churches multiplying***
> ***+***
> ***Leaders NOT multiplying***
> ***=***
> ***LEADERSHIP OVERLOAD*** *(CPM slows or stops)*

When T4T became more widely implemented, we inadvertently discovered that the number of leaders was generally keeping pace with the number of new churches. There were isolated instances of a super-spreader starting and leading numerous groups (and possibly burning out). But by and large, the number of leaders was growing because *every believer was being trained as a trainer.*

Ying himself avoids ever using the term "leader" because he believes it can easily lead to pride. Instead, he just refers to every group leader as a "trainer." Some of his trainers are leading movements of thousands of churches, but they're still just "trainers." He doesn't like to give them titles for fear of pride. "Trainer" just carries with it the basic idea of being a disciple who receives and passes on what he learns.

---

[19] I am indebted to my colleague Bill Fudge for coining this term in regard to CPMs.

The T4T process inherently develops leaders when you do the three thirds well. As your trainers start new generations, leadership questions will naturally arise and they will develop as leaders.

The point is: The T4T process inherently develops leaders when you do the three thirds well. As your trainers start new generations, leadership questions will naturally arise and they will develop as leaders – no matter what title you give them.

T4T helps you emulate something the apostle Paul did well: develop leaders appropriately for each stage from fairly young converts.[20] By giving them assignments and troubleshooting with them along the way, Paul developed leaders rather quickly. At the end of Paul's third journey an interesting verse appears as he prepared to return to Jerusalem:

> And he was accompanied by Sopater of Berea, the son of Pyrrhus, and by Aristarchus and Secundus of the Thessalonians, and Gaius of Derbe, and Timothy, and Tychicus and Trophimus of Asia. (Acts 20:4, NASB)

Look at that verse diagrammed a bit differently:

- At the end of Paul's three journeys (8-10 year period), he was accompanied by leaders representing movements in his major excursions:

    » Gaius of Derbe (Journey One: seven to eight years earlier)

    » Timothy of Lystra-Iconium (Acts 16:1-3; Journey Two: five to seven years earlier)

    » Sopater of Berea (Journey Two: four to six years earlier)

    » Aristarchus and Secundus of Thessalonica (Journey Two: four to six years earlier)

    » Tychicus and Trophimus of Asia (Journey Three: one to four years earlier)

---

[20] See Chapter 17 for a discussion of Paul's prohibition about new converts leading.

Paul's leaders developed so rapidly, that he returned to the original church – Jerusalem – with mature partners who represented the major CPMs that had developed in his three-trip tenure. We could easily list over thirty major partners (not just ordinary people Paul trained) that emerged **out of the harvest** during Paul's three journeys. The movement that started did not need to be fed by a steady stream of leadership from Antioch or Jerusalem; it was homegrown.

His diverse team of partners reflected the effectiveness of giving new leaders an example (Paul) and a pattern of discipleship (Philip. 3:17).

Summary

It is important as a movement launches to guide it in a 9 to 18 month mentorship (or longer). You want to launch, not drop. The mentorship should be long enough to do two things:

1. Help them get to consistent 4th+ generation growth

2. Help them develop as solid leaders

You do not want to control a movement but rather let the Spirit of God control it. But you do want to cooperate with God to help guide it.

The mentorship should be long enough to do two things:

1. Help them get to consistent 4th+ generation growth

Launch; don't drop. Only this will enable the budding discipleship revolution to be long-lived.

These last few chapters unwrap the essentials of the T4T process. How do you adapt it practically for your context? Read on!

2. Help them develop as solid leaders

Be a Doer, not just a Hearer!

Write down how God has spoken to you and what you need to obey as a result:

Part Three
THE APPLICATION OF T4T

CHAPTER 11
Your T4T Package: Vision Casting

The last few chapters have shown you the spirit of a discipleship revolution lifestyle – the process of T4T. Now, how do you actually begin the T4T process in your community?

If T4T is going to be effective in your community, it should help you move them from lostness to multiplying trainers and churches. **T4T should help you and your trainers know what to do at each stage when people say "yes" to moving forward.** It should be an all-in-one package that helps you cooperate with the King in building sustained CPMs. It helps you do your part in the divine-human partnership of kingdom come.

What are the key pieces to a complete T4T package? The remaining chapters will help you discover those pieces and implement T4T effectively in your ministry. As you adapt it, T4T **should** help guide you through the divine-human partnership, so that as God works, you will have a wineskin that can contain what His Spirit produces.

Should, but doesn't
However, there are a number of reasons why T4T sometimes doesn't work:

- Sometimes we don't understand the nuances and stages of T4T. Hence, this book.

- Sometimes we modify T4T so much that we lose the inherent processes that move us through the key stages of a CPM.

- Sometimes we fail to train our trainers adequately to know what to do when people say "yes" at each stage.

It is very possible for you to re-write the T4T curriculum and adapt the process so drastically that you fail to help your trainees move through the stages of a CPM. This chapter and the ones that follow will help you avoid that mistake. We will focus on the specific stages of T4T that enable you to move through the basic parts of a CPM:

1) **Mobilizing the saved** that God will use to start a movement through casting vision

2) **Finding the lost** whom God is preparing to receive the gospel using methods that any new believer can emulate.

3) **Evangelism** that any new believer can do

4) **Discipleship** that any new believer can reproduce

5) **Church formation** that any new believer can emulate

6) **Leadership development** that any new believer can experience and pass on

Every local T4T system needs to be put together or "packaged" in a way to help new believers move through each stage toward CPM. Otherwise they get stuck at a certain point and a CPM fails to emerge. **From this point on in the book, each chapter will give you an additional piece of what your T4T package needs to include**, and then will point you to a number of supplementary resources as examples. By the end of the book, it should be clear to you how to move from one stage to another, how to adapt T4T to your context, and what things you should not violate in the T4T process.

Your Destiny

T4T helps us see our world in a clear dichotomy: lost or saved. The first step in utilizing T4T in your ministry is to **find the believers God will use to launch the movement**. Every believer has a destiny prepared by God. It is both to build him up in Christlikeness and to enable him to walk in good works that fulfill God's mission. It is a destiny that perfectly balances being and doing:

> For those God foreknew he also **predestined to be conformed to the image of his Son**, that he might be the firstborn among many brothers and sisters. (Rom. 8:29, NIV, emphasis added)

> For we are God's handiwork, **created in Christ Jesus to do good works, which God prepared in advance** for us to do. (Eph. 2:10, NIV, emphasis added)

Throughout our world are under-developed and under-utilized believers who need to be called out to live in true conformity to Christ and to fulfill God's purpose to redeem a great multitude for Himself from every tongue, tribe and nation. Each believer is called to help fulfill the purpose of God in his own generation (Acts 13:36).

As God is preparing believers for this, our role is to cast vision to them so that they can see it and fulfill it.

Casting Vision for Being and Doing

Vision casting is a life-style of continually helping brothers and sisters see the potential of who they are and can become in Christ (BEING) and what God wants to do through them (DOING). Since we live in such a fallen world, it is easy for all of us to forget the spiritual reality and destiny God has prepared and walk by sight only. To change that we must spur one another on to walk by faith, not sight.

> And let us consider how we may spur one another on toward love and good deeds, not giving up meeting together, as some are in the habit of doing, but encouraging one another — and all the more as you see the Day approaching. (Heb. 10:24-25, NIV)

Jesus did this often. In John 1 alone, He did this twice.

Simon Peter was brought to Jesus by his brother Andrew. What kind of man was Simon? He was like a wave tossed back and forth, wavering in his affections, but always one of the extremes. I personally imagine that Simon came to Jesus hoping for a fresh start. "Perhaps this is a teacher that won't know the real me and will give me a chance to be different."

But how did Jesus greet Him? "You are Simon the son of John!" (John 1:42). In my mind, I can see Simon's countenance fall. "Oh no, He really knows me! No second chance here."

But what are the next words Jesus speaks? "From now on, I'm going to call you Rock!" Wow! Not only a second chance but a vision of what Peter could become! Not wavering, but solidly firm. Jesus spoke of Simon's future.

Just after this, Philip brought Nathaniel to Jesus. Nathaniel was initially skeptical, but Jesus spoke two words of vision to him:

- "You're a Jew in whom there is no hypocrisy. You're the real deal!" (John 1:47)

- "You're going to see much greater things than this. You're going to have heavenly visions!" (John 1:50-51)

How long do you think it took Jesus to speak those words to Nathaniel? You can take longer if you have time, but you don't need to.

In Acts 11:25-26, Barnabas went to Tarsus to find young disciple Saul (Paul) to bring him to the new church planted in Antioch. What do you think he said to him? I imagine it was something like this:

> Brother Saul, I know that God has put the Gentiles on your heart. Well, it's finally happening! A new church has started in Antioch, a *Gentile* church. Come join me and let's begin teaching them all the things God has designed for them. Perhaps this will be the beginning of movement among the Gentiles!

Saul joined him, and indeed, it became the hub from which a movement started.

Mobilizing Believers to Launch a Movement

Perhaps the single most important start you can make to a CPM strategy utilizing T4T is to mobilize believers from within your context or from a near-culture people group (national believers from another community who speak the same or a similar language). Mobilization means that you cast vision to these believers about what God can do in and through them and then begin to train those who agree to walk forward in the T4T process.

T4T is primarily about **training the saved** for the life and ministry to which God has called them (equipping the saints for work of ministry).

> And He gave some as apostles, and some as prophets, and some as evangelists, and some as pastors and teachers, for the equipping of the saints for the work of service, to the building up of the body of Christ. (Eph. 4:11-12, NASB)

Therefore, a key component of any T4T package is the ability to cast vision to believers for God to develop them in Christlikeness and to use them for His purposes.

In 2007 to 2008, an in-house survey was done of the most fruitful missionaries in one part of Asia. The survey correlated their annual statistical reports on baptisms, new groups and new churches with separate annual performance reviews. The results were surprising. The most important characteristic of the most fruitful workers was NOT evangelism or church planting. Instead, the number one trait of fruitful workers was *their ability to cast vision to local believers and move them onto a kingdom agenda toward CPM.*

In a survey of nine urban CPMs, the majority of their results, some up to 95%, came through believers they mobilized and trained, rather than from lost people they had personally won to the Lord.

In 2010, a research group studied over a hundred CPM-focused teams in Southeast Asia. Teams that had a working partnership with existing national believers were 90% more likely to be effective in baptisms, starting new groups and starting new churches than teams that did not.[21]

Where to Start in Mobilization?

The point is this: spending a significant amount of time mobilizing (casting vision and then training) local believers to partner with you in T4T is a high-value activity in initiating a discipleship *re*-revolution. Where you start depends on your context.

> The number one trait of fruitful CPM workers is *their ability to cast vision to local believers and get them onto a kingdom agenda toward CPM.*

Cross-cultural workers

When you work in a cross-cultural environment, the priority in mobilization is proximity to your people group. Assuming that they are teachable and pursuing the Lord, believers who are closer culturally to your people group will be more effective in this general order. I will compare them with the Ina from my own work, a minority group in an Asian country. Here is the general order of priority:[22]

1. SAME CULTURE: Any Ina believers I can find

2. NATIONAL MINORITY: Any believers from another minority group in my country

3. NATIONAL MAJORITY: Any believers from the majority group in my country

4. FOREIGN ASIAN LANGUAGE SPEAKERS: Any foreign Asians who speak the trade language of my country

5. FOREIGN ASIANS: Any Asians, simply because they can slip into villages without being noticed as much as a Caucasian

6. ANYONE

---

[21] Thanks to my colleague Bryan Galloway for this information.

[22] It was my colleague Bill Fudge who first laid this out succinctly in a similar format.

If you have same-culture believers in your context, spend a lot of time mobilizing, i.e. casting vision and training them. If you have only a few or none, then you need to begin working through the priority list of finding partners. You will have to evaluate what near culture means in your context. For example, someone might find that Jordanian Arab believers are more effective than Egyptian Coptics in reaching Egyptian Arab Muslims.

If you are working with a community that shares your own culture, then almost any believer you mobilize has the potential to be effective since they already know the language and the culture.

Church planters
If you are planting a new church (or now a *movement* of churches!) in another community in your home nation, then you will want to look for any local believers in that community. In addition to the church-planting team you may bring with you, the local believers will be the key God uses to unlock the community since they already have *oikos* relationships there. You can begin right away casting vision for what God can do in and through them. You may want to read this book together as a foundation for that movement. Sometimes hearing it from a third party helps each of you be more objective in wrestling through the issues.

Church leaders and members
If you are trying to apply T4T to your local setting, then your first application would be to discuss the ideas of this book with other church members and staff. You can covenant with a group of people to walk down the discipleship revolution path and learn together. You can be the seed God uses to spark a movement in your town or city. Working through the issues raised in this book together can help to prepare you and your partners for that movement.

Casting Vision

The bridge for mobilizing believers to partner with you in the T4T process is **vision casting**. Just as Jesus did this with His disciples and Paul did with his, we must follow in the same footsteps. Though vision casting will be a part of what you do each week in your regular T4T training, how do you get believers to commit to the T4T relationship in the first place? You have to cast a vision to them of what God can do in and through them.

Since casting vision to potential Christian partners is one of the highest value activities in CPMs, here is a simple acronym to guide you in T4T mobilization. The acronym is **R.E.L.A.T.E.** A much fuller discussion of it can be found in the supplementary materials. Here is an abbreviated version.

R-elationship

All effective influence grows out of relationship. Your goal is to walk in relationship together toward God's purposes, not to use these believers to fulfill your agenda. One is life-giving while the other is manipulative.

The first key to casting vision to local partners is relationship. Get to know them. Love them. Affirm them. Drink a lot of tea or eat a lot of hamburgers with them. Just get to know them in true love. Talk about their vision and your vision together. Talk about the deep things of your heart.

E-valuate the status

Ask these potential partners how they are doing on the path toward fulfilling the vision. Though they may be seeing people come to faith each year, is the current momentum enough to fulfill the vision of reaching their neighborhood, city or state or region in the next few years? Most people find that it isn't.

This is a great time to ask this question: "If we could find a biblical, long-lasting way to get there faster, would you be interested?" Very few people want to say "no" to this.

L-ay out God's vision

Once they see the implications of the path they are on, most people are ready to hear a vision of how it can be different. All of us need to see a vision greater than a human vision. It needs to be faith-filled, yet realistic. You are trying to build faith, but not false hope. You are trying to give them a heavenly vision – God's heart.

An effective way to start is with a three-minute vision casting. Since time is often limited, or you find yourself suddenly thrust into opportunities with local believers, you should be able **to cast a vision to believers in three minutes in the target language at any time!**

> One of the most effective tools in mobilization is to be able **to cast a three-minute vision to believers in the target language at any time!** Many of us know how to share a testimony in 2-3 minutes. Why not our vision?

Suppose you are sitting down in a coffee shop and you see your pastor. He's about to leave but offers you a few minutes to chat. Or you're a cross-cultural worker on the field and you meet a believer on the bus. It's apparent he is about to get off and you only have a few minutes to speak to him. What could you share that could move his heart to follow God's heart for the kingdom to come more fully?

You can share your vision in three minutes or less.

It can be a story of lostness and how that can change.

> In my early work with the Ina, I tried to mobilize many near-culture partners. I frequently shared the story of an old woman about to die in a remote village, but I did not have the language to witness to her. My potential partners did. I challenged them to join me in launching a movement to reach the many who were dying in these villages.

It can be excitement over vision for a CPM or discipleship revolution. You might share something like this:

> I've been reading a book about returning to the original discipleship revolution of the New Testament. [Explain what you have learned in a nutshell] I believe that God can spark a revolution where we live. Would you join me in learning more about this?

What vision is stirring you as you read this book? It probably is something that deeply moves you. As you share it with a potential partner, do not be afraid to transparently show emotion. If God has burdened your heart, He will touch their hearts, too.

> **Application:** Stop and think about what's on your own heart. What moved your heart to reach out to your people or community? What's on your heart as you read this book? Write that down. This is the seed of your three-minute vision casting. Practice it. Memorize it. Get feedback from other believers to see if it moves their hearts.

A-sk them to commit to the next step

In vision casting to believers, the only way you know if they are serious is by asking them to commit to *doing something*. What you ask them to commit to must be appropriate to your relationship and what you've discussed.

Ask people to make some sort of commitment:

- Comeback for our first T4T training Sunday night when we do Session One

- Let's read this book together and discuss it over coffee every Friday morning

- Pray daily about your involvement and let's have lunch in a week

- Let's go prayer-walking on Saturday

- Take a trip with me for the weekend to see an unreached community

Remember: conviction does not equal obedience! You don't know who is obedient until you give them something to commit to. This is the parable of the two sons – one who said "yes" and one who said "no" (Matt. 21:28-32) – all over again. As Jesus cast vision, He repeatedly asked people to respond to what they had heard. So should you.

T-rial group (Daniel Project) – for the reluctant ones

Sometimes, after all of this, the believers you try to mobilize will still say "no." You could walk away with nothing, but you still have one more option. Suggest a trial group, or what I call a "Daniel Project" based on Daniel 1. In that chapter, Daniel and the Hebrew youths are taken to Babylon in captivity and enrolled in the king's leadership development program. It sounded okay except for one problem: eating non-kosher food from the king's table.

Though they were resolved not to eat these foods, the verdict was against them. However, they didn't give up. Instead they appealed to their leaders to let them try things differently with a trial group: a smaller number of people, for a certain period of time, with a different method and an evaluation at the end. When their overseer saw the results, he then expanded the program.

After reading this book, reading the Scriptures, looking at case studies and talking to colleagues, you may be **resolved** in your mind not to go back to the way you used to do ministry. You want to live out the counter-intuitive ways of the kingdom. Yet the local believers you meet differ with you on this subject. What do you do? Do what Daniel did. Ask for a trial group – a Daniel Project.

Many church leaders will be willing to let a "test group" of their members try the T4T process. Instead of asking them to let you train the whole group, you can do something like this:

- Give me 10-20 church members, NOT leaders or even those who are responsible for ministries.

- I can train them myself, but I would love for you to train them with me. You'll be there the whole time.

- Let us try a different method – a CPM method – called T4T.

- We will try it for six months.

- At the end of that time, you evaluate. If you like what you see – i.e. we are getting better results in evangelism and in spiritual maturity – then let us keep going. You can expand it if you like. If you don't like what you see, you can call it off or give us more time.

For reluctant partners, who might say "no" otherwise, ask for a trial group.

E-very training includes more vision casting

As I mentioned in the chapter on the three-thirds process, vision casting should be a part of every meeting. **When training local partners on a continual basis, cast vision EVERY TIME you get together.** Don't assume that one or two vision castings are enough. A short vision-casting element is needed in every training session.

Don't worry about casting a huge CPM vision each time. Rather, just cast a vision for how God wants to reach the lost around your trainees. CPM is too big for many believers to grasp each week. Instead, just give people a vision for their *oikos*, using their Name List. As people witness, and more people come to faith, and they train trainers, their own CPM vision begins to grow. But it all starts with a practical vision for the lost.

TRAIN ANY SIZE
By Ying Kai

If people agree to let you train in their area, don't wait, do it right away. You don't need to recruit helpers. Just go. In my area, I've trained groups of one or two people. But even if it's 20 or 100 people — the biggest group I've trained is 1,500 in one room — I just want to train them. **I want to train any group.** Don't lose time, don't lose chances.

You must cast vision to your trainees again and again because they can easily get discouraged. Sometimes they may need a whole sermon, Bible study or vision-casting message, but the majority of time they need something shorter, something easy to pass on: *a vignette.*

A vision-casting vignette is a short, moving, easy-to-remember image, story or lesson that can be passed on generation by generation. It casts vision for what God can do IN and THROUGH believers, especially in regard to CPM.

Tucked throughout the pages of this book in the main text and in the sidebars are vignettes you can use to build vision in your trainers: Jesus' Great Commission, Heavenly Father's Heart, The Four Calls, plus many Scriptures, examples and testimonies.

As time goes by these vignettes will be passed on from generation to generation.

Gate-keepers and Doers:
Whom do you want to mobilize?

As you find local believers, and they agree to be trained by you, whom do you want to invest in? If you can train everyone, go for it. But if a pastor allows you to train only 10-20 people, whom do you want? Look at the diagram below demonstrating a believer's current ministry responsibilities as well as length of time as a believer.[23] **Choose just one of the four quadrants which you think will exhibit the most fruitful T4T implementers. When you are done, turn the page to find out which quadrant historically is most effective in T4T implementation.**

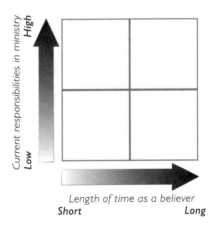

Current responsibilities in ministry — High / Low

Length of time as a believer
Short   Long

Most people in current ministry would guess that the top right quadrant would produce the most productive T4T implementers. But in actuality, CPMs are most often birthed through people in

---

[23] Diagram idea from my colleague Bill Smith.

the lower left quadrant! Is this surprising? An important principle in T4T is that **the most fruitful trainers tend to be ordinary, usually more recent, believers, not current ministry leaders.**

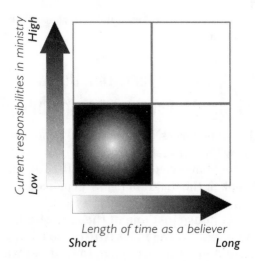

Length of time as a believer
Short   Long

There are a number of reasons for this:

- Current leaders tend to be overly committed already. Many people and ministries are already depending on the way they currently spend their time, so it is difficult to change their ministry patterns.

- Current leaders may be less open to new ideas because they've had so much training already – and much of it very different from CPM thinking.

- Current leaders have more to lose since they are vested in the existing system.

- Current leaders don't know many lost people, or have much time to get to know them. Their main ministry is to the saved.

- The longer a person has been a believer, the fewer contacts he has with non-believers.

It is often important for ministry leaders (gate-keepers) to endorse a CPM approach. But when it comes down to who will usually be most effective, try to invest in the people who have the most potential to become doers in a new paradigm. If you can get everyone to the training, that's best. But if not, always try to get teachable doers.

*An important principle in T4T is that **the most fruitful trainers tend to be ordinary, usually more recent, believers, not current ministry leaders.***

Cast vision to many to find the few who will commit

You will cast vision to many groups of believers. You must in order to find the people God has prepared to launch a movement. Out of the many believers you cast vision to, only a few will commit. It's hard work, yet it's one of the highest value activities of CPMs.

In Ying and Grace Kais' ministry, they did more than just win people to Jesus and train them. They cast the vision of T4T to myriads of existing church leaders and believers. Out of the many they cast vision to, some said "yes." In our work with the Ina, I had to cast vision to *dozens* of near culture partners to find the few who agreed to partner with us.

In order for a CPM to start, you must train dozens, even hundreds, not just a handful to find the fruitful soil persons.

Launch Session One

As believers commit to learn more, it is time to launch your first T4T meeting – Session One. Look at Chapter 5 for a detailed description. Essentially, you want to schedule around two hours to work through the WHY, WHOM and HOW of starting the discipleship *re*-revolution.

THE POWER OF A TESTIMONY

By Ying Kai

God wants to save you and through you all the people who belong to you. He can use even the newest believer to accomplish this.

In Mark 5, Jesus and all his disciples crossed the sea to the people of Gerasene. There was a demon-possessed man who was afraid of Jesus. But Jesus cast the demons out of him. The villagers came outside and were very afraid. But they found that the man was a wholly different person. Before, he was always naked and violent. But now he had clothes on, and he was sitting and listening to Jesus' teaching. When they asked Jesus to leave the town, the man told Jesus, "Lord, wherever you go, I will follow you." That is the best reaction for a new believer to have, right?

But what was in Jesus' heart? He said, "Don't follow me. Go back to your home." Why? "Give them your testimony. Tell them

Continued next page.

- WHY – cast vision for what God can do through them. Use the "Great Commission" vignette or another that will be appropriate.

- WHOM – help them work through their Name List of people who don't know Jesus or are far from God.

- HOW – help them develop a lifestyle to witness to them through a simple bridge that leads to a gospel presentation.

Then send them out to fulfill the vision with an expectation of returning the next week to report to one another.

Repeat this process with as many believers as you can. Begin to fill your calendar with new T4T groups where you are launching Session One.

You're now on your way!

Summary

This is the first step in your T4T package of moving toward a discipleship revolution.

- Actively search for local (or near culture or far culture) believers and cast vision for what God can do in and through them.

- Use the R.E.L.A.T.E. process to mobilize them.

- Be ready with a simple three-minute vision casting at any time.

- Cast vision to many believers and launch as many Session One meetings as possible.

The question is: once they commit to being trained, how will you help them find the lost that God's Spirit is attacking? That's the next chapter.

Be a Doer, not just a Hearer!

Write down how God has spoken to you and what you need to obey as a result:

what the Lord has done for you. Tell them about the Heavenly Father's mercy towards you." For me, that was a new lesson.

First, Jesus trusted him. Why? He was not even psychologically sound. He had just been demon possessed.

Second, how much training did he receive? Almost none! Only one sermon. So would you trust him to share the gospel and train all his people? His home was the Decapolis - the 10 cities. But Jesus trusted him. He said to him, "Go back to your home. Only share your testimony." **New believers can immediately share their testimonies.**

Jesus visited many places where the people were against him. They wanted to throw him off a mountain or stone him. But when Jesus came back to the Decapolis, people came outside and welcomed him. What changed? They had heard this man's testimony. So God works *through* people. All ten cities belonged to the Gerasene demoniac.

CHAPTER 12

Your T4T Package: Gospel Bridges

Now that believers are showing up for Session One, what do you do? You need to help them know how to find the lost people the Spirit is attacking in your community.

So, the second step in applying T4T is to give your new trainees a concrete way to find the lost. You began this in Session One with your introduction of WHO-WHY-HOW. In Session One you also began using the three-thirds process, though it will develop in fullness in the second session.

First Third

As you remember, the first third of a T4T meeting is divided into four parts: pastoral care, worship, accountability and vision casting. Since Session One is just your first meeting, you may not yet do all of these, though you can easily begin with pastoral care ("How are you doing?") and worship. In Session One, you must also include vision casting and accountability.

Vision Casting: WHY

Refer to Chapter 5 for a full discussion of this. The goal of Session One is to have hearts captured by God to live for Him and fulfill His purposes. We do this by starting with God's vision. You can use the "Great Commission" vignette (Go, not come; Everybody, not just some; Make trainers, not just church members – Chapters 2 and 5) or another that will be appropriate.

Accountability: WHOM

Have trainees prayerfully write down the lost members of their *oikos* on their Name List, circling the names of people to witness to this week. You are beginning the accountability process that will lovingly enable you all to cooperate with the Holy Spirit's activity. This Name List should be re-visited every week.

To enable local believers to find the lost people whom the Spirit is attacking have them begin a lifestyle of witnessing FIVE TIMES every week to the people on their list.[24] They should not rule out witnessing to strangers either. If you and the members of your group all begin to witness to five people each week, God is going to do something amazing through you!

For outsiders who are new to the community and have very little *oikos* there, they will have to witness to five strangers each week as they look for persons of peace (See the supplementary material "Essential Elements for CPMs" for a fuller discussion of finding persons of peace.) Sometimes this is best done two by two to encourage each other as you talk to people you don't know.

Final Two Thirds: HOW

In the final two thirds the remaining three parts of a T4T meeting (new lesson, practice, goal-setting with prayer) are blended together. Rather than waiting until the end of the meeting to practice, the trainees practice each new thing they learn as they learn it.

In Session One, the final two thirds are the HOW portion of the meeting. In this section they need two things: a way to *bridge* into gospel conversations and an *effective gospel presentation* to use. This chapter explains how to put effective gospel bridges into your T4T package, while the next chapter does the same thing with gospel presentations.

---

[24] Depending on the persons in the group, this goal may be adjusted up or down. Full-time missionaries often increase it. Home-schooling moms may decrease it. But the norm for people with full-time secular jobs is five times.

Most Christians who have not witnessed much are nervous about bridging into gospel conversations. Your goal in Session One is to help them overcome that.

Finding Those God has Prepared

Your T4T process must help the trainees cooperate with the kingdom dynamics of how God is preparing the hearts of lost people around them to receive the gospel.

As you recall from Chapter 4, all around you, the Holy Spirit is attacking lost people, convicting them of their sin, showing them the need for things to be made right and assuring them that bad things will result if they don't change (John 16:8). Persons of peace are *spiritually* prepared persons. We find them through *spiritual* means. Luke 10 makes it clear that we find these persons of peace through 3P's: presence, power and proclamation.

- Presence – finding those interested in the gospel and lovingly bringing the presence of God to them (Luke 10:5-7)

- Power – crying out for God to work miraculously to reveal Himself through healing, release from spiritual bondage and other interventions (Luke10:9)

- Proclamation – bringing a clear message of salvation that includes an understandable gospel message with a call to commitment (Luke10:9)

We must use spiritual means to find spiritual people. One successful trainer says it this way: "We sift for persons of peace by using the gospel."

In a training session, it became apparent that a long-time colleague and his team were seeing dramatic results in a very "resistant" people group. For seven years, they had labored with **no fruit – no believers and no churches.** How discouraging! At our meeting, he reported that in the eighth year they began to see radically different results. So I asked him: "What changed?"

In embarrassment, he replied, "We started sharing the gospel."

I said, "Excuse me? What did you say?"

Looking me in the eyes, with sadness he said more loudly: "We started sharing the gospel!"

"What do you mean? What did you do the previous seven years?"

"Steve, for seven years, we bought the lie that we had to build relationships first and slowly reveal our Christian identity. It took us years. We saw ourselves as picking up rocks to prepare the field to hear the gospel. We would drop little nuggets of truth, but not really the gospel. As we developed these relationships and got very close to these lost friends, we got nervous about sharing the gospel. We thought, 'What if they reject us?' We began to forget the reason we were there.

"Finally, after seven years of no fruit, we got desperate. We shared the gospel with these friends, and they almost all rejected us. That's when we realized that our approach of 'relationship evangelism' was getting us nowhere. We resolved as a team to share the gospel first, and build relationships afterwards.

"We started sharing everywhere. We bridged into gospel conversations with as many people as we could. A lot of people didn't respond. But we finally began to find some that said 'yes', and it is through these new believers that God is starting to build His kingdom."

For seven years they had been taking on the role that only the Spirit of God can take: picking up rocks (Ezek 11:19). And even then they were rejected. When they finally changed the way they sought for persons of peace, they began to see fruit. Today this missionary is a strong advocate for bridging into gospel conversations very quickly.

Another team was working among a very "antagonistic" people group. The oppression was so difficult that it was easy not to start talking about Jesus — ever. But it's difficult to find spiritually prepared people without spiritual means. Therefore, they established a "five-minute rule" for their team: "In every conversation with a lost person, we will identify ourselves as followers of Jesus within five minutes."

That was their bridge into conversations about Jesus.

Another colleague who was seeing a lot of people come to Christ was asked "Whom do you find to be the most responsive?" He replied, "Those that I share the gospel with. 100% of those I do not share with do not respond."

Find those God is preparing and bridge to the gospel

Your T4T package must include a way to help believers find God-prepared lost people and bridge into gospel conversations. If they are going to witness to five people weekly, how will they start those conversations? They need a bridge to help them move from not talking, or talking about everyday things (sports, weather, family) to talking about Jesus.

What follows are examples of bridges. They are explained further in the supplementary materials.

T4T Classic — Testimony

In T4T "Classic", bridges are very simple. In Session One, the trainer learns how to share his 1-2 minute testimony. The goal is to move someone's heart to listen to the gospel. This is *your* story. But the gospel is THE story.

As soon as the trainer shares his testimony, he **immediately** begins to walk the lost person through T4T Lesson 1 "How to have Assurance of Salvation." The trainer pulls lesson one out of his pocket and teaches the listener how he, too, can come to a saving relationship with God as his Father.

> Congratulations, as a child of the Heavenly Father (Acts 17:28-29) you can have a new relationship with God and receive all of His promises.

As you conclude your testimony, say: "Since I have come into a new relationship with God, He has changed me, made me His child and given me eternal life. According to the Bible, God has made you his child, too. The problem is that until you come into relationship with Him, you are lost. But I can show you how to be saved!"

[Pull out Lesson 1] "The Bible says that we are cut off from Him, but He wants to bring us back into His family so that we won't be lost, but have life with Him forever!"This bridge comes from Acts 17:28-29 in which Paul acknowledges that we are all God's offspring (children). The problem is the Luke 15 problem of the prodigal son who has left his father's home: we are lost sons and daughters cut off from relationship with the Father and outside the security of that eternal relationship.

In a very *positive way*, Ying teaches his trainers to *offer* this new life to the lost around them. Hundreds of thousands of believers in Asia are responding to this bridge. For many of you, a **testimony** is all you need to use for a bridge.

TRT: Training Rural Trainers (Oral T4T)

Out of the Ina work we developed an oral version of T4T. In this version, our goal was to share the gospel via the Creation to Christ story (C2C – more in the chapter on gospel presentations). We got started sharing C2C through a combination of two bridges – miracles and testimony.

Miracles: When evangelists walked into a new village, and people asked why they were there, they often presented themselves as representatives of the Most High God. They offered to pray for people in the name of God's Son Jesus who wanted to show His love to them. When miracles resulted, people wanted to hear the gospel message.

Testimony: Sometimes prior to praying for the needs of people or sometimes after, evangelists shared their testimony in this manner: "I was once bound in darkness to the spirits like you all are. But the Most High God freed me. I want to tell you the story that is changing lives everywhere." Then they shared the Creation to Christ story and prayed for the needs of the people.

It is amazing how **miracles** open the way to share the gospel.

Any3

One of the fastest growing gospel bridges in the Muslim world is called "Any3:" share with anyone, anywhere, any time.[25] The man who developed this is at the center of a fast-growing CPM among Muslim-background believers. He and his national partners grew tired of trying to predict who would be receptive and who wouldn't. **They finally decided to filter for receptive people *using the gospel*.** To do this, they needed a bridge to enable them to share with anyone, anywhere, any time.

This bridge has also been used with Hindus, Buddhists and atheists. With a little adjustment it works well in a number of contexts. And the neat thing is that we've had lost people – who still didn't believe – thank us for witnessing to them. They appreciated us listening to them and then sharing our views in a meaningful interaction of hearts.

Here is Any3 in a nutshell:

Of course, you will begin a conversation getting to know a bit about a person – his family, occupation, etc. But as quickly as possible, you want to get to the point to help identify his religious worldview.

1. **GET TO THE POINT:** Ask the question: **"What religion do you follow?"**

"Are you Hindu, Buddhist, Muslim, ancestor worshiper?" He will tell you what he believes, and you will identify yourself as a Christian or follower of Jesus.

Often they will respond, "But all religions are about the same!" They are trying to smooth over the differences.

For many people, this is a conversation stopper. What can you say after that?

---

[25] Any3 resources can be found on the T4TOnline.org website.

Instead, we usually respond by *agreeing* with him: "Yes, all religions are about the same. We are all trying to deal with our sin problem (or get to heaven, or make enough merit)."

Now you move on to the next concept, "get them to lostness" using their own religion of works-based salvation.

2. **GET THEM TO LOSTNESS:** Ask the question: **"In your religion, how do you get your sins forgiven** (or paid off, or make it to heaven, or make enough merit)?"

Then spend time helping them see their lostness in their own religion. The apostle Paul made it clear that the Law taught him about sin, and he realized his inability to ever reach heaven on his own (Rom. 7:7-10). In a similar way, no religious system can provide assurance of salvation through works (Eph 2:8-9). So ask some questions that help them explore the inadequacy of their works-based religion.

For example with a Muslim, you might let him tell you how well he does upholding the five pillars: Does he pray *five* times *every* day? Does he give alms *as commanded*? Does he fast *completely* during Ramadan? Will he be able to afford to go on the Hajj?

After letting him share about what he does, ask these questions.

a. So how's that going for you?

b. Are your sins paid off yet? [When will you know if you're going to heaven?]

c. Will they be paid off on judgment day? (Or to a Buddhist, how many lifetimes will it take to reach Nirvana?)

What generally happens at this point is that a person realizes there is no certainty in his religious system. At this point, you are ready to share with him your perspective which is not works-based.

3. **GET TO THE GOSPEL:** Say something like this: "**Hmm, well what I believe is a bit different. I know my sins have been forgiven. [And it's not because I'm a good person—who knows, you might be a better person than I am!] Here's how I know my sins have been forgiven . . . GOSPEL PRESENTATION.**

[OR, "God has broken the cycle of me having to make enough merit; OR "I've found freedom from the harassment of spirits. Here's how . . . GOSPEL.]

In Any3 you can let the person's **own religion** be the bridge to show him his lostness and his need for the gospel.

Practice, practice, practice!

Find a bridge that works in your community. Train the trainees in it during Session One. Before teaching them a gospel presentation, have them practice the bridge over and over until they can do it in their sleep. They will not share it five times in the subsequent week if they are not confident doing it in their T4T group.

Just start with ONE!

Whether it's the bridge, or gospel presentation or discipleship lessons, just start with ONE WAY to train your trainers in the beginning. Make

THE CALL FROM BELOW
By Ying Kai

In Luke 16, there is a call from below, from hell. A rich man in hell cries out for someone to warn his family not to come there. There is an urgency. The lost in hell call out for you to share the gospel. We need to share the gospel, and we need to treat it like it's an emergency. Don't wait. Don't waste time. Don't think, "Next time, next time." Don't think, "Tomorrow." If you think like this, you will lose opportunities.

One time at the hospital where I served as chaplain, at around 3:30 P.M., the nurse called me. There was a patient who was in great pain and had no peace. She said, "Will you please help him?"

I went to the ward and visited him. He was around 30 years old. He was a very strong young man, but because he was a drug addict, a policeman sent him to the hospital. He was very uncomfortable and in very much pain. I tried to comfort him. I told him he could talk

Continued next page.

to me, but in my heart, I was thinking, "Right now, should I share the gospel or not? Maybe right now is not a good time." So I just comforted him, prayed for him, and told him, "If you want to talk to me, tell the nurse to call me."

After I prayed, he calmed down. I told him, "Tomorrow I will come back." I was thinking, "Today he is very tired and in great pain, so it's not a good time to share the gospel."

The next day, I went to my office at 7:30 a.m. I looked at the patient list and prayed for all of the patients. After about 30 minutes I went to the ward. I first looked for the drug addict. I thought, "Maybe today will be a good time to share the gospel with him." But I found that his bed was empty. So I went to the nurse and said, "What ward did that man transfer to?"

The nurse looked at the chart and said to me, "Last night he died." Immediately I began to cry! The words rang in my ears. When I meet our Lord someday, He will

Continued next page.

it simple for them to obey and teach someone else. Remember your goal: multiplying generations of trainers and churches.

New believers need just ONE way to learn to do things in the beginning. If you give them more than one way, they get confused and do neither well. In a survey of CPMs from numerous places, a common factor in all of them was the use of just ONE SIMPLE METHOD to get to CPM.

One of our missionary colleagues works among one of the most unreached groups on earth. About a year ago, this people group got its first believers – just a handful. One of the new believers was a man who was *very gifted* at bridging into gospel presentations.

However, none of the people he led to faith could win others to faith. Even though this man was from their own people group, he was so proficient in bridging into the gospel that none of them felt they could measure up. After observing this, the missionary encouraged the man to use just one method for the sake of his brothers and sisters. From that point on, other new believers became effective in witnessing because they had one clear model to imitate.

Start with one bridge into gospel presentations in your T4T package and then use it over and over and over – as long as it is effective. Get proficient.

Summary

As you launch Session One, you need to preserve the three parts of that particular meeting: WHY (cast vision), WHOM (make a Name List) and HOW (teach them a gospel bridge that they practice).

Get a gospel bridge that works in your context and that any new believer can emulate. Have them practice it over and over.

Then encourage each person including yourself to commit to using it five times a week.

ask me, "Where is that person?" I had a chance, but my professional mind thought, "This is not good timing. He needs more time. He needs to be more comfortable. Then I can share the gospel." No. In the span of just one night, I lost a person. So from that day, I resolved to not lose any more chances.

Can you hear the call from below saying, "Who can help our family? Who will share with them?"

Now that you and your trainees know how to bridge into gospel conversations, how do you share the gospel in a way that's effective in your community? That's the next chapter.

Be a Doer, not just a Hearer!

Write down how God has spoken to you and what you need to obey as a result:

CHAPTER 13

Your T4T Package: Gospel Presentation

Before you finish Session One, you want to give your trainees a clear and effective gospel presentation that they can use. The bridge can move a person's heart to listen, but only the gospel can save them.

The Scripture makes it clear that no one can be saved without calling on the name of the Lord. To do that, they must hear the gospel (Acts 2:21; 4:12):

> ¹³For "WHOEVER WILL CALL ON THE NAME OF THE LORD WILL BE SAVED." ¹⁴How then will they call on Him in whom they have not believed? How will they believe in Him whom they have not heard? And how will they hear without a preacher? ¹⁵How will they preach unless they are sent? Just as it is written, "HOW BEAUTIFUL ARE THE FEET OF THOSE WHO BRING GOOD NEWS OF GOOD THINGS!" ¹⁶However, they did not all heed the good news; for Isaiah says, "LORD, WHO HAS BELIEVED OUR REPORT?" ¹⁷So faith comes from hearing, and hearing by the word of Christ. (Rom. 10:13-17, NASB)

In these verses, Paul explains that faith comes by hearing. Hearing what? The message *about Christ* (the gospel).

What is the Gospel?

Many people have a definition of the gospel much broader than what the Scripture gives. Some have defined it as almost any spiritual truth. It is good to share spiritual truth, but that is not necessarily the gospel.

What is the gospel? It is specifically the good news that Jesus Christ provided redemption for us and that we can be saved through faith in Him. The examples below state it succinctly:

> Then He opened their minds to understand the Scriptures, and He said to them, "Thus it is written, **that the Christ would suffer and rise again from the dead the third day, and that repentance for forgiveness of sins would be proclaimed in His name to all the nations,** beginning from Jerusalem. You are witnesses of these things." (Luke 25:45-48, NASB, emphasis added)

> Now I make known to you, brethren, **the gospel** which I preached to you, which also you received, in which also you stand, by which also you are saved, if you hold fast the word which I preached to you, unless you believed in vain. For I delivered to you as of first importance what I also received, **that Christ died for our sins according to the Scriptures, and that He was buried, and that He was raised on the third day according to the Scriptures, and that He appeared to Cephas, then to the twelve.** After that He appeared to more than five hundred brethren at one time, most of whom remain until now, but some have fallen asleep. (1 Cor. 15:1-6, NASB, emphasis added)

What is the gospel? **It is the truth about Jesus dying for our sins, being buried, yet rising again to prove His claims AND that through Him all people can be saved, through repentance and faith.**

ANY gospel presentation that you use in your T4T package must get to these basic truths about Jesus and then show people how to respond. That's the gospel.

Clear and Effective

An important characteristic of the gospel presentation you use in T4T in your context is that it must be understandable by the average lost person and effective in winning them. It should be simple enough, that if God removes the veil from their heart, the gospel will make sense to them – it will really be good news to them.

When anyone hears the message about the kingdom and does not understand it, the evil one comes and snatches away what was sown in his heart. This is the seed sown along the path. (Matt. 13:19, NIV)

We have a responsibility to share the gospel in a way that is not needlessly difficult to grasp – it must be understandable in their worldview. That is why Ying began his typical gospel presentation with a simple declaration: "Congratulations! You are God's child! The problem is that you are lost, but I will show you how to be saved!" This presentation spoke very effectively to the people he was trying to reach.

Addressing the basic worldview of lost people in your community is critical. Your gospel presentation should take the **truth of the gospel** and **apply it** to their worldview as your starting point.

- What is good news for animists? Jesus' power over the spirits.

- What is good news for Buddhists and Hindus? Jesus' power to break the cycles of rebirth and bring them to heaven.

- What is good news for Muslims and Jews? Jesus has the ability to break the system of their futile attempt to gain salvation through good works and give true salvation.

- What is good news for post-moderns? Jesus offers true, eternal relevance. He can really change their lives.

You must share the good news in a way that is understandable and speaks to their need. The gospel is always the same: Jesus' death, burial and resurrection, and salvation through faith in His Name. The manner in which you share it varies from place to place.

What is effective in your context? Find out who, if anyone, is seeing people come to faith consistently. Find out how they are sharing the gospel. You may want to use that gospel presentation or modify it. Or else, find out where people are coming to faith in a culture and worldview similar to your community's. Use or adapt that gospel presentation for your context.

One Simple Reproducible Presentation

A common factor in most CPMs is this: **the use of ONE simple gospel presentation and a call to commitment that any new believer can reproduce.**

*The only way you know a gospel presentation is reproducible is if it is reproduc**ing**.*

Not three. Not two. ONE. Start with one gospel presentation that works. Adapt it as you go if it doesn't seem to be understandable or address the needs of your people's worldview. Tweak and adapt, but USE one.

It needs to be simple and reproducible – able to be used by a new believer. If it is overly complicated, it will never catch on and become part of a viral discipleship revolution.

No effective, reproducible gospel presentation was ever developed in a classroom, study or training room. Great ideas may have begun there. But effective gospel presentations become effective **through repeated trial and error.** Some people want to endlessly tweak and perfect before using. Instead endlessly use it, perfecting it as you go.

Reproducible gospel presentations (as with any method) are developed as new believers try it out. As you see how it easy or difficult it is for them to use it, then tweak it until anyone can use it. The only way you know a reproducible method is if it is reproduc*ing*.

If you use more than one gospel presentation, it is easy for trainees to get confused. Later, when they are proficient, you can expand what they use. But start with one.

This does not rule out supplemental aids such as media (e.g. *JESUS Film*), but every person needs to have a basic gospel presentation: how to witness to anyone, anywhere, any time.

Examples of Gospel Presentations

In the supplementary materials on the website, you will find examples of gospel presentations being used in T4T packages. Included are three highly effective presentations:

- The original **How to have Assurance of Salvation** gospel presentation that Ying used.

- The **Creation to Christ** (C2C) story which was first used to sum up 40 chronological Bible stories in 15 minutes (the story of the Bible). Though it may be the most effective presentation for oral learners, it has now been adapted effectively with good results for almost every worldview. A copy of this story is on page 347.

- The **Any3** gospel presentation that has been a fast, effective way to lead Muslims to faith in a friendly, non-combative conversation.

Of course you can use one of your own gospel presentations: *Four Spiritual Laws, Steps to Peace with God, The Gospel Bridge*, etc. Just make sure the one you use is very reproducible for those you train.

Include a Call to Commitment

Whatever gospel presentation you use in your T4T package you **must include a call to commitment.**

John the Baptist, Jesus, the apostles and other evangelists in Acts repeatedly called people to make a commitment after sharing the good news. **You don't know if someone is ready to receive the gospel until you ask him or call him to respond.**

I often hear people say that we should just wait until the listener, in great conviction, calls out to us: "What must I do to be saved?" That situation is very rare, even in Scripture. Even in the instance quoted in Acts 2:37, Peter and the apostles continued to plead with the people, exhorting them to repent (Acts 2:40)!

Effective evangelism involves effective leadership – to bring people into the kingdom. God convicts, but we must persuade.

Biblical persuasion is calling people to respond to God's conviction. It is not manipulation, but leading people to respond to what God is saying.[26]

Biblical PERSUASION is calling people to respond to God's conviction. It is not manipulation, but leading people to respond to what God is saying.

Now when they heard this, they were pierced to the heart, and said to Peter and the rest of the apostles, "Brethren, what shall we do?" Peter said to them, "Repent, and each of you be baptized in the name of Jesus Christ for the forgiveness of your sins; and you will receive the gift of the Holy Spirit . . ." **And with many other words he solemnly testified and kept on exhorting them**, saying, "Be saved from this perverse generation!" (Acts 2:37-38, 40, NASB, emphasis added)

Therefore, knowing the fear of the Lord, **we persuade men**, but we are made manifest to God; and I hope that we are made manifest also in your consciences. (2 Cor. 5:11, NASB, emphasis added)

People generally will not say "yes" until you call them to respond.

One CPM initiator was witnessing a lot, but no one was coming to faith. He learned that effective evangelists are those who call for commitment or ask the question: "Do you want to follow Jesus now?" Therefore, he changed his approach to witnessing to add a call to commitment at the end of each gospel presentation.

One day, he and a partner were witnessing in a nursing home. They shared the whole gospel with an old woman. She was semi-comatose and very unresponsive. His friend said, "Come on, let's go. She's not interested." As they began to leave, the CPM initiator returned to the bedside and asked: "Grandma, would you like to follow Jesus?"

---

[26] More Scriptures on a biblical model of calling people to commitment can be found in the supplementary materials: "Examples of Calls to Commitment."

"Of course!" she responded. That day she gave her life to Christ, but there had been nothing in her physical demeanor to indicate she was ready. The CPM initiator only discovered this by asking her.

Become a persuader! Ying is an incredible persuader. He witnesses to lost people everywhere *and* he asks people to believe in Jesus. Many of them say "yes." Many of his most effective trainers are people he led to faith and then began to train personally. Ying's philosophy is "don't ask permission, just tell." As he shares the gospel, his philosophy is "don't tell without asking them to believe."

The most effective evangelists ask people to follow Jesus. Remember, 100% of those you don't share the gospel with and call to commitment will not respond.

Just like you did with teaching the gospel bridge, you must take time in Session One to let the trainees practice the gospel presentation over and over until they are confident to share it five times this week. After practicing together, make sure everyone reviews the names they circled on their Name List and then pray for these lost persons and for one another. They should pray for the goal of sharing five complete gospel presentations each week, calling people to commitment.

Once you've done this in Session One, send each other out to begin the revolution!

Summary

The next stage in implementing T4T is to use ONE effective, reproducible gospel presentation WITH a call to commitment. Find one that works in your context.

Then teach this to your trainees as a part of Session One (HOW). Before they leave, they must practice it until they feel confident to use it five times in the subsequent week. When they do, review the names circled on the Name Lists and then re-commission one another in prayer.

Their goal is to share five complete gospel presentations with a call to commitment (when appropriate) each week.

Once people come to faith, how do you help them move through a discipleship process that reproduces generation by generation? Read the next chapter to find out.

Be a Doer, not just a Hearer!

Write down how God has spoken to you and what you need to obey as a result:

CHAPTER 14

Your T4T Package: Discipleship

In the weeks that follow, as your trainees go out to witness, some lost people will say "yes" to following Jesus. Once they do, how do your trainers systematically move them through the discipleship process in a way that can reproduce generation by generation?

Short-term and Long-term Discipleship

Previous chapters emphasized the discipleship *process* that builds a trainer. Most of the stress was on the **three-thirds process**. This chapter focuses on the *content* of the training that every T4T package needs for discipleship – both short term and long term.

Every package needs to include a reproducible set of lessons for **short-term** discipleship that can easily be learned, obeyed and passed on. Your T4T package must have 6-10 biblical short-term discipleship lessons that you begin at Session Two that are appropriate for your context and easy to reproduce. If you find that new believers are not passing the lessons on, they are probably not as reproducible as they need to be.

After completing the short-term discipleship, a **long-term** discipleship process must be introduced that enables the new believers to become self-feeders from the Word and obedient to the Spirit. Long-term discipleship requires a pattern of inductive study and application of the Scripture that they will use for months and years to come.

As you instill discipleship content into your T4T process, you are helping your new believers move into the next stage of a church-planting movement – reproducing discipleship. You are equipping your trainers to help their new believers know how to move forward as they say and do "yes" at each meeting. You are moving them steadily toward Christlikeness and toward fulfilling God's purposes for their generation. (See the supplementary material "Essential Elements for CPMs" for a fuller discussion of how discipleship fits into a CPM plan.)

The Danger of Non-reproducible Lessons

The short and long-term discipleship curriculum set is one of the areas that people adapting T4T are most apt to make **non-**reproducible. Why? Because they want to put an entire Old Testament and New Testament survey plus systematic theology all into 6-10 lessons!

I know. I've been very close to that. The first few sets of curriculum I wrote for the Ina people were intended to give them all they needed to know about life and godliness in eight lessons. They were theologically heavy, overly complicated and full of too many applications for them to obey, much less pass on. To me, a seminary graduate, they appeared pretty simple. To a non-literate person, they were almost incomprehensible! Through trial and error, finding out what does and doesn't work, my team and I kept boiling them down to eight key nuggets that could *start* a new believer on the right track to loving Jesus, loving others well and fulfilling the Great Commission. **Once we gave up trying to put everything into eight sessions, we were free to get simple.** Since this was just the beginning of a discipleship journey together, we could add in the other things as time went by. Once the Ina actually could learn the eight lessons orally and pass them on generation by generation, we knew we had arrived at a good short-term discipleship curriculum.

Don't forget that the 6-10 lessons you use in the beginning are simply that – the beginning. Keep them simple and easy to pass on.

Your T4T Package

You can use a set of lessons straight out of a current T4T curriculum set. On the T4T website are *numerous* sets of curricula in various languages for various worldviews. One of those is probably what you need, or close to it. Take one, use it, and then adapt it as you go. If it is obvious that a few things just won't work in your situation, then adjust them. **But don't let the adjusting and preparing process keep you from training. The fastest way to get a system that works is to put training sessions on your calendar!**

If you include more than 10 basic discipleship lessons for your short-term package, it will be too difficult for most believers to remember and pass on. Instead, you should develop a long-term discipleship pattern after the 6th-10th session and direct the trainees to some Bible passages that will help them grow in the basics of the Christian life (e.g. Mark, Ephesians, etc.).

Non-negotiables for the Short-term Package

Every short-term discipleship curriculum should include some fundamental items like prayer, daily devotions, assurance of salvation, and the Word.[27] However, for the sake of a church-planting movement, there are a few non-negotiables that *must* be included in short-term discipleship in addition to these.

- **Baptism** – Most T4T practitioners get to baptism within the first few hours, days or weeks after a profession of faith. Many are now putting it as the *first* discipleship lesson after salvation.[28] This is probably the single most important act of obedience for solidifying the profession of faith and making true disciples. (See Chapter 15 on baptism.)

---

[27] You can see an explanation from Ying about why he chose his original six lesson in the supplementary materials entitled: "An Overview of the Original Six T4T Lessons."
[28] Ying Kai does not normally put it there. He includes baptism in lesson four as part of church formation. But this is still very soon after salvation.

- **Church** – Every T4T curriculum that is getting to a church-planting movement includes a lesson very early on to intentionally help the group of disciples become a church. Usually this is the 4th or 5th short-term discipleship lesson. That means that T4T groups are usually becoming churches by the 4th or 5th session. Without this lesson, groups will probably not become churches. (See chapter 16 on this subject.)

- **Communion: The Lord's Supper** – Sometimes this is bundled with the church lesson, sometimes it is separate. (See more in chapter 16.) Either way, the Lord's Supper, properly exercised, is one of the most purifying acts of worship in the church and the movement. It helps keep the doctrine and practice of the members pure.

- **Perseverance in persecution** – This may surprise some people, but many young radical believers will face at least light persecution before you think they will. New Testament writers almost always included this as one of their basics of the faith; so should we. Only perseverance will enable this to become a movement. (More on this in chapter 20.) Perseverance and boldness are perhaps the most important factors in helping this generation of believers start a new generation of believers.

- **Great Commission** – Even though reproduction is built into the three-thirds process, it is very helpful to give an entire lesson to the Great Commission to reinforce the need to start successive generations.

Literate versus Oral Approach

One of the decisions you should make early on in building your T4T package is whether to use lessons and training that are more literate in nature or more oral in nature.

Some people have a natural leaning toward using literate or oral formats. **Some CPM initiators use oral means because** *they* **prefer them, NOT because this is what is most effec-**

tive in their context. Choosing one method over the other because this is what we prefer rather than what is most effective and reproducible for our people group is a dangerous approach. We should never let personal preferences *override* methods optimal for reaching our people.

Training using oral methods is like driving a car with the parking brake partially or fully engaged. You can drive the same speed, but it takes more effort. Oral methods inherently have speed dampeners built in for which you must compensate. That usually means, with a few rare exceptions, that it takes more work to make them *reproducible*.

For example, in TRT (Training Rural Trainers which we developed for the Ina), which is story-based and designed for non-literate learners, we had to teach a group to learn a story, memorize a memory verse, learn songs and remember applications. For each story we taught, we might have to practice it 5-10 times before they felt confident and competent to pass it on. In addition, we had to practice the previous weeks' stories from time to time to reinforce them. This takes a lot of time in the training meeting. For a group of trainees to *reproduce* this to others, they have to practice many times, remember the whole training session (story included) and then repeat the same process with their group. It is do-able, but very time intensive. It takes more effort, normally, than literate approaches.

When you train using a written lesson, the educational system in that country has already helped train your group – in literacy. They can read and so can you. When you train them, they can just *read* the Bible story or *follow along* on the lesson sheet. They might need to practice only 1-3 times to really get confident and competent to pass it along to someone else. The

> *Some CPM initiators use oral means because **they** prefer them, NOT because this is what is most effective in their context. Choosing one method over the other because this is what we prefer rather than what is most effective and reproducible in our people group is a dangerous approach. We should never let personal preferences rise above what it will take to reach our people.*

educational system has provided an element to enable your trainers to reproduce with less effort, if you train them right.

Some people describe how easy it is for oral learners to pick up songs, stories and skits. It probably is easier for them than for literate people, but it is never easy. It is *hard work,* generally harder work than a literate approach to make it *reproducible.*

CPMs among non-literate people groups are just as possible as among literate ones. There are a number of CPMs using oral versions of T4T, but it takes a lot of time in the training meetings to make sure it is faithfully passed on. You must use the proper methods and give yourself enough time for practice it the trainees are going to pass it on.

Think about your average 3rd or 4th generation future believer. What type of reproducible method will he need? Bottom line: choose a discipleship curriculum appropriate for your target audience.

How do you choose an oral or literate method? Base your decision on the needs of your group, not your preference. **Think about your average 3rd or 4th generation future believer. What type of reproducible method will *he* need?** Perhaps the people you initially know in your context are educated high school grads finding jobs in your city. You could easily start with a literate T4T model. But when they return to their homes, will they be able to use the same model with parents and grandparents? If not, then you may want to start with an oral method from the beginning.

If the majority of people you will reach in the first few generations are literate, choose a literate model. The reason many people prefer an oral approach is because they love stories. Great! Use stories in your literate model, but keep the training model written and not solely dependent on memorized, orally transmitted lessons. You will find the reproduction cycle goes much faster.

One common misperception about oral methods is that stories are all that is needed. We often remember the stories Jesus told, and therefore assume that stories alone are sufficient. Examine Jesus' interactions. Even though He used stories a lot, He almost always *switched modes* to a didactic application or gave a moral to the story in terms of propositional truth. **Don't assume that oral learners only need stories. They may prefer to learn with stories, but they still need teaching, propositional truth and clear application to show them how to apply the story for their context.** We found in TRT that this was an early mistake we made – not giving clear teaching and application after the story. After we cleaned this up, we found that people became much better doers and could pass on the lessons better. (For more explanation of using oral T4T methods, see the "How to Train Orally" in the supplemental materials on the T4TOnline.org website.)

Bottom line: choose a discipleship curriculum appropriate for your target audience.

Turning Trainees into Trainers

One of the difficulties CPM initiators experienced in T4T in the early years was helping trainees catch on to the three-thirds process. When they looked at the original T4T lessons (the short-term discipleship lessons in the middle third of the meeting), they could not see the reproduction process behind them.

When Ying personally trained a group of local believers in the three thirds, all they needed were the basic lessons because he trained them what to do at each stage. He used the three-thirds process with them. But in sending T4T lessons to other CPM initiators around the world for them to utilize, almost ALL of the *process* of T4T was missed. The T4T lessons were seen as just content, not a lesson plan and process. That's one reason for this book.

As people around the world begin implementing the T4T process, it is easy for them to get bogged down in the content and lose momentum. They focus on how to teach the lessons rather than building a movement. They forget the three thirds and the importance of multiplying generations of trainers.

One way to avoid this problem in your own T4T ministry is to reinforce the three-thirds process by writing each of the short-term discipleship sessions as a three-thirds **lesson plan**. In your lesson plan, you can script each part of the three thirds as a separate lesson *plan* so that the trainer will know what to do at each point. This helps reinforce the three-thirds process, as well as the lesson's content.[29]

You already know the lesson plan for Session One. But what would a lesson plan for Session Two look like? Here is an example of a LESSON PLAN FORMAT that you can easily expand:

First Third of the T4T Meeting (40 minutes)

- **PASTORAL CARE:** Start with a time to genuinely ask one another, "How are you doing?" and pray for, counsel and encourage one another.

- **WORSHIP:** Sing two to three worship songs.

- **ACCOUNTABILITY:** Ask each other these questions based on the previous week. Make sure you share your own testimony of trying to obey this.

  » *Who are you witnessing to? Who has believed?*

  » *Have you done Session One with those who believed? If so, how did it go?*

- **VISION CASTING:** Share the following vignette in five minutes or less:

  » "Heavenly Father's Heart" [write it out here – see Chapter 3].

  » Encourage them that even if they were rebuffed in their witness, God wants to save their household.

---

[29] A good example of a three-thirds lesson plan can be found on the T4TOnline.org website in the Training Rural Trainers –TRT – curriculum. Also see: "How to Train Orally" in the supplementary materials.

Second Third of the T4T Meeting
(40 minutes, but try to do it in less)

- **DISCIPLESHIP LESSON – BAPTISM:** Teach the lesson on baptism [write it out below]. Ensure that you have enough copies for the group members to pass out to their new believers. Make sure each trainer schedules a time to baptize their new believers.

Final Third of the T4T Meeting (40 minutes)

- **PRACTICE**
  - » Have the group practice teaching one another the baptism lesson in pairs. Wander around the group to help answer questions, encourage and gently correct.
  - » Make sure they practice until they are confident and competent to pass it on.
  - » Discuss in the group the three parts of today's meeting and make sure they can do this with their new believers this week.

- **SET GOALS AND PRAY**
  - » Help the group to set appropriate goals
    - If someone in the group has not been baptized, schedule a time to baptize him.
    - Trainees should set goals for witnessing to five more people on their Name List (some of them may be the same ones they witnessed to last week who want to hear more).
    - Trainees should set goals to immediately train anyone who has come to faith. Be sure they have been taught the Who-Why-How Session One as well as the clear gospel presentation. Then teach them the lesson on baptism.
  - » Let the group members briefly share their goals, then pray for one another. If time is running short, do this in pairs or triplets.

Examples of Short-term Discipleship Curricula

In the supplementary resources on the website, "Examples of T4T Curriculum Packages," are some examples of the subjects dealt with in short-term discipleship in various T4T packages. Many of these lessons can be downloaded from the T4T website. Each of them gives a clear example of building initial discipleship in six to ten easily reproducible lessons.

Short-term Discipleship Application

- Determine what the six to ten most important items are for a new believer in your context to grasp to start down the path of following Jesus.

- Get ideas from the other curriculum sets in the supplementary section on the T4TOnline.org website.

- Take existing lessons and tailor them to your people, or build some from scratch. Just make sure they are biblical, appropriate and reproducible.

- Write them as lesson plans (including all three thirds).

- Be ready to adapt them as you find out how easy or difficult it is for your trainees to reproduce them.

Non-negotiables for the Long-term Discipleship Package

The final lesson of your short-term discipleship should be a lesson on how to move into long-term discipleship. To do this effectively, give the group a set of inductive Bible study questions and a guide for which Bible passages to begin studying. Any group can learn to study the Bible inductively. All inductive means is that the *group* learns the answers together as they *ask questions of the text* and ask the Holy Spirit to give them understanding and application.

This does not rule out the role of preaching or teaching. Rather, it is simply a tool the group uses to help themselves become self-feeders. It enables them to truly serve as priests of God. Otherwise, they tend not to study the Word except when a "qualified" Bible teacher or preacher is visiting their group.

You will want to **model** this inductive approach during the lesson that introduces long-term discipleship. You will let the trainees practice the inductive study questions in the practice time until they have confidence to repeat the process with their believers.

Inductive Questions / Pattern

Learning inductively is not easy at first. The group must be taught a *pattern that they will use over and over until it becomes second nature.* Inductive study does not mean that a group leader does not prepare a lesson or share insights. But it takes the pressure off him to be an eloquent teacher in the beginning. He will still share insights and guide learning, but allow the group to dig out much of the truth themselves. It also enables **multiple people** to lead the group through the Bible study time.

You can use any set of accountability questions as long as they 1) are memorable, 2) are effective for uncovering the basic meaning and 3) emphasize application and obedience. Here are some examples. Within each question, you can always ask secondary questions to expand the discussion and application.

The most commonly used questions in T4T are "**SOS**":

- **Say**: What is this passage saying?

- **Obey**: What should we obey from this passage?

- **Share**: Who is someone we can share this message with?

Here is another set of questions:

- What is this passage saying? (And, what do you like?)

- What do you not understand?

- What does it teach us about God?

- What does it tell us to do?

- What can we share with someone else?

Where to start

Once you have a basic set of inductive questions to use then point the group toward a set of biblical passages to start studying. In most cases, you will use a book of the Bible, like Mark. With some oral learners, you may use a set of Bible stories. Choose Scripture passages that will guide the group through basic understanding of the Bible, Jesus and discipleship – something that will give them a basic overview of how to follow Jesus.

For examples of long-term discipleship curricula, see "Examples of T4T Curriculum Packages" in the supplementary materials on the website.

What to do if they cannot read

You may find yourself practicing T4T with oral learners who simply cannot read. How do you help them hear the Word so that they can study and obey it during long-term discipleship?

You will find that in every circumstance, God will provide a way for hungry non-literate believers to hear and obey His Word. Here are some examples:

- Find one person in the group who *can* read and let him read the Bible passage to the others. This reader may be a youth who has been to school.

- Record Bible stories or Bible passages, and let the believers listen to them.

- Help them memorize Bible stories to meditate on during the week

Long-term Discipleship Application

Once you have developed 6-10 short-term discipleship lesson plans, then you should write one more lesson plan. This is the session that introduces the long-term discipleship pattern of inductive Bible study and gives the group a suggestion for which Scripture passages to begin studying.

Therefore, if you have been using the following pattern . . .

- **Session One: WHY** (vision-casting vignette), **WHOM** (make a Name List) and **HOW** (bridge and gospel presentation
  - » This session can be done within minutes of a person's profession of faith.

- **Sessions Two through Nine:** Introduce eight **short-term discipleship** lessons using the three-thirds approach

. . . Then you would need one more lesson plan for your tenth meeting:

- **Session Ten:** An introduction to **inductive Bible study** method of inductive questions to use each week, and a place to start in Scripture for **long-term discipleship**. During Session Ten, you would model this inductive approach and in the subsequent weeks until they feel confident to lead and reproduce it themselves.
  - » They use this approach for the remaining sessions (11th onwards) from that point on.

Remember that your T4T package must help believers move through each stage of short-term and long-term discipleship. Your T4T package must include a reproducible set of short-term lessons that conclude

Your T4T package must include short-term and long-term discipleship.

with an introduction to inductive Bible study that will set the pattern for long-term discipleship.

Two critical milestones in this discipleship process are 1) baptism and 2) forming them into churches. Find out how to cross those hurdles in the next two chapters.

Be a Doer, not just a Hearer!

Write down how God has spoken to you and what you need to obey as a result:

CHAPTER 15

Your T4T Package: Getting to Baptism

A critical milestone in short-term discipleship is the point of baptism. Baptism is the crucial step Jesus gave His followers in solidifying the decision of their heart.

Launching the Discipleship *Re*-Revolution

Unfortunately, the role of baptism is sometimes downplayed for fear of offending the new believer or the culture he lives in. Sometimes we press for a decision, but not a disciple. Dismissing baptism or devaluing baptism creates a huge disservice to those professing faith.

This violates the kingdom principle of the treasure hidden in the field and the pearl of great price: **people will joyfully give all they have to follow Jesus if they see the value of the King and the kingdom life.**

Baptism initiates the discipleship *re*-revolution of kingdom disciples walking in a life of obedience and joy. It helps them consider the value of the King and count the cost of following Him — which is the essential first step to the King's reign.

Sure or Mature?

Some people believe that baptism should be delayed until there is clear evidence that the person is really a follower of Jesus. This delay can be months or even a year or more after a profession of faith. The intention is good: making sure people are growing in Christlikeness. However, delaying baptism is not a biblical approach.

*Baptism is a sign that you are **sure, not mature** in your faith.*

Baptism is a sign that you are sure, not mature in your faith.[30] It is the sign to the new believer and to others around him that he is sure that he wants to follow Jesus. The sign of maturity is the fruit of the Spirit, which will develop over time. If you can remember this one principle, you will **rush** to baptism rather than **delay** baptism. In fact, baptism is a solidifying decision that helps ensure that the new believer **will** lay his old life down and begin walking in a new path of conformity to Christ. By delaying baptism, we delay the means Jesus gave us for effecting firm commitment.

In the early discipleship of the Ina believers, we developed a set of short term lessons. The first one we used after salvation was a lesson on assurance followed by one on baptism. We assumed that the first thing a new believer needed was to know for sure that he was saved and secure. This assumption came from our own discipleship experience, *not* the Bible. As we took new believers through the assurance lesson, an interesting phenomenon recurred: believers had little sense of assurance despite the many Scriptures we taught them.

I scratched my head in puzzlement. I read, and re-read the New Testament looking for answers. In Acts, I discovered that in every instance except for one, it appeared that believers were baptized immediately – the same day they believed. When I read Acts 2:38 it appeared that baptism was a key part of the profession of faith, like in Rom. 10:9-10 – professing with the mouth.

Our new "believers" had no assurance because *they were not completely sure* they wanted to follow Jesus! Since they had not professed Jesus in baptism, they were still wavering in their hearts about their decision. They had no peace of assurance because they really were not taking on the sign of following Jesus yet.

Thereafter, we reversed the first two lessons *from* 1) assurance then 2) baptism *to* 1) baptism then 2) assurance. When we did that, everything changed. People professing Christ were

---

[30] My pastor, Thom Wolf, first taught me this principle.

immediately taught the **first step of obedience – baptism –** and challenged to be baptized very quickly. Some said "no." Many took a deep gulp (counted the cost) and stepped across the line in the sand (baptism). When we took them through the assurance lesson after this, often within hours, they experienced great peace and assurance in their salvation.

We just had to get the order right: **"sure, then assured"**!

Colleagues experiencing CPM results around the world confirm the same thing – the importance of early baptism in developing fervent followers of Jesus. **In your T4T package, you need a short-term discipleship lesson on baptism very early on.**

The Baptism Pattern of Acts — Who, When, Where, How

A biblical view of baptism can be taught well using Acts as a foundation. One reason Acts is so helpful is that it illustrates the command Jesus gave in Matt. 28:19-20 to make disciples by *baptizing* them and teaching them to obey all of Jesus' commands. The command to make disciples carries with it the command for *us* to baptize those *we* lead to faith.

Many of the concerns that Christian leaders have about immediate baptism are answered in Acts in addition to the Great Commission. Acts is a helpful model for overcoming common extra-biblical objections to immediate, believer's baptism. Essentially, there are ten instances of baptism in the book of Acts (Paul's baptism is mentioned twice – Acts 9:18-19 and Acts 22:14-17). The study below can easily become the basis for your own lesson on baptism. However, with most new believers studying just one or two of the passages will suffice.

Study the ten instances in Acts and ask some basic questions about these incidents:

- Who was baptized?

- Who baptized them?

- When were they baptized?

- How and where were they baptized?

    (1) Acts 2:41 – 3,000 baptized in one day after confession of faith

    (2) Acts 8:6-13 Samaritans, former demon-possessed/sorcerers/sick

    (3) Acts 8:36-38 Ethiopian eunuch traveling on road

    (4) Acts 9:18-19 Saul the persecutor

    (5) Acts 10:47-48 Gentiles, Peter commanded companions not to wait

    (6) Acts 16:13-15 Women by the riverside

    (7) Acts 16:33 Roman jailer and his family

    (8) Acts 18:8 Ruler of the synagogue, his family and many believers

    (9) Acts 19:1-5 John's baptism was not enough

    (10) Acts 22:14-17 "Why are you waiting?" (Ananias speaking to Saul)

The answers to these questions are very revealing:

- Who was baptized?

    » New believers who had just professed faith in Jesus Christ, generally hours before

    » **Lesson**: Baptism is the first step of obedience for people professing Christ, and is probably best equated with the outward confession of the mouth (Rom. 10:9-10)

- Who baptized them?

    » In most cases, it appears that it was the person leading them to faith

> » **Lesson:** Baptizing others is commanded for all believers fulfilling the Great Commission. Ordination or special certification does not seem to be called for in Scripture, but rather obedience to the Great Commission. Any believer can baptize others in the mission of leading them to faith.

- When were they baptized?

> » Immediately. In all instances except for Saul, it appears that they were baptized the *same day they believed.* In Saul's instance, he fasted three days until he was baptized.

> » **Lesson:** Immediate baptism is the command (Matt. 28:19-20; Acts 2:38) and pattern of Scripture. The sooner, the better. Baptism seems to solidify their decision to follow Jesus and encourage new believers toward boldness.

- **How and where were they baptized?**

> » In water through immersion. They were baptized wherever they could find water, not necessarily a dedicated baptistery[31]. In the clear instances (like the eunuch), they went *down into* the water. Immersion / submersion is the meaning of the Greek word *baptizo.*

> » **Lesson:** Immersion is the biblical mode that best pictures the spiritual reality of being buried with Christ and raised to new life (Rom. 6:4). Baptism can occur wherever one can find enough water for immersion.

An excellent example of a discipleship lesson on baptism is the "Acts Hammer of Baptism" by George Tupper. It can be found in "Baptism Resources" in the supplementary materials on the website T4TOnline.org. While we have to use resources like

---

[31] There is nothing wrong with a dedicated baptistery. It is just that this is not required for baptism.

this for existing Christian leaders, most new believers have no stereotype about baptism, and are willing to be baptized when they see it commanded from Scripture.

Why This is True —
Baptism as a Profession of Faith

One of the reasons that baptism is so important is the function it was intended to play from the New Testament time onward. Baptism is clearly commanded from Scripture for all believers (Matt. 28:19-20; Acts 2:38) and the Great Commission makes it very clear that all disciples are authorized to baptize. Why is this command so important?

In our recent history, various modes of demonstrating a desire to profess Christ have arisen: walking down an aisle; raising a hand; standing up in a crowd; praying a prayer. All of these modes arose as good attempts to help those who were believing in their heart to *act on this belief* by demonstrating a commitment. The most notable example of this is walking down the aisle of a church in front of everyone watching. None of these is wrong.

There is a danger in these, however: they can easily take the place of baptism as *the* profession (confession) of faith. In the Scripture and in history, baptism has been the sign of publicly professing faith in Christ. With other modes of professing faith coming into vogue, baptism can take a backseat and therefore be delayed. However, if we continue to see baptism as *the primary means* of professing faith in front of witnesses, we will place it very near the time of one's personal decision to follow Christ.

Look at the parallelism of these passages.

> "The time is fulfilled, and the kingdom of God is at hand; **repent and believe** in the gospel." (Mark 1:15, NASB, emphasis added)

> **Repent and be baptized** every one of you in the name of Jesus Christ for the forgiveness of your sins, and you will receive the gift of the Holy Spirit. For the promise is for you and for your

children and for all who are far off, everyone whom the Lord our God calls to himself. (Acts 2:38, NASB, emphasis added)

Therefore **repent and return**, so that your sins may be wiped away, in order that times of refreshing may come from the presence of the Lord (Acts 3:19, NASB, emphasis added)

That if you **confess with your mouth** Jesus as Lord, **and believe in your heart** that God raised Him from the dead, you will be saved; for with the heart a person believes, resulting in righteousness, and with the mouth he confesses, resulting in salvation. (Rom. 10:9-10, NASB, emphasis added)

Corresponding to that, **baptism now saves you**—not the removal of dirt from the flesh, but **an appeal to God for a good conscience**--through the resurrection of Jesus Christ (1 Pet. 3:21, NASB, emphasis added)

In the texts above, the call for people to believe consisted of some version of 1) repenting and believing inwardly, and 2) professing it outwardly. "Repent and be baptized" of Acts 2:38 is parallel to "Repent and return" of Acts 3:19 or "Believe in your heart and confess with your mouth" of Rom. 10:9-10.

Baptism is important because it is the profession of faith that we make outwardly. Until then, it is easy for a person to waver in his heart, but baptism creates a clear decision: "I am following Jesus." Baptism helps people who believe in their heart to call upon the name of the Lord outwardly.

This is why the biblical writers connected baptism so closely to the actual point of regeneration of a heart.

Because it is such an outward act baptism helps to seal a person's inward decision to follow Christ. There is no doubt: the inward cry of a person's heart for salvation is where rebirth takes place. Baptism is an outward act to help make that inward decision sure. Remember, it is a sign that you are sure, not mature.

Baptism is similar to what happened to Abraham in the Old Testament when he was circumcised.

> We have been saying that Abraham's faith was credited to him as righteousness. Under what circumstances was it credited? Was it after he was circumcised, or before? It was not after, but before! And he received the sign of circumcision, **a seal of the righteousness** that he had by faith while he was still uncircumcised. (Rom. 4:9-11, NIV, emphasis added)

First, he believed and received righteousness. His salvation came through faith in God. This was an inward decision (of his heart). Second, he received the sign of circumcision to seal his commitment. When he took this step, there was no longer any doubt about his allegiance to God. Up to this point, it would be easy for Abraham to deny his faith or turn back, because there was not a no-turning-back step he had taken yet. *If there was any doubt in Abraham's heart before about following God, or any wavering of commitment, this put all doubts to rest!* In that sense, circumcision *sealed* his decision to be a follower of the LORD God. It didn't save him, but it made him firm. There was no turning back now. Any non-Israelite could easily confirm Abraham's commitment if he chose to.

Baptism fulfills a similar role for disciples in the New Covenant. It helps confirm the decision of our heart so that we waver no longer. Turning back is much harder. Baptism is a line in the sand. Prior to it, a person professing faith can easily turn back. After baptism, it is much harder to turn back.

If you want firm followers of Jesus, get them baptized.

Allegiance Shift

Baptism represents an allegiance shift that a new believer has made from his old gods and beliefs. It clearly delineates that Jesus is not one god among many that you believe in, but that He is the ONLY God that you follow. Baptism helps to reduce the tendency toward syncretism, adding Jesus as one more god among many.

It is very helpful at baptism to help believers renounce the old allegiances of their previous religion. One way to do this is by asking questions at the time they are baptized. Some questions often asked are[32]:

1. Have you decided to follow Jesus and Him only?

2. Do you know that He has forgiven you of all of your sins?

3. Are you telling all of these witnesses that you will follow Jesus and never turn back?

4. When they come into your house, and drag you away, and throw you into prison and threaten to kill you, will you still follow Jesus? [Or "When people ridicule you and mistreat you, will you still follow Jesus?"]

A critical part of baptism is **helping people make a conscious allegiance shift**. The great missionary of old to the Lisu people in China, J. O. Frasier, struggled with Lisu converts reverting back to old idolatrous ways, sometimes even after baptism. A breakthrough came for him when he helped families finally tear down idol altars, throw away amulets and destroy any temptations to revert to idolatry.

If you are working with people who would be tempted to revert to their old religion, it can be immensely helpful at the time of the baptism to go with them to remove any temptations from their home and life – altars, idols, amulets, books, etc. It helps them not revert in times of weakness or temptation – a sickness, a religious holiday or a cultural rite of passage.

If this is an issue for your people group, it is easy to make this a part of your T4T baptism lesson.

For practical ideas on where to baptize or who can baptize, see the "Baptism Resources" in the supplementary resources at T4TOnline.org.

---

[32] See "Baptism Resources" in the supplementary resources on the website T4TOnline.org for other examples of questions.

Baptism and Boldness

The single most important factor, outside of the Holy Spirit, in helping new believers become bold in their faith and witness may be baptism. It is wonderful how the Spirit of God blesses them in their first act of obedience. They begin to reap the promises of Acts 2:

> Repent and be baptized every one of you in the name of Jesus Christ for the forgiveness of your sins, and **you will receive the gift of the Holy Spirit**. For the promise is for you and for your children and for all who are far off, everyone whom the Lord our God calls to himself. (Acts 2:38-39, ESV, emphasis added)

If you want bold, firm followers of Jesus, encourage them to take on the sign of following Jesus as quickly as possible: **baptism.** *It's the way of Jesus.*

When believers willingly surrender all to follow Jesus through baptism, the Spirit takes greater control of them. In the book of Acts, disciples were often filled with the Spirit. The sign that was always demonstrated in Acts was **speaking the word of God with boldness** (Acts 4:31).[33] Baptism helps believers become bold.

If you want bold, firm followers of Jesus, encourage them to take on the sign of following Jesus as quickly as possible: **baptism.** It's the way of Jesus.

Add a Baptism Lesson to Your T4T Package

Simply adding a baptism lesson, often as the first one after salvation, can make all the difference in this regard. Once a person professes Christ upon hearing the gospel, be ready to walk him through the baptism lesson as soon as possible.

---

[33] Dr. Jack McGorman, my New Testament professor at Southwestern Baptist Theological Seminary, first brought this to my attention.

A typical T4T pattern when lost people profess faith in Jesus is this:

1. **Immediately do Session One with him/them** – WHY-WHOM-HOW. This can be done in the first few minutes after their salvation. Coach them through some appropriate ways to begin sharing what just happened to them and the best people to share this with first.

2. **Follow this with a lesson on baptism** at the same time or within hours (or a day or two). As they answer the baptism questions, help them realize that others may persecute them for their faith but Jesus will stand with them.

One missionary who is at the center of a CPM was seeing many people come to faith and churches planted. Professions of faith were high, but baptisms were low. The missionary came to realize that he had no dedicated lesson on baptism immediately after profession. He added in a simple lesson on baptism and then trained his key leaders in this, who also trained the members of their churches. Within weeks and months, baptisms skyrocketed to new highs. It didn't take a lot of extra work, just some focused attention.

If you want firm followers of Jesus, get them baptized immediately.

Once you have done that, you have crossed the first major milestone toward a discipleship *re*-revolution. The second is right behind it: helping a group of new believers become a church. Read on to find out how to cross this milestone.

Be a Doer, not just a Hearer!

Write down how God has spoken to you and what you need to obey as a result:

CHAPTER 16

Your T4T Package: Forming Churches

You've begun the T4T process. You've cast vision to many believers and begun several T4T groups.

You've trained them in Session One (WHY-WHOM-HOW) and they are now witnessing and starting new T4T groups.

You've started them down the path of short-term discipleship. You've gone through several lessons in your early discipleship already including the important one on baptism. Your trainees are starting to become trainers because they're forming their new believers into T4T groups and passing on the discipleship lessons in a three-thirds format.

But where do churches fit into this mix? When do these groups become churches, if ever?

New believers must be gathered into churches. This is God's design from the beginning of history. Church planting is not our value because it is a pragmatic way to reach people. It is our value because this was the purpose of creation – the preparation of a bride for the Son (Eph. 1:23; Eph. 3:21; Eph. 5:27; Rev. 19:7-8, Rev. 21:9)! Living in community as church is the King's way to equip His people to be what they were designed to be and do what they were called to do.

Your T4T package should purposefully form groups into churches at a key stage in the short-term discipleship process. This is a second critical milestone for a discipleship re-revolution to emerge as a church-planting movement. Your

T4T package should include a lesson at about Session Four or Five to help the group purposefully become church.

Often these groups become churches that meet in houses or other convenient places. Sometimes they become home groups of a larger church but carry out the functions of the Body of Christ. The essential point is to help the new believers become a part of the Body of Christ in a reproducible form that fits into their community.

There are two guidelines that govern CPM churches:

- **BIBLICAL:** Is this model and/or each aspect of church consistent with the Scripture?

There is no single biblical model of what a church must be. We see numerous examples of culturally adapted models in the Scripture. For example various churches had culturally appropriate leadership models. Pastors, elders, and overseers were all examples of this, depending on the context. But each fulfilled the biblical mandate of having leaders to serve as overseers.

In the same way, T4T does not propose one model of church as THE biblical model. Many models of church can be biblical. So the question is not: "Is this **the** biblical model?" but rather "Is this model (and its elements) **consistent with** scriptural teaching?

- **CULTURALLY REPRODUCIBLE:** Is this model of church something an average new believer can start and organize?

Since many models of church can faithfully serve the scriptural teaching, the secondary question becomes: "Which of the many biblically faithful models (or elements) should we implement?" The answer is: the one that is most culturally appropriate and reproducible in our community. The general guideline is this: "Could an average young believer start and organize such a church?" Otherwise, church planting will be relegated to a few highly trained individuals.

With these two guidelines in mind, T4T tries to help believers start simple types of churches that enable believers to faithfully follow Jesus as the body of Christ. This is not a critique of other forms of churches. There is room in the kingdom community for many types of churches. In initiating CPMs, however, for the sake of reaching all of the lost, we advocate CPM churches that are relevant and reproducible. That type of church will need to emphasize small group meetings in locations that are easy to find such as homes, coffee shops and parks rather than in locations that are costly to purchase or build.

Four Helps in Getting to Church

You must have a clear step in your early T4T discipleship at which you help a group of believers consciously become a church. To establish reproducing churches or small groups, there are four practices that we have found especially helpful. The goal is to help the training group purposefully become church.

1. Know what you are trying to achieve: a CLEAR DEFINITION of when a group becomes a church.

It is difficult to start a church if you do not have a clear idea in mind of when a group moves from being a cell group or Bible study to a church.

> **Scenario**: A group has been meeting independently of any church for three months. They have great worship times and deeply moving Bible studies. They listen to the Word and try to obey whatever it says. They are making plans to visit a nursing home to minister to the needs of people there. Are they a church?

There's probably not enough information there for you to make a call. Is it a church or a great Bible study group? If your definition of when a group becomes church is not clear, you might be tempted to call this group a church. The first step in starting churches is establishing a clear definition of what a church is – the basic essentials of a church.

Clear definition

Acts provides a concrete example that can be helpful here:

> **Activity:** Read Acts 2:36-47. Try not to make things too complicated. Boiled down, what made this group a church? Write down your answer.

Here is an example of a definition of church created from the Acts 2 passage. It emphasizes the 3 C's of church: Covenant, Characteristics, Caring leaders.

- **COVENANT:** a group of baptized believers (Mt.18:20; Acts 2:41) who recognize themselves as Christ's body and are committed to meeting together regularly (Acts 2:46)

- **CHARACTERISTICS:** they regularly *abide* in Christ through the characteristics of church:

  » **Worship:** exalting & enjoying God's presence

  » **Fellowship:** loving care for one another
    - Including **giving offerings** to meet needs and as an act of worship

  » **Prayer**

  » **Word:** Studying and OBEYING the Scripture as authoritative

  » **The Lord's Supper**[34]

  » They live out a commitment to **share the gospel** to the world and **minister** to the needs of others

- **CARING LEADERS:** As the church develops, leaders are appointed according to biblical standards (Titus 1:5-9) and exercise mutual accountability, including church discipline.

---

[34] For more information on the importance of the Lord's Supper in new churches, see "Church Formation Resources" in the supplemental resources on the T4TOnline.org website.

For the sake of church planting, the 3 C's are in order of priority. The most important C is **"Covenant."** The group sees itself as church (identity) and has made a commitment (covenant) to follow Jesus together. (Do not read into this that they have to have a written covenant.)

The second part of the definition is **"Characteristics."** A group may call itself a church, but if it repeatedly lacks the basic functions or characteristics of a church, it is not really a church. If an animal barks, wags its tail and walks on all fours, you may call it a duck, but it is really a dog.

Finally, a healthy church will eventually develop **"Caring Leaders."** It is possible to have a church before caring leaders develop. A good example of this is at the end of Paul's first journey. In Acts 14:21-23, Paul and Barnabas visited the churches they had just planted in the previous weeks and months. But for the sake of the long-term health of the churches, caring leaders should be raised up.

The first step in starting churches through T4T is: ***Know what you are trying to achieve: a clear definition of when a group becomes a church.***

2. From the beginning when you start a training group, MODEL the parts of church life mentioned above. You can do this through the three-thirds process of training trainers.

A church planter was having a hard time helping the groups he was training to become churches. As he described his training groups, the process sounded like a sterile classroom experience. As the group worked through the lessons, it was very cerebral and not very warm. In this classroom environment he was teaching them to start something *different* in their homes. There was a disconnect between what he was modeling and what he was teaching them to do. By changing his training meetings into a format similar to what he would want the churches to look like, it would be much easier to help these groups actually become churches.

The easiest way to transition a new training group into a church is to start living as church and modeling church from the very first meeting. That way, when you get to the T4T lesson on church, it is what you have already been living out together. If you do all the seven parts of the three thirds in a Spirit-filled loving manner, you will already be very close to living as church.

Do your best from the first T4T meeting to model what you will eventually want this new church to look like. Don't make it feel like a sterile training until you get to the session on church. The lesson on church should come as no surprise. You don't want to spend 4-5 weeks together as a "class" and then announce: "Today we will have the lesson on church and become a church" and completely change how you meet together. *Becoming a church should be the next natural step in the progression of meeting together.*

3. Make sure you have a SPECIFIC LESSON (OR LESSONS) ON CHURCH and its ordinances in your T4T package.

If you have a clear definition of church and are modeling church-like meetings each training session, then it is easy to help the group become a church when you go through the "church" lesson in your short-term discipleship package. If you want quickly reproducing churches, then include one or two lessons on becoming a church by about Session Four or Five. [In the supplemental resources on the website "Church Formation Resources" are examples of church lessons.]

Have a specific goal in mind when you go through the church lesson: *This week we will commit to become a church and will add in any missing characteristics of a church.*

When a T4T group goes through the lesson(s) on church, one of two things usually happens:

1 step: A group recognizes that it **is** a church and is practicing the characteristics of church. At this point it takes the final step by committing to be a church together (gains identity and covenant).

2 steps: More often, a group recognizes that it is deficient in some of the characteristics of church. It takes two conscious steps forward to 1) add in those characteristics (e.g. Lord's Supper, offerings) and then 2) commit to becoming church together.

4. Use CHURCH HEALTH MAPPING to help a group evaluate if they have all the elements of church life.[35]

A great diagnostic tool called Church Health Mapping (or Church Circles) can be used with a group, or the leaders of a group or network of groups, to help them determine if the group is a church. The tool helps them spot deficiencies and correct these. It also helps them see which groups may not be church yet.

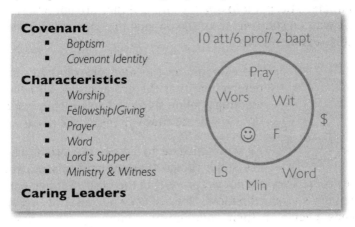

The basic idea of church circles is best illustrated with one group. In this example, you have a group meeting together. At this point draw a circle with a dotted line to represent a group meeting.

If the group calls itself a church or sees itself as a church (covenant identity), then make the dotted line a solid line.

---

[35] Thanks to Jeff Sundell and Nathan Shank for the concept of church-health mapping that is now being adapted and widely used in many areas.

Above the circle, write three numbers representing the number of people attending the group, the number of them who have professed faith in Christ and the number who have been baptized. In this scenario you have 10 attendees, six professing believers and two who have been baptized. These numbers tell you and your partners a lot. Apparently more needs to be done to share the gospel with existing attendees. In addition, the baptism ratio is very low. They may need a lesson on baptism, or the importance of baptism may need a stronger application point.

10 att / 6 prof / 2 bapt

You have just assessed the first component of church: Covenant.

Now it is time to assess the second component of church: Characteristics. Go back to your simplified definition of church (Help #1) and give a one word description or symbol to each characteristic. If a church is consistently practicing the characteristic, put it *inside* the circle. If they are not practicing it or wait on someone from the outside to come do it for them, put it *outside* the circle.

10 att / 6 prof / 2 bapt

For example, in the next diagram, you have determined that the group prays, witnesses, worships, fellowships and has caring leaders "☺". So you put those all inside the circle.

As you continue to assess the group, there are some things that are still missing from the group. They are not yet practicing the Lord's Supper, one of the Lord's two ordinances. Nor are they purposefully serving needy people in their community – ministry. They haven't started giving offerings yet. Even though they do have Bible study sometimes (Word), they rely on an outside teacher to do it. He only comes through once a month. So they're not really feeding themselves from the Word yet. Therefore you put all these things outside the circle.

10 att / 6 prof / 2 bapt

At this point, it is relatively easy to see what is blocking the group from really becoming a church. They have a covenant, but could improve by winning the rest of the attendees and getting everyone baptized. Adding in the Lord's Supper and offerings would greatly strengthen the church. It's important for this group to gain confidence in how to study and apply the Word on their own. You'll need to help them also see how to serve the needs of people outside their immediate circle.

Though they are deficient, you now see a way to transform this group into a church, and they see it too! It is a wonderfully empowering process to let the group prayerfully brainstorm about how to add each of the elements into the circle. These become clear action plans for the group.

You can use the church health mapping process on its own, or you can include it as a part of the lesson on church. As you and your trainers begin to start multiple churches, mapping all the churches in this way will help you understand the specifics of each church and areas that need strengthening.

Application: Forming Churches

You must train your trainers to purposefully help groups become churches at a key stage in the short-term discipleship process by having a specific lesson(s) on becoming church.

If you are clear in your definition and you model church life during each meeting, then the lesson on church will be a natural next step. Church-health mapping can also help you in that process.

And you will have passed the next major milestone toward a discipleship *re*-revolution. Think about how exhilarating it is when successive generations of trainers are all forming their groups into churches at about the fourth or fifth meeting! That is when church-planting movements emerge!

No church lesson? Then expect very few churches!

Church lesson early on? Then expect new generations of churches!

Bottom line: you must train your trainers to purposefully help T4T groups to become churches at a key stage in the short-term discipleship process by having a specific lesson(s) on becoming church.

No church lesson? Very few churches!

Church lesson early on? New generations of churches!

As churches develop, the development of church leaders is critical. The multiplication of leaders is the key to sustaining the church-planting movement. Yet how can you do this when the majority of your believers are relatively new to the faith? Read the next chapter to find out.

Be a Doer, not just a Hearer!

Write down how God has spoken to you and what you need to obey as a result:

CHAPTER 17

Your T4T Package: Reproducing Leaders

Your discipleship model is moving along nicely. People are coming to faith and T4T groups are becoming churches. Yet where do the church leaders come from? Your T4T package must include specific ways to help leaders multiply along with the multiplication of churches.

Before explaining what must be in your T4T package, we need to explore the counter-intuitive nature of developing leaders in the kingdom. If you don't understand this, your movement will stall very quickly.

Leadership Multiplication Movements

Sustained CPMs are in essence *leadership multiplication movements*. The development and multiplication of leaders is what the Spirit uses to drive the movement. This is the spiritual engine of sustained CPMs. CPMs can start without effective leadership development and multiplication, but they will be short-lived without it. You must have a system in place that results in generations of *reproducing leaders*.

Prior to T4T, leadership overload was a common malady of CPMs. With the effective implementation of T4T, this problem has been largely overcome. That is because T4T inherently develops and multiplies leaders in the three-thirds process.

As mentioned in Chapter 4, believers mature more rapidly when they are given responsibilities for service immediately (Eph. 4:11-16). Remember that T4T uses loving accountability to help trainees become trainers who 1) follow Jesus and 2) fish for men. Because *everyone* is encouraged to pass on what he learns to others, everyone is given the opportunity to grow as a leader.

In T4T you do not typically *choose* leaders, they *choose themselves* in the proving process of obedience. They become leaders by starting their own groups and taking responsibility for them. This does not mean that you leave the leadership development process up to them entirely. As you will see, you need to devote a lot of attention to *speaking vision* into their lives and *helping to appoint* them to appropriate leadership responsibilities in the beginning, until there is a holy climate that fosters spiritual leadership aspirations.

Beginning Needs vs. Later Needs

An important premise in leadership development is this: **what a new leader of a small home church needs in terms of character and skills is very different from what a mature leader of a large church needs.** Both are leaders, but the character set and skill set vary significantly. Keep this in mind in your quest for a CPM. *In developing new leaders, you should be looking for the most basic qualifications for spiritual leadership that are appropriate to that stage.*

The leader of a church of 500 members will need much more in terms of character (patience, spiritual vision, self-discipline) and skills (management ability, teaching ability, time usage, handling interpersonal conflict) than a leader of a church of 20. *What a leader needs in the beginning (character and skills) will be different from what he may need at a later stage.*

The Development Process

How do we develop new leaders in CPMs? We do it in same manner Jesus and Paul did – through lots of proving opportunities. Think about how the actual process of Jesus choosing the first four disciples contrasts with our mental picture of them simply leaving their nets to follow a person they had never met before.

Such a view is naïve. There is much more involved in picking these men when we compare the four gospels together.

> **Exercise: Read each of the passages below that relate to Jesus choosing the twelve apostles. After reading each passage, answer the two questions below.**
>
> - **First** encounters - John 1:35-51
>
> - **Second** call to them at the seashore- Mark 1:16-20, Luke 5:1-11
>
> - **Final** selection of the Twelve – Luke 6:12-16; Mark 3:13-19
>
>   1. How did Jesus discern that they were the right men?
>
>   2. How did he develop them at that stage?

Stage One: First Encounters - John 1:35-51

Long before Jesus called the four brothers to leave their boats and follow Him, He had a number of encounters with them. The first one occurred when John the Baptist referred Jesus to them.

Though they began to show interest in Jesus, Jesus wasn't ready to call them to full-time "followship" or make them apostles. Instead, He probed them with small requests or statements. He watched how they responded to these small requests or statements.

How did Jesus develop them? He gave them small things to obey – stay with Me tonight, go get your brother, think about what you can become. Plus, He began to spend *sporadic time with them* observing their lives as they observed His. At this point, Jesus did not yet make great demands on the disciples.

Stage Two: Creating Disciples in the Seashore Call – Mark 1:16-20, Luke 5:1-11

The famous story we all know about Jesus calling the four men – Andrew, Peter, James and John – who were business partners came weeks or months after John 1. These men knew Jesus and had spent time with Him. Knowing this helps explain how Jesus

THE PRAYER LIFE OF YING KAI

With reluctance, Ying discussed with a group of missionaries his personal prayer life. He gave illustrations of unsuccessful witnessing, and in fact being rebuffed by evil spirits, when he witnessed without previously praying through the situation and praying for the individual. He described even such mundane events as working as a hospital chaplain and failing to pray for the patient before he went into the room when he intended to witness. He described situations of failure in witness in which he went back and prayed for more than an hour for the individual that had rebuffed his witness.

When various participants asked him further about the practicality of always praying in advance, he described his DAILY practice of rising early and often praying one to two hours for his ministry every single day. He then pulled up his pants legs and showed two calloused knees to the group. With his "big trainers" he insists they become persons of prayer,

Continued next page.

could walk up to them and essentially say: "Okay guys, it's time. Leave your business and follow Me full time." Knowing what they knew about Jesus at this point, they counted the cost and decided it was worth it.

How did Jesus discern they were the right men? He had already spent time with them. When He probed them with larger requests (take Me out in your boat; let down your nets; leave your nets to follow Me), they repeatedly obeyed.

How did He develop them? By giving them greater tasks to fulfill and by spending uninterrupted time with them. This was when He began to give them much more attention.

Stage Three: Choosing the Twelve – Luke 6:12-16; Mark 3:13-19

But realize that the Twelve were not yet apostles. In actuality, Jesus had many more men and women who were disciples of His than merely the Twelve (Luke 6:12). But it was time to raise up twelve men to become "apostles" who would receive more authority and take on more leadership responsibility. They were being given more of a leadership role. Even after choosing the apostles, Jesus continued to invest in many other disciples (e.g. the 72 disciples of Luke 10), but the Twelve received His greatest investment.

How did Jesus discern that these were the right men? Through an evening of prayer and fasting (Luke 6:12).

How did He develop them at this point? By giving them more attention and increasing their ministry responsibilities (Mark 3:14-15).

Lessons for us

Jesus developed these men fairly rapidly, even without them being indwelt by the Holy Spirit. But it didn't happen immediately. There was a proving process. In T4T we have the same opportunity for developing leaders.

What can we learn from how Jesus discerned the right men and developed them?

- **Give new disciples small assignments and see who is faithful, then increase responsibility. (Matt. 25:21)**

- **It is easier to take a faithful man and teach him skills, than to take a skillful man and teach him faithfulness.**[36]

This is very easy to do in T4T. In the beginning, you don't expect your new trainees to lead a movement. You are just trying to see who is good soil. Who will obey the Word? Who will begin to witness? Then will they start a new group with their new converts?

Then will they train them? *You ease them into leadership responsibilities.*

and he communicates to them that it would be best if they pray at least two hours every morning prior to going out to begin their other ministries.

When Ying was asked about praying for others, he indicated that he ALWAYS prays for others when asked. When the subject of healings came up, he indicated that he would ask God in advance what to pray for people and he would pray what God communicated to him was God's intention for that situation. Ying has no reluctance whatsoever in following this pattern to pray for healing, pray for deliverance, pray for freedom from sinful habits, pray for the restoration of relationships, and pray for a myriad of other results. It is because he ALWAYS prays first to ask God what to pray that he has no reluctance to publicly or privately "put God on the spot" to pray for dramatic results.

From "Why T4T is Successful" by Bill Smith

---

[36] This is a statement that my pastor and mentor Thom Wolf taught me early in ministry that has held true for me the last 25 years.

- **As people prove faithful, give them more time and attention.** The best leaders/trainers are developed on the job.

As it becomes apparent where the good soil is, **then** you begin to give those people more attention. A common leadership mistake we make is by spending 90% of our time with the 10% who are the least responsive. We cajole them and do whatever we can to move them off center. Successful CPM practitioners do what Jesus did – spend the majority of their time with the minority who are most fruitful.

The fruitful ones need extra attention because they are taking on increased responsibilities and the problems that accompany them. They need to be developed on the job. Your T4T system must build in times to help them grow. We will discuss the mechanisms for that later in this chapter.

- **God often chooses those that seem to be unlikely leadership prospects because these persons long for Him and are teachable (1 Sam. 22:2; 1 Chr. 11:10ff)**

- **What people can become may not be what they are now; we must see their potential, and speak to them about it. (e.g. Peter the rock – John 1:42)**

In CPMs the leaders of the movement rise up out of the harvest (e.g. just like David's mighty men in the wilderness – 1 Sam. 22:2). My colleague Kevin Greeson says: "Men of peace do not descend from heaven but rise up from hell!" The future leaders of the movement were men with sin-filled lives yesterday. They are sinful with lives full of problems, but they are hungry for change. As you pray with them and spend time with them you will come to see the potential underneath their apparent sins and problems.

If you don't see their potential, and speak to them about it, who will? These men and women will often rise up to the vision you speak to them as you faithfully develop them along the way. It is risky. But hungry people will often push through the barriers to rise to the occasion. Jesus described them as "violent" or "forceful" men who let nothing stand in their way of acquiring the treasure in the field (Matt. 11:12; Luke 16:16; see Matt. 23:13 for the reason why they had to be violent).

> From the days of John the Baptist until now, the kingdom of heaven has been forcefully advancing, and forceful men lay hold of it. (Matt. 11:12, NIV)

T4T gives you many opportunities to help them develop and observe their faithfulness in a safe environment. You're there to catch them when they stumble and assist them at each step of the way. It's on-the-job training.

Post-Pentecost

As referenced in Chapter 4, Paul developed his leaders much more rapidly than Jesus did because he worked in a post-Pentecost situation whereas Jesus worked in a pre-Pentecost situation. Once the Spirit was given, even the Twelve developed much more rapidly and showed remarkable boldness (Acts 2). Paul trusted the role of the Spirit to mature his leaders *as he developed them along the way.*

In CPMs we operate from a post-Pentecost perspective. We use the developmental leadership principles of Jesus but benefit from the *presence of Jesus in the life of each believer through His Spirit. You* do not have to be constantly present for your trainers to *be with Jesus.* Instead, your role is to help them learn how to listen to and respond to Jesus.

Leadership development post-Pentecost, therefore, is even more rapid than when Jesus walked with His disciples on earth.

> "Truly, truly, I say to you, he who believes in Me, the works that I do, he will do also; and **greater works** than these he will do; because I go to the Father." (John 14:12, NASB, emphasis added)

Basic Qualifications: Crete vs. Ephesus

One of the most common objections to CPMs is that fairly new believers are developed as leaders of groups and churches. This seems to contradict what Paul says about the qualifications of overseers:

He must not be a recent convert, or he may become conceited and fall under the same judgment as the devil. (1 Tim. 3:6, NIV)

The list of leadership qualifications given in Titus 1 is the list to use in NEW CHURCH situations.

However, this is not the only list of qualifications for overseers that Paul gave. Remember, you must develop *biblical* expectations for leaders *appropriate to their stage of responsibility and development.* The prohibition about new converts above is very important – **for the right setting.**

Paul actually gives *two* lists of qualifications for church leaders (elders or overseers) in his epistles – Titus 1:5-9 and 1 Timothy 3:1-7. Both lists are important, but they are appropriate for completely different contexts.

In Titus, Paul and Titus had just completed a church-planting trip to the island of Crete.[37] The language of Titus 1 makes it clear that there are a number of new churches (weeks and months old) around the island in the various cities. Paul has left Titus behind in the apostolic role of completing the foundation for the movement in Crete (1:5). The final step is appointing leaders of these new churches. Remember that *all of the believers* are young in their faith at this point. Out of this group, Paul gives Titus clear guidelines for the type of men to pick. **Therefore, the list given in Titus 1 is the list to use in *NEW CHURCH* situations.**

Contrast this with the list in 1 Timothy 3. When Paul writes Timothy, he instructs him on what to look for in new leaders who felt God calling them to serve as overseers. The church and this CPM are mature, probably 10-15 years old! **Therefore, the list given in 1 Timothy 3 is the list to use for *MATURE CHURCH* situations.**

This explains the differences between the two lists.

---

[37] Acts does not speak about this. Most scholars believe this happened after Paul's first trial in Rome. He may have been released and then traveled for a while. During this time, he made the Crete tour. Later he was re-imprisoned in Rome. This is a strong possibility, though we cannot be certain of the timing.

Lessons from Crete and Ephesus

Overseer Qualifications	New Church Crete - Titus 1:5-9 "Appoint"	Mature Church Ephesus - 1 Tim. 3:1-7 "Aspire"
Character	Above reproach	Above reproach
	True to one wife	True to one wife
	Not wild living	Respectable
	Not rebellious	Not contentious
	Not self-willed	
	Not quick-tempered	Gentle
	Not addicted to wine	Not addicted to wine
	Not violent	Not violent
	Not greedy	Free from love of money
	Hospitable	Hospitable
	Love what is good	Good reputation with outsiders
	Sensible	Prudent
	Just	
	Devout/(devoted to God)	**NOT a new convert (so not become conceited)**
	Self-controlled	Temperate
Skill	**HOLD FAST** the Word in order to exhort	Able to **TEACH** the Word
	Children who believe	Manage household / Children under control
	(True to one wife?)	(True to one wife?)

Character First: The first obvious lesson from the two lists is the focus on *character* over *skills.* In looking for the basic qualifications for church leadership, character is paramount.

What a contrast to what we often look for: educational credentials, experience, ability to preach eloquently, etc. If we can get people with *growing character,* then we have good material from which to develop the appropriate skill sets.

The key differences
What is remarkable about these two lists are the four key differences. In new church situations, this is helpful. It enables

us to adjust our expectations for new leaders in new groups and movements.

Difference 1: "Appoint" versus "Aspire"

In the mature CPM in the province of Asia (Ephesus as the epicenter), a spiritual environment had developed not too different from the one you may have grown up in. Believers and churches were maturing. Leaders were prevalent. Many godly examples of leadership were evident to younger believers on a weekly basis. As these younger believers followed the Lord, He put on their hearts a desire to serve Him in greater ways – as church leaders or missionaries. They felt a "call" from God – just like you may have:

> It is a trustworthy statement: if any man **aspires** to the office of overseer, it is a fine work he desires to do. (1 Tim. 3:1, NASB, emphasis added)

Out of the many who aspired, Timothy had to discern if they were *qualified* to lead at this level yet.

In contrast, in the emerging movement on Crete, the new believers had very little concept of what a church leader looked like. They had no aspirations to lead. Therefore, until a spiritual climate of leadership aspiration was developed, it was Titus' responsibility to *appoint* or choose new leaders. He was going to have to look for qualified men to speak to them about their potential and help them ease into leadership.

> For this reason I left you in Crete, that you would set in order what remains and **appoint** elders in every city as I directed you. (Titus 1:5, NASB, emphasis added)

The word in the Greek for "appoint" here is very similar to the meaning of the word for "appoint" in Acts 14:23:

> When they had **appointed** elders for them in every church, having prayed with fasting, they commended them to the Lord in whom they had believed. (Acts 14:23, NASB, emphasis added)

Toward the end of their first journey, with churches that were weeks and months old, Paul and Barnabas did exactly what Paul was asking Titus to do: appointed new believers to lead the new churches. In the beginning of a CPM or a new church start, you must be very proactive in choosing and developing leaders. You do it as they begin to prove themselves to be leaders by their faithfulness and fruitfulness. You must take some risks and then "commend them to God's care." Some will not make it (e.g. Judas), but that is a risk you must take if leaders will develop. They will not aspire; you must appoint.

One principle that can help is to appoint **multiple leaders in each church.** That is the meaning behind the Greek in Acts 14:23: Paul and Barnabas appointed multiple elders in each church they started. Because your new leaders are still fairly young believers with not many skills, this helps them share the load and reduces the fear factor. It provides a safer environment in which to grow.

Difference 2: Not a New Convert

A second major difference between the two lists is that Paul removes the prohibition ("not a new convert") for the Cretan situation. Why? Because all he had were new converts, just like Acts 14:23! When all you have are new converts, you must develop some of them to lead the others.

When all you have are new converts, you must develop some of them to lead the others.

Paul removes the new convert leadership prohibition from the Titus list, but does add "devout" which is not in Timothy's list. In essence what he means is this: "Titus, even though you may have to appoint a new convert as leader, make sure he is devout – devoted to Jesus."

Why the prohibition against new converts in 1 Tim. 3:6? Paul says, "*he may become conceited and fall under the same judgment as the devil.*"

Paul essentially says: "In a mature church, don't you dare make a new convert a leader of a mature group. He'll become proud and then fall quickly!"

The corollary is this:

> **In a new church with all new believers, the prohibition for new converts is removed. You are free to develop new converts to lead – out of necessity.**

Difference 3: The "No Longers" of Titus 1

Look at the qualifications in Titus' list. Note how many of them begin with "not."

- Not wild living
- Not rebellious
- Not self-willed
- Not quick-tempered
- Not addicted to wine
- Not violent
- Not greedy

In the Greek, another way to translate "not" in a context like this is "no longer." Look at how the list changes:

- No longer living wild
- No longer rebelling
- No longer living for oneself
- No longer quick to get angry
- No longer addicted to alcohol
- No longer violent
- No longer living for money

The implication of the "nots" or "no longers" is that many of these people *used to be that way*. Look at what kind of starting material they came from:

Even one of their own prophets has said, "Cretans are always liars, evil brutes, lazy gluttons." This testimony is true. Therefore, rebuke them sharply, so that they will be sound in the faith. (Titus 1:12-13, NIV)

Titus wasn't starting from great material. He wasn't working with moral Jews or God-fearers who obeyed the Old Testament Law (Titus 3:3). He was dealing with recently carnal pagans turned children of God! So, the instruction Paul gave him was this: "Look for people who are getting their lives cleaned up from a trashy past: people who are no longer selfish hedonists, drunkards, fighters, rebels or materialists. Find people who are changing."

In Ephesus, on the contrary, the qualifications were stricter. Look at the contrasts. Timothy receives a "matured" version of Titus' list.

Crete (earlier)	Ephesus (later)
No longer living wild	Worthy of respect
Not quick-tempered or harsh	Gentle
Not greedy	Free from even the love of money

That's a lesson for us in choosing leaders in new churches: look for the "no longers." They are not perfect or mature yet, but they are growing in godly character. Therefore, they can prove to be examples to the flock (1 Peter 5:3). They are people that other new believers can emulate in life transformation.

Difference 4: "Hold Fast" the Word versus "Able to Teach" the Word

There is at least one very important skill that church leaders need: they need to be able to handle the Word of God well and guide their flock to understand and obey it. This is a non-negotiable. (The other skill is the ability to manage their household.)

THE POWER OF THANKSGIVING TO CHANGE A LIFE

By Ying Kai

When I was younger, I was the kind of person that always lost my temper. In my childhood I always stuttered. I could not even speak a whole sentence, so my attitude was very bad, and I always used my fists. One day my father said, "We know you always lose your temper and we can't stop you. But the next time you want to lose your temper, stop and pray for three minutes. After you pray for three minutes if you still want to lose your temper, okay, no problem."

I said, "Dad, if I was able to wait and pray for three minutes, then I think I would not lose my temper. But it's impossible." When I got offended, I could not wait even one second. I prayed for myself, and many other people prayed for me but there was no change.

Before I got married to Grace she knew that my temper was not very

Continued next page.

The difference in the two lists, however, is their ability in relation to the Word.

> **Holding fast the faithful word** which is in accordance with the teaching, so that he will be able both to exhort in sound doctrine and to refute those who contradict. (Titus 1:9, NASB, emphasis added)

> **Able to teach** .... (1 Tim. 3:2, NASB, emphasis added)

The only way leaders can faithfully lead their churches and keep them within doctrinal purity and moral uprightness is by helping them value the Scripture as their authority and obey whatever it says. Holding the word as authoritative and obeying whatever it says are the twin river banks to keep the movement flowing within doctrinal orthodoxy and moral purity.[38]

In a new church situation, a new convert is not yet able to teach the Word, at least not eloquently. However, in a mature church a basic skill is the ability to teach the meaning of God's word to the flock.

What **is** required in a new church? The new leader must **hold fast the Word** so that he can use it as the authority for encouraging and correcting the flock. He may not be able to teach well yet (a skill he will learn) but he

---

[38] See "Banks of a Movement" in the supplemental resources on the T4TOnline.org website for more.

must **value** the Word and go to it for answers. With the Scripture as his guide, he can exhort/encourage and refute people with sound doctrine. Sound doctrine means that he finds answers from the Word, not from others sources.

With leaders in new church situations, use the Titus qualifications: make sure they love the Word and rely on it as their authority for leading the flock.

Case Study on Developing Young Believers as Leaders

In our work there came a point at which the outside national partners were starting quite a few churches among the Ina people. In addition, the new Ina believers were beginning to start new churches themselves. The difficulty we had at this point was developing and appointing new Ina believers to lead the churches. They still wanted the mature national partners to lead them, and the mature national partners wanted to lead them also!

At a training meeting I had with my national partners, this issue came to a head. We began to troubleshoot why very few Ina leaders were emerging. We knew this could kill the emerging movement. It became apparent to me in the course of our discussion that my national partners had extra-biblical views on who could lead and how to develop them.

good. But she thought that maybe she would get lucky and I would not fight with her. But when we got married, we fought every day. I always lost my temper with her. After each time we would kneel down together to pray for my bad temper. But I was unable to change. It was very hard. After each explosion, I swore there would be no next time. When there was a next time I would hate myself. No matter how much remorse I felt, there was no change.

At that time we were studying in seminary. One day, when I came home, Grace was already there. This day she was very different. She was very happy! I said, "What happened?"

She said, "Today God talked to me and told me how to pray for you. I gave thanks to the Lord for your bad attitude. I praised the Lord."

I said, "What?! For good things you thank the Lord and praise Him. But for bad things?" Then the Lord gave me the verse Psalm 22:3:

Continued next page.

Yet You are holy, O You who are enthroned upon the praises of Israel.

God is enthroned on the praises of your heart. If you praise him, God will live in your heart! The Bible says give thanks for everything.

Always giving thanks to God the Father **for everything**, *in the name of our Lord Jesus Christ.* (Eph 5:20, NIV, emphasis added)

That means for good things **and** for bad things, **not only** for good things.

My wife said, "God created you and he loves you. You are my husband and even if you lose your temper every day I will thank God because I know God will love you. He'll change you. He'll help you. You cannot do anything by yourself. You've tried everything. But today you need to kneel down and pray with me. Give thanks to the Lord; praise the Lord for your bad attitude."

For me it was very strange. I did not really believe yet, but I prayed to God. "God, I know it's very strange but I'll try to give thanks to you because You created me.

Continued next page.

At this time, we probably had 30-40 new churches. I took them through the study of the leadership qualifications of 1 Timothy 3 and Titus 1. I stressed the importance of character over skills. In their minds, however, the character they were looking for was like what they saw in their leaders back home in the sending churches – mature, godly men (1 Timothy 3)! Of course the Ina believers couldn't measure up to those leaders from the sending churches who had walked with the Lord for many years.

When I realized this, I took the national partners through this dialogue:

"You need to appoint multiple Ina leaders in each church (Acts 14:23)."

"We don't have anyone qualified!" they responded.

"Hmm, okay. But do any of you have any liars in your churches?"

Many hands went up. "Oh, we have a lot! You wouldn't believe how much the Ina people lie."

"Okay," I responded. "Do any of you have any drunkards or gluttons in your churches?"

Again, many hands went up. "You wouldn't believe it. Ina men get drunk *every night!*"

"Okay," I responded. "Do any of you have lazy brutes in your churches who make their wives and kids do all the work?"

Now most of the hands went up. "These men are so lazy. They make their wives do all the work and won't lift one finger to help them!"

"Do you have men that are just plain mean?" Many hands raised again, and lots of murmuring.

"Great!" I responded. "You've got a great group of men from which to pick leaders."I could see the puzzlement on their faces. They figured I had finally gone mad. Together we read out loud the verses in Titus just after the elder qualifications:

> Even one of their own prophets has said, "Cretans are always liars, evil brutes, lazy gluttons." This testimony is true. Therefore, rebuke them sharply, so that they will be sound in the faith. (Titus 1:12-13 NIV, emphasis added)

I explained to them: "Paul told Titus to pick men who were growing in character. These men were all liars, mean people, lazy drunkards and gluttons. ***But they were changing***. On the outside, they didn't look too good yet, but things were changing. So let me ask you some questions: "Do any of you have men who *used to* get drunk every night, but no longer do?" A few hands went up.

My attitude was bad and I always lost my temper but I give thanks to you because I belong to you. I know in myself I cannot change or heal myself so I pray to you. Today let me know that I am nothing; only You can help me." I tried to just give thanks to the Lord and praise him. So I praised and sang and praised and sang. Every day I did this.

One day my wife told me to come and look at the calendar. Every day since we were married she had marked each day when I lost my temper. Some days it was three times, some days five times. Then she said, "How many days do you think it has been since you lost your temper and fought with me? Six months!"

I had prayed for 26 years and many other people prayed for me. I asked, asked, asked but now I only sang to the Lord and praised the Lord. God changed my mind; He changed my attitude. So when you praise the Lord he'll change everything. Grace said, "When you praise the Lord, that means you honor God and his power." If God does not

Continued next page.

give His permission then nothing can happen that does happen. Today whoever you meet, whatever happens, it's because God gave permission for it to happen.

So I learned this, and I now teach my trainers to give thanks for everything and praise the Lord.

"Do any of you have men who have stopped being mean all the time, but are starting to be nice to people?" More hands. "Do any of you have men that are finally getting up and helping their wives and kids with the chores?" Even more hands.

"Great! Choose those men to lead. They will be a good example to other men about how Jesus can start changing their lives."

As reluctant as they were, these partners caught on. They began to list the names of these men who were growing in godliness. I sent them out with the instructions to lay hands on these men and appoint them to their new responsibilities. They needed to pick at least two in each church.

When they returned for the next training, they had appointed multiple elders in each church. **We finally had a group of Ina leaders to invest in for the future. All because the church planters had adjusted their expectations and used the right qualifications for the right stage of the work.**

Your T4T Package:
T4T as a Leadership Development Process

Now that you have adjusted your expectations to the counter-intuitive ways of developing leaders in the King's reign, how can the T4T process help you choose and develop these leaders along the way? What needs to be in your basic T4T package?

There are three avenues for doing this based on the level of leadership responsibility they have. Leaders tend to be at one of three stages in responsibility.

- TRAINERS

- MID-LEVEL TRAINERS

- BIG TRAINERS

Each stage can be developed through a different aspect of the T4T process.

TRAINERS (Church leaders): **Avenue for development is the first third of each meeting over 9-18 months.**

In Chapter 10 you learned the importance of staying with a T4T group for at least 9-18 months to develop leadership during the pastoral care component of the first third of the meeting. If you give them adequate time to respond to "How are you doing?" you will be able to respond to leadership questions that arise as they train trainers who train trainers.

Keeping the three-thirds process all along the way enables you and other generations of trainers to develop leaders on the job – in the midst of leading.

Keeping the three-thirds process all along the way enables you and other generations of trainers to develop leaders on the job – in the midst of leading. Rather than choosing and preparing leaders before they lead, you are building a movement in which leaders prove themselves and find an opportunity to develop while they minister. **If this becomes an expectation at every new generation of T4T groups, there is no limit to the number of leaders that can be developed and multiplied.**

MID-LEVEL TRAINERS (leading multiple generations): **Avenue for leadership development is mid-level retreats.**

As generations develop, some of the leaders (represented by the grey circles) of the groups

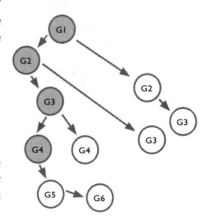

begin to oversee multiple generations of churches. As they prove themselves to be fruitful, bearing multiple generations, they emerge as mid-level trainers.

Because of the *increased responsibility, they need extra attention.* They need you and other leaders to come alongside them to encourage them and equip them.

The most effective way to do that in T4T is by pulling aside these mid-level trainers periodically for retreats to rest, be refreshed, be encouraged and be equipped for the next stage. They are the paths of the movement through which whole streams of new churches are starting. Give them special attention to help sustain them.

Depending on your context, a mid-level leaders retreat could take place for one day (e.g. one Saturday each month) or for an extended time (4-10 days) during a long weekend, a holiday period or down time (such as after harvest season).

When Ying first began to give reports on his emerging CPM, he mentioned "training centers" in these reports. For instance, the report for January in one area might be: "1503 new believers, 174 new churches, eight active training centers in which 85 people were trained." This last phrase mentioning training centers and people trained was puzzling. Ying was not referring to people receiving basic T4T training.

> Mid-level trainers generally become mid-level by producing fruit illustrated by multi-generational groups. Train them through mid-level retreats.

Instead Ying was saying this: "The movement is growing. We've had many new believers and churches start in which believers are receiving T4T training. In addition, we have eight places where we are doing mid-level training for leaders. 85 mid-level trainers were trained this month."

What Ying was doing was taking aside these mid-level trainers and their big trainer (the one who led that network of churches) for 4-10 days in a private setting where they stayed together. During this period of time, he did the basic three thirds with them in a new way.

In a six-day retreat, he might spend two days helping them look back, rest (sleep!), assess, get counseling, debrief, worship, pray, care for each other, etc.

The second two days he or someone else would just feed them from the Word. For example, he might teach them the book of Colossians – not for them to pass on but just to receive into their souls.

The last two days would be spent thinking about the future and making plans for the next period of time.[39]

As time went by, he and/or his big trainers would gather these mid-level trainers together as often as possible, but on average 3-4 times a year.

Every context is different. You may only have a weekend free with your mid-level trainers. But find a time when you can pull them aside to rest, hear fresh vision, receive personal counseling, be fed from the Word, pray and plan for the future. You cannot afford to neglect it.

> As the budding movement begins to exceed your personal control, how do you keep it in the banks of biblical orthodoxy and morality? Read the **"The Banks of a Movement"** in the supplemental resources to find out how.

Plan to organize your entire meeting with the same three-thirds principle:

- Look back: personal care, worship, vision, accountability, counseling, rest, personal devotions, prayer, etc.

- Look up: teaching from the Word to feed their souls. They are used to feeding others, so take time to feed them.

- Look forward: planning, praying together, making decisions, etc.

---

[39] In the supplemental resources "Leadership Development Resources" on the T4TOnline.org website is a guide for mid-level training conferences that Ying Kai wrote. It gives a very detailed description of how Ying conducts these retreats.

The ticking clock

When a movement begins, it takes off rapidly. As the clock starts ticking, you need to begin planning your first mid-level retreat long before you have mid-level trainers. Stay ahead of the CPM curve. Anticipate the needs. Don't let leadership overload kill the movement.

BIG TRAINERS (Those who lead a whole stream of a movement): **Avenue for leadership development is M.A.W.L.**

Every CPM develops a number of "streams" through which the growth is flowing. These are usually different segments of work that begin through different relationship networks and have expanded greatly. In general, one or two believers (who were probably persons of peace originally) spearhead the efforts of that whole stream of believers and churches. They not only oversee multiple generations of churches, but some of them have the gifts and vision to keep the movement going forward. We call these people Big Trainers.

These are the people that enable the initial CPM initiators (missionaries, original church planters, etc.) to disengage from active oversight of a CPM stream. They have the special gifting or quality like Timothy or Titus to lead a movement.

The way to train them is the way Jesus and Paul trained their big leaders: M.A.W.L. – Model, Assist, Watch and Leave. Essentially, what this means is that you take special interest in mentoring the big trainer in a way appropriate to each stage. You can MAWL people not just in the overall development of their ministry, but also in specific tasks. To learn more about the MAWL process, see the supplemental resources ("Leadership Development Resources") on the T4TOnline.org website.

Your goal with Big Trainers is to enable them to lead parts of the CPM without your constant attention including leading mid-level trainers retreats. You find them through much prayer and fasting.

For a discussion of other leadership issues in T4T, see the supplemental resources "Leadership Development Resources" on the T4TOnline.org website.

Summary

Leadership multiplication is the engine the Spirit uses to sustain a movement.

Developing leaders in CPMs is a process similar to the one Jesus used in choosing the Twelve. Leaders are developed in the midst of proving themselves in ministry.

In addition, we must use the appropriate set of leadership qualifications (from Titus 1) for choosing leaders in a new church setting.

Finally, your T4T process must include avenues for developing three types of leaders on the job: trainers, mid-level trainers and big trainers.

Does your T4T package have such leadership development plans in place?

You've now thought through both the process and package of T4T for your ministry from mobilizing believers to winning the lost to short and long-term discipling to forming churches to leadership development – generation by generation.

What is adaptable, and what's not? Read the next chapter to find out.

Be a Doer, not just a Hearer!

Write down how God has spoken to you and what you need to obey as a result:

CHAPTER 18

Your T4T Package:
What's Adaptable and What's Not

This book has primarily been about how to initiate CPMs through the discipleship *re*-revolution process of T4T.

The **principles** of the kingdom (initiating CPMs) are **timeless**.

The practical **methods** of implementing the principles are **adaptable**.

The first purpose in this book was to help you understand the *ways that God works in His kingdom* so that you would learn how to raise your sails to align with the wind of His Spirit.

The second purpose was to give you a practical tool or method that would help you implement these principles. T4T is one very proven and adaptable method (or process) for implementing the principles of a CPM. It helps you do your part in the human-divine partnership.

God is willing. Are you?

The Danger of Confusion

Don't confuse: CPM and T4T. CPM is a movement; T4T is a method. I believe that 50-100 years from now, the CPM principles discussed in this book will be valid for another generation. The prayer for that aspect of this book has been to share cross-generational truths as in Psalm 78:

> That the generation to come might know, even the children yet to be born, That they may arise and tell them to their children. (Ps. 78:6, NASB)

At the same time, there are parts of this book that will be outdated before it goes to print, for we are forever learning and adapting how to initiate CPMs, particularly in the area of T4T.

Because T4T is a method (or process), it *is* adaptable. There are two dangers in implementing a method like T4T:

- **Exalt the method as unchangeable.** There is "power" in the method; therefore you must implement it exactly as given. Don't change a thing.

- **Adapt the method in a way that violates the underlying principles.** The other extreme, however, is that you adapt the method according to your preferences, ignorant of the underlying kingdom principles. As you adapt, you make it more "logical" and actually begin violating the underlying counter-intuitive kingdom principles.

If you do not understand the ways of the kingdom, you certainly will not welcome it when it arrives, and may even find yourself opposing it! If you do not understand CPMs, you will be tempted to follow one of these two courses:

- **Exalting the method:** you slavishly implement T4T exactly as Ying Kai did it for his context and cannot figure out why you do not get the same results.[40]

- **Violating the principles:** you endlessly adapt, tweak and modify everything about T4T. In the end you have a process that is more about teaching your particular set of lessons than developing trainers and a movement. You think you adapted it faithfully and cannot figure out why you do not get the same results as Ying.

T4T is not a law. It is a method. Therefore, you *must* make some adaptations unless your situation is virtually identical

---

[40] As I mentioned earlier, I don't know of anyone getting the same results as broadly and as quickly as Ying. Part of the reason is Ying's context and the great numbers of people and groups he, his wife and leaders tirelessly train. However, many T4T implementers are seeing rapid multi-generational growth.

to Ying's. Chapters 11-17 of this book describe many adaptations and applications.

So, what is adaptable and what is not? What needs to be in any basic T4T package? Let's draw all of this together now.

Here are some recommendations:

Evaluate the context of your ministry (worldview, literacy rate, exposure to the gospel, etc.).

- That way you will know how to adapt the various pieces of your T4T package.

- This doesn't have to take years! Get on with the next step.

Plug and play appropriate reproducible components into the T4T package.

- Make sure that each part of your T4T package flows naturally into the next stage of building a movement.

Personalize your T4T package for your context, then call it what you want.

Never, ever violate the three-thirds process – the heart of training a trainer – unless you find a more effective way to train trainers who train trainers to train trainers.

Implement it! Then make adjustments as you see what reproduces and what does not. Start mobilizing believers to train (or winning the lost and then training them) even though you don't have all of your lesson plans adapted yet.

If you're not getting new generations of believers and churches, critically examine everything you do, get wise counsel and then make adjustments.

If you're not getting new generations of believers and churches, critically examine everything you do, get wise counsel and then make adjustments.

What's Adaptable

Remember that your T4T package must enable believers at each generation to know how to move to the next stage of a CPM when they say "yes" at the previous one. In the list below, the first stage is in parentheses because it applies to you, but **not** to successive generations of new believers.

1. **(Mobilizing the saved** that God will use to start a movement through casting vision)

2. **Finding the lost** in whom God is at work, in ways any new believer can emulate

3. **Evangelism** that any new believer can do

4. **Discipleship** that any new believer can emulate

5. **Church starting** that any new believer can reproduce

6. **Leadership development** that any new believer can experience and pass on

Each of these stages (after the first) should naturally lead to the following stage. And then the whole process should reproduce itself generation by generation until at least four generations of believers and churches have occurred. Remember that the whole process is not completely sequential. Most of these things are happening simultaneously:

If you are going to use components someone else wrote, or will use some you and your team write, make sure they fulfill these three criteria:
1) Biblical,
2) effective for your context and
3) reproducible for your context.

For example, while you are doing your short-term discipleship, churches are starting at about Session Four. Before you finish your short-term discipleship, you have probably raised up your first leaders. Before you finish your short-term discipleship, many of the first generation are repeating the process by finding new lost people, evangelizing and discipling them.

Yet, you still need a clear process of how to initiate each new part of the plan. You must know what to do when someone says "yes" at each stage. Your T4T package should include components that do this. Every T4T package should include the following components. If you are going to use components someone else wrote, or some you and your team will write, make sure they fulfill these three criteria: 1) biblical, 2) effective for your context and 3) reproducible for your context. Complete T4T curriculum packages can be found on the T4T website.

Critical Components

The outline below summarizes what you've learned in the previous seven chapters. Each of the bullet points below marks a critical component that you will need to include in your T4T package.

- Mobilizing the Saved: a way to **cast vision to the saved** for T4T training (3-Minute Vision Casting PLUS Session One) [see Chapter 11]

- **Session One** should include [see Chapter 5]:

  » WHY: vision-casting piece [see Chapter 11]

  » WHOM: a way to build an *oikos* Name List

  » HOW: a loving evangelism method which includes a **bridge** [see Chapter 12], a **gospel presentation** [see Chapter 13] with a call to commitment. These must equip new believers to share with five people weekly.

- **6-10 Short-Term Discipleship Lessons** that give the basic things a believer needs to start growing in Christ. [Chapter 14] Some lessons that should not be left out are:

  » Baptism [see Chapter 15]

  » Lord's Supper

  » **1-2 lessons on becoming a church** with a clear plan to help them covenant to become (or join) a church [Chapter 16]

> » Perseverance in persecution [see Chapter 20]

> » Great Commission Vision

Vision-casting vignettes for the first 1/3 of each training meeting, especially the first few weeks. [see Chapter 11, plus supplemental resources on vision-casting vignettes]

Included should be **Accountability Questions** that progressively move the groups to fourth generation believers and churches and beyond. [see Chapter 7]

- **Launch Long-Term Discipleship: Lesson introducing inductive Bible study** and a plan for what to study first. (Goal is to help them become self-feeders.) [see Chapter 14]

  A **recommended study plan** such as the Gospel of Mark, 40 chronological Bible stories, etc.

- A plan to develop **church leaders** (trainers) in the first third of each training session: Most people who start a group will become leaders by default but you may have to be fairly directive at first. [see Chapter 17]

  > » **Mid-level leadership retreats** or training days [see Chapter 17]

  > » A plan to **MAWL (Model, Assist, Watch and Leave) big trainers** [see Chapter 17]

- **Progress-tracking system:** Accountability should be in place for G4 growth (right accountability questions) and records kept to make sure that new generations are starting. You need a system for tracking to make sure this happens. You need a system for good reporting so that you can evaluate progress.

What NOT to Adapt

As you adapt things like gospel presentations and discipleship lesson, remember that they must be **1) biblical, 2) effective for your context and 3) reproducible for new believers.**

There are a number of processes that you should not adapt, or do so only with great wisdom:

- The three parts of the training process including the bold parts that get you to reproduction.

    » Although it is possible to make changes to the order of the seven components, do not leave out the BOLD parts if you want reproduction: Accountability, Vision Casting, Practice, Setting Goals with Prayer.

- Make sure you have a clear gospel presentation that is shared often with a call to commitment. No CPMs start without a lot of gospel witnessing person to person or mouth to ear.

- Do not fail to have 1-2 clear lessons on church that launch the group to the stage of becoming a church. (See possible adaptations for churched contexts in the next chapter.)

- Make sure that you have vision-casting vignettes that are easy to pass on

- Make sure your accountability questions progressively move people toward four generations.

    » WITNESS: Who are you witnessing to? Who has believed?

    » STARTER: When are you training them in the same process?

    » TRAINER: How are these new believers doing witnessing to and winning others?

    » TRAINER OF TRAINERS: When are they training their groups?

    » TRAINER OF TRAINERS WHO TRAINS TRAINERS: How are the trainers, that you are training, doing training in their new groups?

- Keep the movement obedience-based, centered around the two great commands and Great Commission (or Mark 1:17 Followers & Fishers).

  » A loving environment is critical – love for God and love for one another. Life-on-life loving relationships are paramount in training trainers. Love will keep the movement from becoming sterile and works focused. Therefore, accountability must be in place not only for evangelism/training, but for personal godliness that demonstrates a heart for God.

    > "**I know your deeds and your toil and perseverance**, and that you cannot tolerate evil men, and you put to the test those who call themselves apostles, and they are not, and you found them to be false; and you have perseverance and have endured for My name's sake, and have not grown weary. **But I have this against you, that you have left your first love**." (Rev. 2:2-4, NASB, emphasis added; Jesus speaking to the church at the center of the greatest New Testament CPM.)

- Challenge trainers to start more than one group as the weeks progress. The power of at least two groups per trainer will help generate movements.

- Make sure trainers at each stage know how to progress from one component to the next seamlessly. They must know what to do when people say "yes" at each stage.

  » Realize that the evangelism phase will often be more than one witnessing encounter. Always have a simple gospel overview that you can share in one sitting to lead people to faith. Consider having an **expanded gospel track** (several weeks) for the evangelism phase when people are interested, but need more time. (e.g. Creation to Christ expanded)

If you adapt the appropriate components and retain the CPM processes (non-adaptable portions), you should be on track with an effective CPM plan.

CPM and T4T. One is a movement of God. The other is a process or method for positioning ourselves to live out the principles of this movement. Keep the eternal principles of the kingdom. Don't lose them or adapt them. At the same time, take, adapt and apply the methods of T4T to help you live the principles of CPM. Adapt them, but don't lose the essence. Only then will the discipleship *re*-revolution start.

> *CPM and T4T. One is a movement of God. The other is a process or method for positioning ourselves to live out the principles of this movement. Keep the eternal principles of the kingdom. Don't lose them or adapt them.*

Can CPMs emerge in a churched or post-churched culture such as North America, Australia, New Zealand, Europe or Latin America? Read the next chapter to find out.

Be a Doer, not just a Hearer!

Write down how God has spoken to you and what you need to obey as a result:

CHAPTER 19

T4T for the Churched or Post-Churched

Can T4T work in a churched or post-churched culture such as the United States, Europe or Latin America?

The answer is: Yes.

CPMs can emerge in any context. You have to adapt the application of CPM principles to your own community's worldview and culture. When you do so effectively a *model* will emerge that others can see. After that happens it will make common sense to many. But until an effective model emerges, skepticism will reign.

In any context, an understanding of CPM principles of the kingdom is necessary. Then begins a period of experimentation, and trial and error until successful adaptations emerge. At this point, a culturally appropriate model emerges.

I believe that CPMs have developed first in Asia, then Africa, because of a desperation to take risks and try new ways of doing things due to the sheer mass of lostness faced by missionaries and national leaders there. *The inability to use traditional church planting models in many limited-access nations has driven us to find ways to equip new believers to reproduce quickly in small churches that can spread endlessly without outside leadership or financial support.*

The serendipity in this is the recovery of some principles and methods of the original discipleship revolution that can be used in any context. *We* were forced there by necessity. But many others in open or churched nations can reap the benefit of the principles and methods.

Yet, for CPMs to emerge in any churched setting, believers must shed hindrances that traditions can bring, be willing to receive some ridicule in the beginning and persevere in faith to see generations of lost people reached.

Some feel that in churched cultures, where persecution is almost non-existent, a CPM cannot emerge. On the contrary, the moment a CPM emerges, all sorts of persecution will arise because of the radical nature of the movement. One church-planting network in the USA is moving more and more in the CPM direction. Even prior to this, they have been branded as "cult-like" or a "sect" by some because of their radical desire to love Jesus by 1) following Jesus and 2) fishing for men.

> Remember: **What's radical today will be commonplace tomorrow.** There was a time when CPMs were unusual in Asia and Africa. Now it seems like everyone is talking about them.
>
> There is a day coming (already emerging) when good CPM models will be evident in churched and post-churched cultures.

Others say things like this: "When we first went to a house church in our churched culture, we thought something was missing. It just didn't *feel* like church. Now after planting house churches overseas in which we experienced such great community and spiritual stimulation, we laugh at our first impressions back home. We would never go back to our previous way."

Remember: **What's radical today will be commonplace tomorrow.**[41] There was a time when CPMs were unusual in Asia and Africa. Now it seems like everyone is talking about them.

There is a day coming (already emerging) when good CPM models will be evident in churched and post-churched cultures. In the current cry for authenticity by a new generation, CPM churches may fill a critical need. Here are some lessons, in no particular order, from those who are pursuing CPMs in churched cultures.

---

[41] Anonymous saying. Variant used at least as early as 1969 by attorney Preston A. Trimble in article, "Well, Here It Is Tomorrow Already" in American Bar Association Journal. August 1969.

Key Adaptations

- **Multiply celebrations.** Many people just expect to be a part of a larger worship time with good preaching. Don't fight it but use it (plus, preaching has an important role in the right contexts). Continue to have large celebrations periodically (weekly or monthly). Use a church facility if you have one. But knowing that all churches (celebrations) have a natural size limit, launch new celebration gatherings of home groups in other parts of your city or area.

- **Let small groups function as house churches — whatever you call them.** Allow your home group meetings to take on church-like qualities: baptism, Lord's Supper, offerings, etc. – even if you don't call them churches. They can continue being connected to the larger church, or some may launch into whole new churches or church networks depending on the need. Your goal is to empower them to start movements with your blessing and support. Give them autonomy within the larger vision. (See the case study at the end of this chapter for an example of avoiding the term "church" in the beginning.)

- **Launch rather than multiply.** Make a subtle shift in how you do small groups. Rather than inviting new believers to the main group and eventually multiplying, encourage small group members to launch new groups with their *oikos* as people come to faith.

- **For launches, shorten or eliminate the leadership-training phase needed to lead a small group.** Your T4T group process *is* their training. Take a risk. When people lead others to faith, encourage them to launch a new group while they continue to come to your group for T4T training. Many churches use a leadership-training phase where a potential leader is mentored first, then becomes a co-leader and eventually leads his own group. Eliminate this lengthy "safe" approach for new launches. Continue the leadership-training phase, but just realize it will happen on-the-job *while the person comes to your T4T group AND leads his own group.*

- **Focus on the lost, especially persons of peace, NOT transfer or reclamation growth.** Every CPM in the world does one thing well: evangelizes a lot of lost people. In many churched cultures, the majority of church growth is 1) transfer growth – church members joining another church – or 2) reclamation growth (reclamation of people that are unchurched, but used to go to church even as children).

  » **Develop a culture of going to where the lost are.** Find persons of peace; don't make them find you. This requires a new atmosphere of boldness to share the gospel and a new atmosphere of love to go to where the lost are. The emerging movements in churched cultures are reaching addicts, prostitutes, homeless, atheists, intellectuals, party-ers, secular businessmen, etc. Churches are springing up at times and places normally unheard of.

  » **Help people re-define who is lost in their *oikos*.** See the case study at the end of this chapter for an example of identifying "lost" people as people "far from God."

- **Go off-site for evangelism, training and church.** One CPM initiator who is seeing promising CPM results in the Bible belt in America mentioned that his most fruitful T4T training happens in diners, coffee shops and homes, not in the church facility. By training a group of businessmen in a diner, they can easily visualize doing the same thing with lost friends. The same is true of a home. But when training happens in the church facility, the sterility and artificial nature of the facility create barriers in the minds of trainees: "What will this look like in a different setting?" If you want groups and churches to meet in homes, train in homes. If you want groups and churches to meet in diners, train in diners.

» In the same way, evangelism has to happen in bars, restaurants, diners, coffee shops, businesses, parks and homes at the times people are available – *wherever* people discuss life issues in meaningful ways. In addition, much evangelism fails because we are not available *when* lost people are available which is usually in the evenings and weekends.

- **Consider longer evangelism tracks that can easily morph into small groups.** If people in your area are leery of gospel confrontations (which are often not very loving), empower your church members to launch new groups with lost people – discovery groups or discovery studies. These can meet for 6-10 weeks (or more) to use inductive methods that help the lost people uncover the truths of the Scripture. Using the three-thirds meeting process allows them to begin passing on the Bible stories or passages to other lost friends. At least by the final session, a call is issued for people to come to faith. The group then morphs into a house church or home group that lives out the three-thirds process.

- **Provide an umbrella.** Because ridicule is very likely in the beginning of a movement in your area, give the new groups or house churches an *umbrella of covering.* This helps explain to other more traditional churches what is happening and helps them accept it (not publicly criticize it). Even though you may be planting numerous house churches, you can call them by another name and include them as a part of your overall church structure. In this manner, they receive a covering as they implement ordinances and reach into new areas. Members are able to say, "We are part of 'XYZ network' of churches." This kind of covering helps build identity and confidence in the new believers even though they are not a part of a "traditional" church.

- **Don't talk about it too much in the beginning – give it a chance to grow.** In areas where there is a high likelihood of persecution, ridicule or others wanting to come in to influence the budding movement (even steal sheep), it's helpful not to advertise what is happening too much. Give the budding movement a chance to grow. There will come a time that you can share more publicly about it, and it won't detrimentally affect it.

- **Do a Daniel Project.** Don't dismantle the current program and services of your church to launch a CPM model if it will tear the church apart. Instead, start a Daniel Project [see Chapter 11] with a few people who are hungry for something different. Choose people who are not leaders nor have huge time obligations to the church. Start the project with newer believers and use a much purer T4T approach.

- **Divest yourself of low value activities. Instead, cast vision, witness and train.** One reason more CPMs do not yet emerge in churched cultures is because church and ministry leaders are already so heavily committed to other tasks. If you want to initiate a CPM, find ways to divest yourself of low-value activities (activities that do not contribute much to CPM) and invest in the high value activities. Give yourself time to witness to the lost, cast vision to the saved and train everyone who is willing to listen. CPMs only develop with **significant time given to high value activities.** One person asked if it was possible for him to help launch a CPM when only giving 5-10 hours a week to CPM activities as a full-time minister. The answer is "no." Whoever is overseeing the start of a CPM must give more attention to it at least until there are other leaders who are giving major time to guiding the movement.

- **Train everyone.** Re-think your current church meetings. You probably already have significant numbers of believers in worship services, Bible studies, Sunday School and home groups. Start an initiative to turn many of these meetings into training-focused sessions. Consider kicking this off with a weekend or week-long retreat going through principles from the Scriptures and helps from this book. You may even want to have your members read this book together. Keep the same meetings going; don't necessarily stop them. But be purposeful in training everyone to win and train others.

- **Adapt home groups to the three-thirds process by adding in the BOLD parts.** One church network made a simple change to their home groups: they re-tooled the meeting format to the three thirds emphasizing the seven components, especially the **bold** parts that they had been neglecting. This was not traumatic for them. It was not a radical change – they were already meeting in home groups and doing some of the seven components. Rather it was a step forward for them. They initiated it by re-training all their home group leaders, explaining how this was a progression for them toward the vision of reaching all people in their city.

- **Turn church facilities into training centers.** We are not advocating selling off your properties and dispersing your church members (unless the Lord tells you to do so, of course!). Many pastors are already heavily vested in the current system and would not begin down the CPM path if it meant this. However, you (ministry leader or pastor) can easily make the shift to CPM by shifting your horizon from pastoring people to pastoring pastors. You can shift your horizon from your church facility being a church meeting place to becoming a training center at the epicenter of a movement! Begin to view your congregational members as future leaders and pastors through whom a movement will be launched. Most will not become trainers of trainers, but some will [see Chapter 6]. Eventually your church facility will become a training base to reach the world.

- **Willingness to go bi-vocational for the sake of a movement.** I made a move personally that I think transformed the beginnings of our church in Los Angeles from a potential movement to just one church – just the opposite direction we are advocating! Before our church "started" our small church planting team was growing as we reached out to university students and folks in our neighborhood. We sat around the living room playing guitars, worshipping, praying, challenging each other from the Word, etc. When we "started the church" we pushed aside the couches and arranged chairs in rows even though we still met in the same house! The group had a very natural family feeling prior to that point. But the picture of church in our minds was something more organized and structured – even though we were seen as pretty innovative at the time. In my mind, though I was bi-vocational, I dreamed of becoming the full-time pastor one day. How much better if we had just started new groups meeting in other homes, coffee shops and parks rather than increasing space in our living room, then moving to a school building and finally into our own dedicated facility! We had the potential to launch a movement, but we moved into our perception of what church should be. I think that if I were to do it over again, I would plan to be bi-vocational as long as possible and try to shepherd a movement of Jesus-loving followers who meet wherever they can find space, and then probably get everyone together every few weeks to continue casting vision, sharing worship and giving more directional teaching. A willingness to sacrifice full-time support for the sake of a movement may be the most strategic move you can make. Many early movements in England and the USA were started and shepherded by bi-vocational leaders.

- **Start from scratch.** Start with no investment in the current church system (i.e. responsibilities). Start something from scratch (bi-vocationally probably) by going where lost people are and winning them. In addition, you may find some believers who have become unchurched and are willing to encounter Jesus through an alternative approach. They, too, may be willing to walk this path with you. This is easiest in less-churched areas of churched countries, such as the Pacific Northwest in the U.S. From there, it may be easier to build a model that works well in more churched areas. However, in two instances in the USA, movements are starting in the heart of churched culture – Texas and North Carolina.

- **Cast a vision.** Eventually, when a CPM begins to emerge in a churched culture, believers in your network will soon bump up against more traditional Christians who may voice opinions that inject non-CPM DNA into the movement. As hard as you try, there is no way to keep your believers isolated from them. This happens all over the world. CPM believers bump into traditional believers and a whole variety of sparks fly. How can you preserve the DNA of the movement knowing that they will bump into other believers? One way is to **cast a vision for why you are doing what you are doing.** This vision casting should be encouraging and rallying in nature, never caustic or belittling. Rather, develop a simple vision-casting vignette that says something like this:

> *"In this world, there are all types of believers and churches. Jesus' Bride is marvelous! You will meet many other believers out there, and many of them may live differently or live as church differently than we do. That's normal. They have reasons for why they live that way. It's not necessarily better or worse -- just different. We are different because of our vision. Our vision is to see our city reached, and we think it will happen fastest if we structure ourselves this way and emphasize these things [fill in the ideas]. So, when you meet other believers, enjoy your fellowship. Encourage them and let them encourage you. But inside remember why we live the way we do – that God's kingdom may come fully to our city (or area)."*

CASE STUDY: T4T in the USA

Over a 12-month span of time leading up to the writing of this book, a T4T movement has been emerging in North Carolina (USA) in a very churched area. It has gone from zero to 30+ groups in one year and continues to expand in reaching lost people. The initiator was a successful CPM practitioner in South Asia who took the same T4T principles he had used in Asia and adapted them for a move back to the USA. This is a summary of T4T adaptations from his perspective:[42]

Transitioning from practicing T4T in Asia to a churched culture, we had to grapple with pre-existing forms of church. **Our FIRST adjustment: We moved away from terms like "house church," "simple church" and "organic church," and we ended up calling the T4T process the Discipleship Cycle.** This described the T4T process well but wasn't loaded with meaning. It actually left the T4T process as an unknown, which allowed us to focus on **moving forward** instead of deconstructing current understandings of church.

Every week we would meet using the three-thirds structure for our meetings with the content being that every believer needs to know with whom to share in the community, how to share his testimony and the gospel, and if the person with whom he shared believed, how he would disciple him. In the beginning, we prayed weekly for our lost friends in our *oikos* and consistently held everyone accountable to share their testimonies, but, for the most part, no one was doing this. The reason was that many of the long-time Christians in the group did not know any lost people.

That led to a SECOND adjustment: redefining "lostness" to give everyone a clear idea of where to start. We had a two-fold answer for this question:

1. We quit using the term "lost" and began to ask people if they knew 10 people **"far from God."** The reasoning behind this phrase was that people could think of individuals who had grown up in church but now lived a worldly lifestyle, no longer attending church. At this point our trainees could write down many names because of the change of terminology. This was a huge breakthrough for all of the groups.

---

[42] Thanks to my colleague Jeff Sundell who is adapting T4T in North Carolina.

2. **We asked them to identify one person out of 10 on their lists whose life God was stirring up somehow (accepted Christ recently, life in turmoil, special needs, etc.).** We then told them to share their testimonies with that person and members of his household. God was obviously working in this whole "house of peace." To help these new houses of peace become indigenous when they believed, a local pastor encouraged us to start baptizing family members in their own context -- in one instance, in a horse trough in a trailer park on a snowy day.

The THIRD adjustment we made with our T4T groups and churches was to begin finding ways to get into the homes of people who were far from God to lead evangelistic Bible studies. We stopped inviting people to church and started inviting them to Jesus. This became a new mantra for us because, as our folks shared their stories, their default was still to invite people to church and not to invite them to Jesus. Now when people came to faith, this made discipleship *our* responsibility. We do not discourage people from going to church, but we do encourage our trainers to keep discipling these people in a small T4T group regardless of what type of church they become a part of.

Reap the Promise of Scribes in the Kingdom

Remember the parable of the scribe who comes into the kingdom (Chapter 4):

> And Jesus said to them, "Therefore every scribe who has become a disciple of the kingdom of heaven is like a head of a household, who brings out of his treasure things new and old." (Matt. 13:52, NASB)

In Chapter 4, the application we made was:

> T4T helps us not only start from scratch in winning new believers, but gives a practical process to mobilize existing believers with lots of Bible knowledge to live out the counter-intuitive ways of the kingdom. When they do, they can be

great force multipliers. Mobilizing and training existing Christians is also a high value in CPMs all over the world.

Churched and post-churched cultures are filled with "scribes" who are full of Bible knowledge. When people like this come to understand the true nature of the King and the kingdom, they have a huge storehouse of Scripture they bring a new lens to. Out of this storehouse they are able to mature rapidly and offer great resources.

> *Churched cultures are filled with "scribes" who are full of Bible knowledge.*
>
> *When people like this come to understand the true nature of the King and the kingdom, they offer great potential for church-planting movements!*

Of all the places in the world ripest for great church-planting movements, churched cultures should be at the top! May you reap the promises of many scribes coming into and accelerating the kingdom where you live!

The question remains, whether you are in a churched or unchurched setting, what will it cost you for a CPM to develop? Are you willing to pay the price? Read the next chapter to learn more.

Be a Doer, not just a Hearer!

Write down how God has spoken to you and what you need to obey as a result:

CHAPTER 20

Death — Persevering to See a CPM

There is a spiritual trigger required for every CPM: death. All of the previously mentioned plans, methods and expectations can be ready to launch, but until the trigger is pulled, nothing really occurs. This is the trigger: to be willing to persevere through much to see a CPM. You must be willing to suffer and even die to boldly make Christ known.

The Spiritual Trigger: Death

Truly, truly, I say to you, unless a grain of wheat falls into the earth and dies, it remains alone; but if it dies, it bears much fruit. (John 12:24, NASB)

The final kingdom principle of this book is this: **the only way to fruitfulness is through giving up our lives – death.** It was the way Jesus had to walk – the way of the cross for atonement. It is the way we must walk – the way of the cross – to fulfill the proclamation of that atonement. Death (whether physical death or a life of sacrifice) is the spiritual trigger that God seems to use to birth the life of a movement. The bold, sacrificial believer lays down his life of self-focus and personal dreams, and from the ground emerges the sprouts of a revolutionary discipleship movement. You must persevere to see a movement.

Consider these statements by Paul:

Now I rejoice in my sufferings for your sake, and in my flesh I do my share on behalf of His body, which is the church, in filling up what is lacking in Christ's afflictions. (Col. 1:24, NASB)

So death works in us, but life in you. (2 Cor. 4:12, NASB)

Christ did His part to purchase our redemption. We must do our part to proclaim it to the world.

What is lacking in Christ's afflictions? Nothing for atonement. Much yet, however, for the fulfillment of the Great Commission. Christ did His part to purchase our redemption. We must do our part to proclaim it to the world. Christ did not shrink back. Do we? We have received eternal life; what do we have to lose?

Paul essentially said this to his churches:

> I knew ahead of time it would be tough to proclaim the gospel to you, but how could I do otherwise? Christ compelled me. You were lost, so we came with news of salvation. The moment we opened our mouths verbal abuse was hurled at us, and eventually rocks were hurled at us. We were hunted down and imprisoned. We were beaten, but the Word of God was not imprisoned. Because we counted the cost and joyfully opened our mouths, you received eternal life! So, death was at work in our mortal bodies, but life in your spiritual bodies!

Until someone is willing to boldly risk living out and launching the disciple-making commands of the King, regardless of the personal cost, movements lay dormant. There are no exceptions. Every CPM has come at great personal cost to the CPM initiators – both outsiders and insiders. Every CPM resulted when a person of peace gladly received Jesus and decided to be the first in his community to make Jesus known, even though it would be very unpopular – even life-threatening.

The way of the cross is the triggering effect of movements. Persecution will come to every movement. It's not a matter of IF but HOW LONG before it starts.

Who Suffers in Movements?

Suffering for proclaiming the gospel and living the life of the discipleship revolution is not limited to a few. It affects many.

The CPM initiators suffer

Begin to boldly strive to birth a movement and see what happens. We often ask CPM initiators: "Do you *really* want to initiate a CPM – if it means suffering, even death?" Push aside the grandeur of dreams for a moment. One underground church leader was helping me prepare national church planters in a very restricted-access nation. I had painted the vision and the method. She got up and said: "Brother Steve has given you a heavenly vision. Let me show you the earthly reality!" She then began to talk about the difficulties they would face the moment they walked into the new towns and villages they were heading to.

Don't lose the vision; just push it aside for a moment. Open your eyes. If this goes as you pray, you will bear the brand-marks in your body.

> From now on let no one cause trouble for me, for I bear on my body the brand-marks of Jesus. (Gal. 6:17, NASB)

However, they are worth it! A great number of CPM initiators at the center of CPMs are suffering because of their work. Ying has come close to death before. My family and I bear the brand-marks in our bodies. Undeniably, He is worth it!

Their families suffer

This feels like hitting below the belt. Often the enemy attacks those you love rather than attacking you directly. If he can stop you by attacking your family, he will do it. Countless family members of CPM initiators bear in their bodies and minds the brand-marks of Jesus.

I remember when my three sons were being singled out in the national school they attended and bullied and mistreated. I remember thinking: "Okay, Satan, come after me, but not after my boys! That's not fair fighting." But he doesn't fight fair. My wife and I had to come to a point of resolving that even if our boys suffered for the sake of us proclaiming the gospel, it was worth it. Not easy, but worth it. We shed many a tear – I still do when I remember those days. But our sons would not trade

BOLDNESS TO SHARE WITH A DIFFICULT FATHER

By Ying Kai

Years ago, I heard a testimony from a bright, well-educated Chinese-American young man in our church in Texas.

He said, "Last week, pastor, you told us, 'Don't waste time. Think of your family and any person who doesn't believe in Jesus. Send them a letter, or a story, or your testimony to them.'" So he went home and first thought of his father, who was not a believer. He said, "I have already believed in Jesus for over 11 years. But I have never shared with my father because I am nervous." Previously, his father was a powerful general in Taiwan. For the last ten years he had lived in Washington, D.C. For 11 years, this young man had still not shared with his father. He said, "I prayed for my father every day, and asked, 'God, send some people to save my father, but not me, because

Continued next page.

a day of the lives they lived overseas. They would tell you in a heartbeat: "It was worth it!"

Yes, it's worth it.

New believers suffer

This is perhaps the most difficult one. In many areas of the world, if missionaries are caught sharing the gospel, they get kicked out of the country. Not so for new believers. They have to stay and bear the consequences. This one fact alone causes many a missionary to shrink back from being bold or encouraging new believers to be bold.

In non-mission contexts, the effect is still the same. When we see new believers suffer because of a plan we helped initiate, we feel guilty and are tempted to pull back. We fear they are not mature enough to endure such difficulty.

In the months leading up to the publishing of this book, the national leaders of the Kais' work have suffered major persecution – one even tortured to death. Yet they would tell you it is worth it.

At the time that reports of great breakthroughs were beginning among the Ina people, another set of reports also trickled in – reports about our national partners:

- Brother Zaccheus and his partner where in jail being tortured.

- Brothers J & Y were on the run after being chased by an angry mob.

- Red Canyon Team was dispersed and several of them were in jail.

- Green Valley Team was missing – no word for days.

As the reports came in, it felt like a weight progressively pushing down my shoulders and countenance. Each day, as reports continued to trickle in, I neared my breaking point. My teammates feared bringing any more bad news to me – fearful that I might lose it.

One morning in my quiet time, I was expressing my deep burden to the Lord, asking why my men needed to suffer so. In that moment, I felt Him clearly say to me: "Steve, these are *MY MEN*, not *YOURS*. I will take care of them." In that moment, all the weight of worry was lifted from my shoulders, and I was free from the snare the enemy had set for me. As it happened, shortly thereafter, my colleagues came in to bring me the worst news to-date. They were so nervous to tell me. I told them: "Just give it to me." They did, and it just rolled off my shoulders – to their great surprise.

In all, 75% of our 33 national partners were arrested, beaten and expelled from their regions. One came close to death. After 2-3 months in the

I cannot talk to my father. He will get very mad at me.'

But pastor, last week you gave us the message. So I went home, I prayed for my father. Then I began to write out my testimony. It was three pages. On Monday morning, I put it in the mailbox and I prayed over the letter. I said, 'Holy Spirit, bring the letter to my father's hand.' Wednesday night, my father called me from Washington D.C. His first sentence was 'Are you a Christian?' I said, 'Yes.' 'How long?' he asked. I told him, 'II years.' 'Why didn't you tell me?' he asked. I said, 'Because I was afraid that you would be mad at me.' He said, 'That means you would go to heaven and your father would go to hell?!'"

That day, on the phone, he shared the gospel with his father. That night, he led his father to trust Christ. He said, "I prayed for my father for II years, but the responsibility was in my hands. God was waiting for me to share the Gospel with my father."

So, that's the Heavenly Father's heart. He works through you. When you

Continued next page.

> train, encourage every trainer, "All the names in your Name List, God will work through you to save them." So, if they know God's heart, they are confident. They won't have any worries, and they won't be nervous, because they'll have faith.

Ina areas, we had to withdraw them for a season. They left the areas and returned home. A couple of months later I had my first reunion with them.

Nervousness crept over my heart. What would I say to these men? They had suffered and I had not. They bore in their bodies the brand-marks of Jesus; I did not. How could I show my face to them? It was because of my vision – the vision I had imparted to them – that they had suffered.

I prayed and searched the Scripture for how to approach them. The day finally came for me to meet them again but I was still at a loss for what I would say. I journeyed several hours up into the mountains of their home churches. I was ushered into a simple two-room house built on a mountainside, one room behind the other. I entered the back room, but no one was there. But on the back wall was a large wardrobe – very Narnia feeling.

As my host opened the door to the wardrobe sounds of singing tumbled upon me. I stepped through the wardrobe, not into another world, but into a soundproofed room built into the mountainside. As I walked into the light, my national partners stood in a circle, hands clasped dancing joyfully. From their lips spilled forth the words of their song:

Who are we to be considered worthy of suffering for Your Name?!

Tears of joy streamed down their faces as they worshiped their King, oblivious to my presence. In that moment, the Spirit said to me: "Steve, you don't need to say anything. They have a greater joy because of what they have suffered."

That is the way of the cross. It is worth it. As I sat with my brothers, wept with them, laughed with them and heard their stories, the picture grew more complete. They had gone to their respective locations. They had lovingly looked for persons of peace and preached the gospel to whole families. They prayed for the sick and many were healed. Still, the salvations were few until the persecution began. When Ina non-believers saw that the national partners were willing to suffer for what they preached, the Ina began to put their faith in the Lord. They felt, "If it's worth them suffering for, it must be worth us suffering for also!"

Over the coming months and years, the new Ina believers followed the pattern of sacrifice and boldness set for them. Many, many more of them suffered. One died. They will tell you to this day. The King is worth it. The kingdom is worth it.

One of my most cherished possessions is a video recording of an Ina woman singing the words of John 3:16. She sings it twice, unable to get through parts because she is so choked up with gratitude. It's as if her eyes say:

> And he died for all, that those who live should no longer live for themselves but for him who died for them and was raised again. (2 Cor. 5:17, NIV)

It's worth it.

Acts Persecution Study

How do you personally, your family and the new believers count the cost? It begins by focusing on the value of the King and his kingdom. He is the pearl of great price, the treasure hidden in the field.

A very practical way to do this is to take people through a study of persecution in Acts. I did something similar with my national partners before they ever went to share the gospel. It prepared us all immensely for what was ahead. Here is an example of one:[43]

Nine Passages in Acts to study (in nine small groups; or individually as desired)

1) 3:1 - 4:31   Peter heals a beggar
2) 5:12-42   Many healed, the apostles arrested and angel released them
3) 6:8 - 8:4   Stephen stoned and church scattered

---

[43] My colleague Neill Mims developed the first form of this particular study.

4) 12:1-24   James killed; Peter imprisoned
5) 13:13-52   Barnabas and Saul #1
6) 14:1-28   Paul and Barnabas #2 (several stories)
7) 16:16-40   Paul and Silas in Philippi
8) 17:1-9   Paul and Silas in Thessalonica
                            and Berea
9) 18:1-17   Paul and Silas in Corinth

Six Questions to ask of each passage and report back to the group:

1. How did they start talking and what did they say?
2. What prompted the persecution?
3. What type of persecution resulted and by whom?
4. What happened after that?
5. What was the overall response to persecution by these preachers of the gospel?
6. What was the effect on the local believers?

When a group returns from doing this study, put all of their answers up side by side in nine columns. As you do, a number of similarities emerge. At the very top one truth becomes very obvious: **if you share the gospel, you will be persecuted.** The corollary is probably true: if you don't want to be persecuted, keep silent.

> In every instance in Acts, talking about Jesus prompted persecution. If you talk about Jesus boldly, you'll probably be persecuted.

From there, the similarities begin diverging. Sometimes God intervenes miraculously; sometimes not. Sometimes they escape; at other times they are beaten, even die.

Then they merge back together. Almost always, the result is increased joy and power IF the believers respond to the persecution with boldness and sacrifice. Almost always there are references to *more* people coming to faith because of their sacrifice.

The responses of those persecuted are varied: running away; standing and taking their licks; praying for persecutors; hiding; loving their enemies visibly; witnessing to their persecutors; rejoicing and praising God. There is no single response to persecution except this: trust the Holy Spirit to show you what to say and how to respond:

> But when they arrest you, do not worry about what to say or how to say it. At that time you will be given what to say. (Matt. 10:19, NIV)

We use this Bible study to prepare ourselves and our colleagues to count the cost. It helps us know the range of things God might tell us to do when persecuted. Sometimes God might tell us to run, sometimes to stand and take it.

Fear is Contagious, But So is Faith

In conversations with many believers who have been imprisoned and beaten, their response is almost always unanimous. "I was afraid of being persecuted *before* the time came. But when I went through it, God was with me. It wasn't nearly as difficult as I imagined it would be."

It is the fear of persecution that paralyzes, not the persecution itself.

Make no mistake: *Persecution does not breed CPMs; boldness and perseverance in the face of persecution does.* Persecution can kill the budding faith, like the rocky soil of the parable:

THE MAN BEHIND THE METHOD

One important point, after observing Ying Kai train some missionaries for several days, concerns the issue of a holy life-giving power to the ministry. Yes, Ying provides simple tools and he does insist that people teach his lessons just the way he teaches them and he does tell his local converts not to use any other books than the Bible.

However, the bottom line is that it is not the tools that are the key. It is the modeling, holy life, intense focus on heaven, hell, judgment, and the need for salvation that are some of the keys to his effectiveness.

All this is to say that those who "catch his spirit" and model it in front of new believers are more likely to see the same type of results than those who came, copied the lessons and plan to go back and just repeat the methodology.

From "Why T4T is Successful" by Bill Smith

When affliction or persecution arises, because of the word, immediately he falls away. (Matt. 13:21, NASB)

GOD'S PROTECTION WHEN TRAINING

by Ying Kai

God will protect you in everything. Every day before you begin working you must pray and you will feel the difference. God will protect you. One time a man invited me to train the managers and leaders in his factory. There were over 40 people and I was so happy to train them. But when I finished the police were outside waiting for me. I thought that maybe my work in this country was already finished! In this country, there are many different types of factories. One type is built by the government and the rent is very cheap for the owner. The government prepares everything. The owner just has to invest the money for making the products. In those kinds of factories the government will send one person to be a manager who is a member of the political party.

The factory I was in was like this. The government informant listened to my training

Continued next page.

The fear of persecution can paralyze believers from living and speaking boldly for Jesus. They've figured out the corollary of the Acts persecution study: if you don't say anything, you may not be persecuted.

Fear is contagious. It spreads through a group of believers and paralyzes them all. Any time I see a group of believers not witnessing or reproducing, the first thing I examine is their boldness. In the majority of cases, this is the problem.

Fear is contagious, but so is faith! One good-soil believer who trusts God's providential care can live a life of boldness that will inspire many others. A group can be transformed from fearful paralysis to faith-filled boldness by one person.

Three Ways to Encourage Boldness

T4T can help you and your believers live out John 12:24.

> Truly, truly, I say to you, unless a grain of wheat falls into the earth and dies, it remains alone; but if it dies, it bears much fruit. (John 12:24, NASB)

In T4T training, you must demonstrate boldness and share testimonies of boldness to encourage your trainers to act on what they are hearing. Every time I hear Ying train I am amazed at how many testimonies of boldness he shares.

In another context, a church planter who went out to a particular county to plant churches was arrested and thrown into a military prison. The first day, fear gripped his heart, because as a former soldier he knew the types of things army officers do to people in prison in his country. Before the day was out, he made up his mind to live in faith. He stood with his hands on the bars of his prison door and said in a trembling voice to the guards outside:

"If you don't release me from this prison, the blood of 50,000 lost people will be on your head."

He was scared to death to say it, but he did it anyway. **Boldness is acting in spite of fear.** After he said this, he realized God was with him. He could do this. The next day he said it more loudly:

"If you don't release me from this prison, the blood of 50,000 lost people will be on your head!"

As the days progressed, he stood by his prison door and shouted at the top of his lungs:

"If you don't release me from this prison, the blood of 50,000 lost people will be on your head!"

Eventually, the jailors were so perturbed that they took him out of prison, escorted him to the border of the county and sent him away! This brother had the opportunity that first day to live in boldness or in fear. He chose boldness.

and then called the police. The police came after the training but they were very nice to me. They led me to the regional officer's office. The regional officer was very mad! He was ordering people to leave, and I started to leave, too, but he said to me, "You stay!" So of course I stayed.

I prayed, "Oh, Lord, help me! I don't want to go to jail." After everyone else had left, the officer told me to close the door.

I closed the door and he said, "Don't do this again. You know, you are lucky because I am a Christian. I'm giving you a warning. I'm a party member but two years ago I got cancer. Six times the doctor told me that I was dying but finally a couple of years ago two pastors came to the hospital to visit me and pray for me. God healed me!

"From now on, just ask the factory owner to rent an apartment for your training. I'll give you permission to train there but don't do it in the factory."

So God protected me.

In T4T, you must include a lesson on boldness and perseverance. It can be similar to the Acts persecution study. In T4T loving, encouraging accountability helps you to move from fear to faith. You must also model for your trainees a lifestyle of boldness, perseverance and sacrifice. In T4T helping people to create a Name List and begin witnessing to them moves them from timidity to boldness.

Boldness is acting in spite of fear.

In addition, there are three practices that have helped encourage boldness in many believers:

1. **Baptize immediately.** The sooner their baptism, the bolder new believers become. This is the first chance for them to count the cost.

2. **Memorize and trust the promises of Scripture.** Encourage them to memorize promises about God taking care of them, and then to hold onto those promises in difficult times.

3. **Count the cost.** Help them to count the cost and have a realistic understanding of pursuing God's heart. It sobers them so that they can joyfully sell all to have the treasure in the field.

When you have brothers and sisters who undergo persecution after you train them, you can comfort yourself in remembering that together you all counted the cost. You entered the difficulty with eyes wide open. And they are reaping a special blessing that only comes in persecution. They are gaining more of the treasure:

If you are reviled for the name of Christ, you are blessed, because the Spirit of glory and of God rests on you. (1 Pet. 4:14, NASB)

For momentary, light affliction is producing for us an eternal weight of glory far beyond all comparison. (2 Cor. 4:17, NASB)

Persevere to See a Movement

The examples of Ying and Grace and a multitude of other church-planting movement practitioners demonstrate the incredibly hard work and perseverance it takes to cooperate with God in initiating CPMs. Besides enduring persecution, successful CPM initiators sacrifice a lot of time to initiate the CPM. They re-direct the hours in their week to focus on high-value activities of CPMs and reduce their investment in low-value activities. Without a significant time investment in the high value kingdom activities, no CPM will get off the ground. Paul described his investment in the Ephesian CPM this way:

> Therefore be on the alert, remembering that night and day for a period of three years I did not cease to admonish each one with tears. (Acts 20:31, NASB)

A casual or undisciplined stab at this will never work. You must be committed to kingdom movements and invest a lot of time in them if this is the direction you are going to go. You must demonstrate incredible perseverance to change mindsets in yourself and believers around you and launch a discipleship _re-_revolution. And you must persevere through every obstacle and persecution.

Persecution does not breed CPMs; boldness and perseverance in the face of persecution do!

Yet, it's worth it! He's worth it!

You may not have yet seen a discipleship re-revolution. Take heart! That's true of most places prior to a breakthrough. There is a way for a movement to become a reality. Read the final chapter to find out how.

Be a Doer, not just a Hearer!

Write down how God has spoken to you and what you need to obey as a result:

CHAPTER 21

Precedent and Promise

You can master every lesson in this book, and yet a lack of faith can still stop you.

As a CPM trainer and hub for CPM conversations, I regularly get requests from missionaries and mission leaders, church planters, and church leaders to send them case studies of CPMs. Their preference is for a case study that exactly matches their situation. I get requests like this:[44]

> *Do you have an example of a CPM among educated, post-modern Middle-Eastern Arabs living in Western Europe?*

Hmm! I check my files. Nope. No case study for such a group. Sometimes their response, whether verbalized or not, conveys:

> *Well, that proves it! A CPM can't happen among my people group!*

Their logic makes no sense. The absence of a case study proves nothing other than we don't have a CPM among that people group yet!

So, I send them a few case studies of CPMs in China. I often get this response: "Don't send me these case studies. Of course CPMS can occur there; that's *China!*"

> What they don't realize is that some of the first CPM initiators in China in the late 1990s were told when they arrived: "It takes\an average of four years to win a Chinese atheist to the Lord."

---

[44] I don't give the actual place names for security reasons.

So, I send them a case study from India, perhaps the longest-lived and largest CPM in the world, along with some other Indian case studies. They look at them and respond: "Don't send me these case studies. Of course CPMs can happen there. That's India. So many people speak English there!

> What they don't realize is that the area in which the large CPM emerged was until recently called the "Graveyard of Missionaries" because of its unresponsiveness.

So I send them case studies from several urban CPMs. But the response is: "Don't send me these. Of course CPMs can happen in cities. There's so much anonymity! You can get away with anything there."

> What they don't realize is that just two or three years ago, senior leaders of mission organizations were scratching their heads in search of ways to reach cities and were declaring that we had no examples of CPMs in these spiritual deserts!

About this time, I'm getting a little frustrated. They express to me that they really want some good case studies for reaching Muslims. So I send them a case study of the largest Muslim-background CPM in the world. But the response is: "Don't give me this. That's South Asia. It's easy there!"

> What they don't realize is one of the monthly uses of offerings by national believers in that movement is to rebuild burned down homes of persecuted Christians and assist Christian women who have been raped by their persecutors.

So I send them two case studies from Southeast Asian Muslim-background CPMs. The response this time is: "They're not *real* Muslims!"

> What they don't realize is that the very areas in which these CPMs are thriving have been the traditional seedbeds and training grounds for Muslim terrorist groups.

Finally, I send them an extremely confidential case study of a Muslim-background CPM in one of the most restricted areas of the Middle East. The response I finally get on this one is: "They must be lying!" I've been told this several times.

At this I throw up my hands and give up. I realize that for some people no amount of case studies will convince them. There is a basic disconnect in their faith in the very nature of God and His heart to reach the nations.

Someone Has to be First

There are a number of places for which we have no examples of CPMs – yet. The number and diversity of places for which we DO have CPMs grows yearly. My own awareness of new movements astounds me each year. Just a few years ago, I could count 10-15 CPMs. This past year I felt pretty confident about 30-35. But interactions with other CPM trainers and mission leaders indicate that the number is much, much higher. What we know of is just a fraction of what God is really up to.

> And there are also many other things which Jesus did, which if they were written in detail, I suppose that even the world itself would not contain the books that would be written. (John 21:25, NASB)

You must live with an assumption that God is doing more than you are aware of even when your heart doubts.

Today, with young missionaries coming to the field, we prepare them to go to places like East Asia, South Asia and Southeast Asia *expecting that CPMs will develop.* It's not hard to because we have good examples of other CPMs in the same type of locale. We have **precedent**.

But there was a time when there were no CPMs in those places.

> There was a time when there were no CPMs in China; *someone had to be first.*

> There was a time when there were no CPMs in India; *someone had to be first.*

> There was a time when there were no CPMs in Southeast Asia; *someone had to be first.*

There may be no CPM where you live. Fine! Someone has to be first. Be that first one! In the beginning, when there is no PRECEDENT, SOMEONE has to be FIRST.

Precedent

Fortunately, in some places in the world, we *do* have precedents for CPMs. These precedents are a great encouragement to other church planters to believe that CPMs are possible and to give them a model for what it can look like. This is illustrated well in 2 Samuel.

> [15]Now when the Philistines were at war again with Israel, David went down and his servants with him; and as they fought against the Philistines, David became weary. [16]Then **Ishbi-benob, who was among the descendants of the giant,** the weight of whose spear was three hundred shekels of bronze in weight, was girded with a new sword, and he intended to kill David. [17]But Abishai the son of Zeruiah helped him, and struck the Philistine and killed him. Then the men of David swore to him, saying, "You shall not go out again with us to battle, so that you do not extinguish the lamp of Israel."
>
> [18]Now it came about after this that there was war again with the Philistines at Gob; then Sibbecai the Hushathite struck down **Saph, who was among the descendants of the giant**.
>
> [19]There was war with the Philistines again at Gob, and Elhanan the son of Jaare-oregim the Bethlehemite killed **Goliath the Gittite**, the shaft of whose spear was like a weaver's beam.
>
> [20]There was war at Gath again, where there was **a man of great stature** who had six fingers on each hand and six toes on each foot, twenty-four in number; and **he also had been born to the giant**. [21]When he defied Israel, Jonathan the son of Shimei, David's brother, struck him down.
>
> [22]**These four were born to the giant in Gath, and they fell by the hand of David and by the hand of his servants.** (2 Sam. 21:15-22, NASB, emphasis added)

This is a remarkable record: four giants killed by the hand of David's followers. Imagine the situation with the first one Ishbi-benob. The text says he was a descendant of "the giant" – most likely Goliath. David is in battle against one of Goliath's sons. The giant has payback in mind. He spots David in the battle line and rushes toward him with a new sword, intending to kill David and avenge his father's death.

There may be no CPM where you live. Fine! Someone has to be first. Be that first one! In the beginning, when there is no PRECEDENT, SOMEONE has to be FIRST.

But David is not the one who slays him. Instead, Abishai, one of the army commanders does.

Shortly thereafter, another descendant of Goliath, Saph, fights against the Israelites. David doesn't slay him either. Sibbecai does.

Later, a descendant of Goliath, bearing Goliath's name, fights Israel. David doesn't slay him either. Elhanan does.

Finally, the greatest of the descendants who remains nameless fights against Israel. But David doesn't slay him. His nephew Jonathan does.

When you have PRECEDENT, you know how to find victory. The precedent gives you a model and the courage to attempt the same thing.

What's happening here? Why is it that four men in succession can slay vengeful giants when, less than a generation earlier, the entire nation of Israel (including the tallest man in Israel – Saul) cowered in fear? What was the difference? How did they learn to slay giants?

They had precedent

David showed them how to slay giants; now they had a model and the faith to reproduce it. They knew how to beat giants! One after another, these men, even David's nephew, slew giants that a generation before would have paralyzed an entire army.

That's the power of precedent. When you have precedent, you know how to find victory in your context. The precedent gives you a model and the courage to attempt the same thing.

Remember: What seems radical today will be commonplace tomorrow. There was a time when CPMs were unusual in Asia and Africa. Now it seems like everyone is talking about them. And they are emerging at a faster rate than ever. That's the power of precedent.

But what do you do when you have no precedent?

Promise

There was a time in Israel when there was no precedent for killing giants. Less than a generation earlier, Israel was paralyzed with the very thought of approaching a giant in hand-to-hand combat. 1 Samuel 17 records the well-known story. Goliath was a giant of a man who stood over nine feet tall (v.4) and whose armor weighed 125 pounds (v.5)!

Saul stood head and shoulders above all the men of Israel (1 Sam. 9:2), yet in his own strength he cowered in fear. For weeks, the people of Israel camping in the Valley of Elah followed his example, paralyzed by fear (1 Sam. 17:10-11, 23-24). Each day Goliath would taunt and challenge them. Each day they would flee from the battle line. They lived in a *lifestyle* of fear and lack of faith.

When David, fresh from the pastures and sheep pens, saw this scene unfold, he was appalled. Coming in with an outsider's perspective, the irrational fear and lack of faith seemed ludicrous to him.

What had David been doing in the sheep pens and pastures that prepared him for this day?

- Meditating upon the majesty and promises of God, and writing these down in songs (Psalms).

- Fighting off lions and bears to protect his sheep (vv.34-36)

In his mind, the standoff with the giant made no sense. *The giant stood no chance*, but the people couldn't see it! They couldn't see it because there was no precedent for killing giants.

David believed the promise that God would overcome this giant because he knew what God desired; he understood the heart of God. God had promised to give His people the land and to give them victory over their enemies. As a man after God's own heart, David *knew* God's heart, so he believed the promise. This giant was *uncircumcised – outside the promise of the covenant (v.26)*. In David's mind, it was Goliath against God. Goliath didn't stand a chance.

What do you do when you have no precedent? All you have is a promise. The promise is enough!

David believed the promise also because he had *personal precedent*. He had never killed a giant, but he *had* killed lions and bears. How could this giant be any different if God wanted to protect His own flock (v.36)?

Three times in the passage, David quotes the promise – to himself, to the people of God and to the enemy. He didn't have a precedent, but he did have a promise. And it was enough.

> The day is coming in your context where there will be first, then second, then third CPMs. The day is coming that people will say of your context: "Don't give me a CPM case study from there; that's _____ country!"

To himself: As David inquires of the men around him, he is sounding them out and musing to himself:

> "What will be done for the man who kills this Philistine and takes away the reproach from Israel? For who is this uncircumcised Philistine, that he should taunt the armies of the living God?" (1 Sam. 17:26, NASB)

David comes to terms personally with the promise. God *can* deliver this giant up, and why shouldn't David be the one to accomplish it?

To the people of God: As David stands before Saul and his officers, he has come to terms with the promise personally, and now declares it to the people of God, "God can do this, and He will use me!"

> "Your servant has killed both the lion and the bear; and this uncircumcised Philistine will be like one of them, since he has taunted the armies of the living God." (1 Sam. 17:36, NASB)

David encourages them to take heart and take a risk with him.

What do you do when you have no precedent? All you have is a PROMISE, and the promise is enough!

To the enemy: Now David approaches Goliath. Closer and closer he gets and the giant begins taunting him. "You think I'm a dog that you bring that stick after me? I'm going to give your flesh to the birds of the sky today, boy!"

This has to be unnerving. What's going through David's mind? We are not told, but he begins to shout the promise out loud to the enemy:

> "You come to me with a sword, a spear, and a javelin, but I come to you in the name of the LORD of hosts, the God of the armies of Israel, whom you have taunted. This day the LORD will deliver you up into my hands, and I will strike you down and remove your head from you. And I will give the dead bodies of the army of the Philistines this day to the birds of the sky and the wild beasts of the earth, that all the earth may know that there is a God in Israel, and that all this assembly may know that the LORD does not deliver by sword or by spear; for the battle is the LORD'S and He will give you into our hands." (1 Sam. 17:45-47, NASB)

Whether fear was creeping into David's heart or not, we don't know. But his heart meditated on the promise of God in the face of the enemy. Goliath intended to give David's body to the birds. David intended to give not only Goliath's body, but the bodies of all the Philistine army to the birds!

The Promise is Enough

At the end of the day, if you have no precedent for a discipleship *re*-revolution, and all you have is a promise, it is enough. David acted on the promise and became a giant killer. His example served as a precedent (model) for others to learn from. What's radical today will be commonplace tomorrow.

Fifteen years ago, modern-day CPMs were mostly just a dream. Today, CPMs are a reality, almost taken for granted, in a number of contexts. Why? That's the power of precedent.

In India, a few individuals held onto a promise and birthed one of the first CPMs that we know of in modern times. In China, another group held onto a promise and birthed one of the first CPMs that we know of in that country. And so the drama has unfolded around the world. A few faith-filled individuals have defied the paralyzed ranks and pressed forward with nothing but a promise.

And now we say things like: "Don't give me a CPM case study from there; that's China!" It wasn't always that way. Someone had to be first. That's the power of precedent.

The day is coming when there will be a first, then second, then third CPM in your own context. The day is coming that people will say of your situation: "Don't give me a CPM case study from there; that's _____!"

But when you don't yet have a precedent, the promise of Scripture is clear: God will harvest a great multitude for Himself from every people group and He will launch discipleship revolutions that will rock the world (e.g. Matt. 24:14, Rev. 7:9, John 4:35, Matt. 9:37-38, Mark 1:15-17, Matt. 13:23, Matt. 13:31-32, Mark 4:26-29; Acts 19:10).

Do you think God wants you to pray for something He doesn't intend to fulfill? The promise is clear. Live your life based on it.

Do you think God wants you to pray for something He doesn't intend to fulfill? The promise is clear. Live your life based on it.

He wants to fulfill it in your place, at this time, through you!

Epilogue: Forgotten Precedent

Sometimes there *is* precedent from history but we have forgotten it. CPMs are not simply a modern-day phenomenon. All throughout church history, there have been CPM-like movements – discipleship revolutions.

Sometimes, there *is* precedent from history but we have forgotten it. Such was the case with the story of David and Goliath.

Some, 400 years earlier, Caleb, at the age of 85, drove out three giants from the mountain God had promised him (Josh. 15:14). All evidence from the ancient record indicated that the race of giants he defeated were a larger race than the one that David and his men defeated.

Yet 40 years before that, Moses and the Israelites defeated Og of Bashan (Num. 21:33-35). Og, according to Scripture, appears to have been bigger still. He slept in a 13-foot bed (Deut. 3:11; remember Goliath was only nine feet tall). Og was so frightening that the Lord appeared to Moses to personally give him the promise of deliverance, announcing:

> "Do not fear him, for I have given him into your hand, and all his people and his land; and you shall do to him as you did to Sihon, king of the Amorites, who lived at Heshbon." (Num. 21:34, NASB)

Moses had a promise from God. And he had personal precedent on a smaller scale (Sihon). It was enough.

Did the army of Israel, camped in the Valley of Elah, taunted by the giant Goliath remember these stories from 400 years earlier?

If they did, they apparently dismissed them as irrelevant:

- *That can't happen here. Our situation is different.*

- *That can't happen through us. Moses and Caleb were special.*

- ***That can't happen today;*** *it's ancient history. God no longer works that way.*

If they had forgotten them, it was their loss. It was a precedent that could have encouraged them to fight the battle and trust God to deliver them.

Did David know those stories? We don't know. If so, then perhaps they helped him as he ran toward the battle line. He had precedent.

If they were forgotten stories, stored in musty scrolls in a tabernacle, unavailable to a common shepherd boy, it didn't matter. **David knew his God. The promise was enough.**

Be a Doer, not just a Hearer!

Write down how God has spoken to you and what you need to obey as a result:

INDEX

SCRIPTURE INDEX

CREATION TO CHRIST

A Summary of the Bible's Basic Message

I would like to share with you a story that is changing the lives of people around the world.

PART1 - True Story from the Bible:

This is a summary story of the Most High God's relationship with the world. This story is from a book called the Bible. Men did not make up the Bible. It is the word of the Most High God. The Most High God is more powerful than any ancestor, person, government or god that people worship. This story is true and reliable because it is the word of the Most High God.

PART 2 – Created for a Relationship With God

Creator: There is only one God, and He is the Most High God. He existed in the beginning before there was anything else. The Most High God is the Creator. He created everything on earth and in heaven and is all powerful over everything. When God began to create things, He just used His words. He spoke and everything came to being. He created angels to worship and serve Him. They were very beautiful. He also created everything we can see -- the sky, land, water, mountains, oceans, sun, moon, stars, all plant and animals. Finally, He created man according to His image. God created man to enjoy all that He has created. God created everything and saw that it was good.

God and Man in Relationship: God placed the man and woman in a beautiful garden to live. They had a very good relationship with Him and with each other. He told them to take care of the garden and enjoy everything. He gave them a special command: they could eat from every tree in the garden except one. If they ate from that one tree, they would be punished and die. The man and woman listened to God and had a wonderful relationship with Him in the garden. *God created us to have a wonderful relationship with Him forever!*

PART 3 – People are Separated from God

Fall of the Devil: However, do you remember the angels God created? One of the angels was very smart and beautiful. This angel became very proud. He wanted to be like God and to have the other angels to worship him instead of God. Only God deserves all the worship and service. Therefore God cast the disobedient angel, the devil, and the other angels who listened to him out of heaven. These bad angels are known as demons.

Disobeying: One day, the devil tempted woman to eat the food from the tree that was forbidden. The woman listened to the devil and ate the fruit. Then she gave it to her husband to eat. Both of them disobeyed God's command. **Disobeying God's command is sin**. God is righteous and holy. He must punish sin. God cast the man and the woman out of the garden, and their relationship with God was broken. Human beings and God were now separated forever.

All Have Sinned: Like the first man and the woman, all people like us since then have sinned by not listening to God's commands and are separated from God. The result of sin is eternal punishment in hell. *We cannot live forever with God as we were designed.*

PART 4 – People Can't Come Back to God

10 Commands: Over time, the number of people on earth multiplied. Yet God loved them very much and wanted them to have a relationship with Him. He gave them 10 commandments to follow. Remember God is perfect and holy, so we must be perfect and holy to live with him. The 10 commandments teach people how to relate to God and how to relate to people. Some of the commands were: do not worship other gods or make idols; honor your parents; do not lie, steal, murder or commit adultery. However, no one was able to obey all of these commands.

Sacrifices: So, each time they sinned, God allowed them to repent of their sins and offer a blood sacrifice to take the place of their punishment. This sacrifice was shedding the blood of a perfect animal like a lamb. If they would repent and offer the blood sacrifice, God would forgive them and let the animal die in their place. **Only by the shedding of blood can a person's sin be forgiven**. However, people kept sinning and the sin sacrifice became a ritual rather than something from their heart. God became tired of their insincere acts. People were still separated from God. *We cannot come back to God on our own no matter what we do.*

PART 5 - Jesus Comes to Earth

God Sends Jesus: However, God still loved us very much. Therefore He gave us a perfect way to reconnect to Him. God sent Jesus to show us the way back to Himself. Who is Jesus? Jesus is God's one and only son.

Teacher: When Jesus was on earth, He was a wise teacher. Many people would come to hear Him teach about how they could return to God.

Storm: Jesus was also a powerful **miracle worker.** On one occasion, He was with some of His followers crossing a large lake on a boat. It was late at night. While Jesus was sleeping, a powerful storm arose on the lake. Jesus' followers were very afraid. They awakened Jesus and said, "We are about to die!" Jesus rebuked the wind and said to the waves, "Quiet! Be still!" Immediately the wind and rained stopped. **Jesus' power is greater than the powers of the world.**

Feed 5000: On another occasion over 5,000 people came to listen to Jesus teach about God. When evening came they had not eaten and were hungry. Altogether they only had five loaves of bread and two fish. Jesus used the five loaves of bread and two fish to feed over 5,000 people. **Jesus' power is able to satisfy man's needs.**

Demon-possessed Man: Another time, Jesus saw a man with many demons inside him. The man was very powerful and dangerous. Yet Jesus loved the man and cast the demons out of him. **Jesus is more powerful than the evil spiritual world.**

Raising the Dead: Finally, on another occasion, Jesus' good friend became sick and died. Jesus was not with him. Several days later Jesus arrived at His friend's house. Jesus felt very sad. His friend was already in the tomb. Jesus went to the front of the tomb and said, "Friend, come out." His friend was rose up and walked out of the tomb alive! **Jesus' power is greater than death.**

Love: *Jesus did all these things because He loves people and wants us all to come back to God.*

PART 6 - Jesus, The Perfect Sacrifice

Perfect: Unlike us, Jesus never sinned. He obeyed His Father in heaven perfectly. He alone never deserved to be punished.

Cross: Therefore most people loved Jesus. However, there some religious leaders were jealous of Jesus. These men arrested Jesus and decided to kill Him. They placed Jesus on a large cross which is two large pieces of wood shaped in a "T". They took His hands and His feet and nailed them to the cross. His precious blood flowed from His hands, feet and body. Jesus suffered much pain on the cross.

Substitute: Jesus is the perfect sacrifice. Jesus was perfect and did not deserve to die. Instead, Jesus died for all mankind. God loves us and allowed Jesus to die on the cross in our place. Only through the shedding of Jesus' precious blood was God able to forgive our sin. Jesus death demonstrates God's love towards us.

Resurrection: After Jesus died, he was placed in a secure tomb. However this story doesn't end here. On the third day Jesus rose from the dead and showed Himself to His followers! Then He returned to His Father in heaven. *Jesus took our punishment and now provides a way for us to come back to God!*

PART 7 – The Wandering Son

Before He left the earth, Jesus told a story to his followers about a father and his sons.

A Son Leaves: The father had two sons. The younger one said to his father, "Father, give me my share of the inheritance." So he divided his property between them. The younger son got together all he had, set off for a distant country and there wasted his wealth in wild living. After he had spent everything, he began to be in need. So he went and got a lowly job feeding pigs. He longed to fill his stomach with the pods that the pigs were eating, but no one gave him anything.

Comes to His Senses: One day he came to his senses. He said, "How many of my father's hired men have food to spare, and here I am starving to death! I will set out and go back to my father and say to him: 'Father, I have sinned against heaven and against you. I am no longer worthy to be called your son; make me like one of your hired men.'"

Repents: So he got up and went to his father. But while he was still a long way off, his father saw him and was filled with compassion for him. He ran to his son, threw his arms around him and kissed him. The son said to him, "Father, I have sinned against heaven and against you. I am no longer worthy to be called your son."

Restored: But the father said to his servants, "Quick! Bring the best robe and put it on him. Put a ring on his finger and sandals on his feet. Bring the fattened calf and kill it. Let's have a feast and celebrate. For this son of mine was dead and is alive again; he was lost and is found." So they began to celebrate.

PART 8: How to come back to God

Jesus Brings Us Back: We are all like the younger son. We all have left God and are forever separated from Him. We all must repent of our sins and return to God. Only Jesus can lead us back to God's side and make us His son or daughter. We can live with Him forever in heaven.

Jesus said, **"I am the way, the truth, and the life. No one comes to the Father except through me." John 14:6**

Question: We must go through Jesus to return to God. How can we go through Jesus? You must admit to God that you have sinned against Him. You must believe that Jesus died in your place. You put your trust in Jesus to bring you back and give you eternal life as God's son or daughter. From that point on, you let Jesus be your Master and obey His word.

***Do you want to let Jesus bring you back to God?**

How to Come Back to God

The whole Creation to Christ story is summarized in one verse: **"For God so loved the world that he gave his one and only Son, that whoever believes [trusts] in him shall not perish but have eternal life." John 3:16**

To come back to God, you must put your faith (trust) in Jesus. To do that, we must turn from our old sinful life and ask God to forgive us. **"If we confess our sins, he is faithful and just and will forgive us our sins and purify us from all unrighteousness." 1 John 1:9** He is a treasure worth joyfully giving your life to gain!

Therefore, to return to God you must <u>repent</u> (turn from) your sins and <u>believe</u> in Jesus as your new Master.

Prayer: God wants you, your family and friends to return to Him. To return, you must believe in your heart and confess . . .

> **"God, I know you love me, but I have sinned against you.**
>
> **However, Jesus is the perfect sacrifice for my sin. I believe and trust in Jesus to take my punishment.**
>
> **I confess I have sinned and am sorry. God please forgive me.**
>
> **I put my trust in You Jesus and ask you to lead me back to God.**
>
> **I agree to joyfully obey You as my Master from this moment on as I read the Bible.**

Thank you for my new and eternal life as your child."

You can talk to God through prayer and He will hear you. If you truly mean it, then you may want to sign below to remember that today you came back to God!

NAME_____ DATE_____

Assurance

If you truly turned back to God, you are now God's child. You have a brand new life! The Bible says:

"I write these things to you who believe in the name of the Son of God so that you may know that you have eternal life." **1 John 5:13**

No matter what happens, you are now God's child forever! He wants you to rest assured that you have a new life and nothing can separate you again!

It is important now to meet with other believers, read God's Word and pray to Him regularly to grow in your new relationship with God.

Go Tell and Train Five

God's plan is not only to bring you back but to bring back your family and friends through you. God is waiting for your whole family to believe in Him. Go home and tell your family and friends this good news. God loves them too! **Write down the names of at least five people you want to tell this story to this week. Whom do you think most would like to hear this?**

_____   _____

_____   _____

_____   _____

Let's practice telling the story together several times and then pray for the people you will tell. If they decide to follow Jesus, train them to repeat the process the next week with five of their friends or family. I am giving you five copies of this lesson that you can give to them.

I will meet again with you soon to see how you are doing with this, and I will train you in the next step in growing in your new relationship with God.